Strengthening Your Stepfamily

RebuildingBooks
Relationships – Divorce – and Beyond

Strengthening Your Stepfamily

Elizabeth Einstein, M.A., MFT
Linda Albert, Ph.D.

Impact **Publishers**®
ATASCADERO, CALIFORNIA

ATTENTION ORGANIZATIONS AND CORPORATIONS:

This book is available at quantity discounts on bulk purchases for educational, business, or sales promotional use. For further information, please contact Impact Publishers, P.O. Box 6016, Atascadero, California 93423-6016. Phone 805-466-5917, e-mail: info@impactpublishers.com

Parts of this book are based upon an earlier book by Elizabeth Einstein and Linda Albert, *Strengthening Your Stepfamily,* © 1986, published by AGS® American Guidance Service, Inc.

All cartoons by John Bush were created exclusively for this book except for seven (© 1997) which are used with permission of AGS Publishing — STEP. Like the text, all rights are reserved under international and Pan-American Copyright Conventions. Reproduction without express written permission of Impact Publishers is prohibited.

Library of Congress Cataloging-in-Publication Data

Einstein, Elizabeth.
    Stengthening your stepfamily / Elizabeth Einstein, Linda Albert.
      p. cm. — (Rebuilding books)
    Includes bibliographical references and index.
    ISBN 1-886230-62-5 (alk. paper)
    1. Stepfamilies.   I. Albert, Linda.   II. Title. III. Series:
RebuildingBooks.
    HQ759.92.S365 2006
    646.7'8—dc22

                    2005018547

Cover design by K.A. White Design, San Luis Obispo, California
Printed in the United States of America on acid-free recycled paper.

Published by
Impact ✍ Publishers®
POST OFFICE BOX 6016
ATASCADERO, CALIFORNIA 93423-6016
www.impactpublishers.com

Contents

Introduction 1

1 A Different Kind of Family 9

2 Clearing the Path to Stepfamily Success 19
    The Stepfamily Workshop — Session One 31

3 Letting Go of the Past 35
    The Stepfamily Workshop — Session Two 49

4 Your Stepfamily Journey 53

5 Creating a Comfortable Stepfamily 69
    The Stepfamily Workshop — Session Three 77

6 Strengthening Your Couple Relationship I:
Dealing With the Past 83

7 Strengthening Your Couple Relationship II:
Making Practical Decisions Together 93

8 Strengthening Your Couple Relationship III:
Building Intimacy and Communication 99
    The Stepfamily Workshop — Session Four 111

9 Recreating Roles and Relationships 119

10 Overcoming Stepfamily Obstacles 135
    The Stepfamily Workshop — Session Five 151

11 Stepfamilies and Discipline 157

12 Why Children Misbehave 176
    The Stepfamily Workshop — Session Six 193

13 Your Stepchild's Challenges I:
Healing Young Hearts 197

14 Your Stepchild's Challenges II:
Dealing with Differences 203

15 Your Stepchild's Challenges III:
Coping with Changes 215
    The Stepfamily Workshop — Session Seven 229

16 Hope! The Heart of Your Stepfamily 235

The Stepfamily Workshop — Session Eight 247

References 251

Stepfamily Resources and Training 255

Index 257

Acknowledgements

Just like building a successful stepfamily, following a calling and creating a book is a collaborative effort. The first edition of *Strengthening Your Stepfamily* with my co-author was such an effort. My appreciation to Linda for finding our first publisher and providing her expertise from the world of education on our original and, ultimately very popular, stepfamily education kit published by American Guidance Service. Since her retirement, she pursues other interests.

After being deeply involved in the stepfamily education world for over 20 years, I felt more qualified to produce this revised edition than the first time around. But I could not have done this alone. While I take full responsibility for this expanded edition, without my wonderful new editor's expertise and excellent editing eye, it wouldn't be the fine book it's become. My appreciation to Robert Alberti, the founder of Impact Publishers, with whom I've corresponded for many years about publishing possibilities. Perhaps he realized the only way to get rid of me was to do this project — and, hopefully, future ones. Thank you Bob for *all* of your great guidance and patience.

Time teaches many lessons and timing is everything! Just as taking time is the basis for stepfamily success, time has taught me much more about the complexities of stepfamily living. After growing up as a stepchild, raising two biological sons and two sets of stepchildren, my stepfamily adventure started professionally when I wrote an article for *Human Behavior* magazine in 1980. Ever since, I've taken the "road less traveled" to follow a calling to strengthen stepfamilies, carrying out that commitment by writing, teaching, making media appearances, and working with families as a marriage and family therapist.

When I wrote my first books on stepfamilies, little formal research existed. Back then, much of what I knew was rooted in personal experience or that of the many stepfamilies I interviewed as a journalist; since then, hundreds of researchers have since validated what those families taught me.

My great lesson about time and timing is the same one that you must understand from the start: Making a stepfamily is a process and it takes time — a long time. It's tempting to make finding a new partner and remarriage your priority, but it could be a great mistake! This "too close, too soon" syndrome could set you up to become one of the too many stepfamilies that end prematurely, putting your children through yet another cycle of divorce. But even time alone is not enough. While time may help you heal, it's *what you do with that time* that truly matters in the long run.

Use time wisely! Take time to understand your part in the ended relationship, or why you still harbor intense feelings if your partner died. Take time to learn to become a better parent to your children and to help them heal. Take time to come to know you better. Take time to begin dreams you may have left behind and ponder a plan for the future. And take time to learn in advance about the challenges of stepfamily living and what you must do to build a healthy remarriage and successful stepfamily. It is my hope that this new revised and expanded edition supports you as you create a very special stepfamily.

My gratitude goes to the many others who, throughout the years I've worked with stepfamilies, have supported my work in so many different ways. It's possible I would never have taken this path except for strong encouragement by

Clarke Thomas, Senior Editor at the Pittsburgh Post-Gazette who read an early draft of my first stepfamily book at Bread Loaf Writers Conference many years ago. "You must write that book," he insisted as we walked the wooded path of Robert Frost in Vermont. Great appreciation to my beloved mentor, the late Virginia Satir, who taught me to trust process and to have the courage to follow my calling continues; still, I feel her presence. Above all, my deepest thanks to John Visher and the late Emily Visher, founders of the national Stepfamily Association of America. Already, they'd devoted their lives to making the stepfamily visible in the early eighties when they gave generously of their time and encouraged me to write my first book on stepfamilies.

Throughout the years, many other collaborators and friends supported me in various ways as I've traveled teaching *Strengthening Stepfamilies* workshops. I thank these generous and gracious people and all those whom I forget to name here: Julie Baumgardner, Barbara Berendzen, Sue Bissell, George Bodine, Gloria Clark, Bernice Hagen, Frank Halse, Jr., Nicki Palmer, Meg Rafanelli, Thomas Seibt, Diane Sollee, Tracey Soska, Billie Stewart. All of you have believed in me and the importance of my work with stepfamilies the entire time. My appreciation to you is deep.

And, of course, without living in a stepfamily for most of my life, my path would have been very different. I'm glad for how it's been! Thank you to my dear stepfather, Ben and to my beloved sons, Chris and Jeff. Thank you to **all** my stepchildren: Cynthia and Lynn, Beverly, Brenda and Kurt. I have learned from all of you. This book is for you.

— Elizabeth Einstein
Ithaca, New York

Introduction

$\mathbf{A}$re you living in a stepfamily? Are you considering a new marriage and wonder what the best approach to creating a successful stepfamily might be? Have you moved past the honeymoon phase and realize that some challenges are creating tension, making the adjustment to your new family harder than you thought it would be? Maybe you've heard of the high remarriage divorce rate and want to learn skills and gain insights to avoid becoming just another statistic. Stepfamily living can be very difficult — especially at first — and you may not be prepared to face the challenges. You're not alone! There is a trail map for success.

See if you identify with either of these scenarios.

When they met and began dating, both John and Amy had custody of their children. John's first wife had died nine months before, about the same time Amy separated from her husband. Both were doing the best they could to take care of their children, but still wanted to spend a lot of time alone together. John wined and dined Amy and she found their courtship exciting. Though her former husband called frequently and wanted to talk about what happened, she put him off, preferring to be with her new love. Once Amy's divorce was final, she and John married. After a brief honeymoon, they returned to live in John's house with her three children and his two.

Amy and John dreamed they could make marriage better the second time around. But as they settled into the first few weeks of stepfamily living, the couple found themselves repeating the patterns of their previous lifestyles. Things became even more difficult when Amy's former husband called to discuss unresolved issues about the children. Too often their telephone conversations ended in arguments. John often felt resentful and jealous when Amy spent a lot of time talking with her ex-husband. But he didn't tell Amy what he felt, nor did she tell him how guilty she had begun to feel for not loving his children the way she did her own. Privately, neither believed their relationship could hold up if such feelings were brought into the open. Amy's children wanted to spend more time alone with her, but they kept quiet, fearing they would upset their new stepfather. Even though they were angry, they also worried that he, too, might leave. No one talked about any of these feelings and little trust developed among family members. Within months, child-rearing problems intensified. Dealing with discipline became a major issue between the couple. Amy believed in strict rules and severe punishment; John felt that if the children were allowed to make their own decisions, they would do fine. While he threatened them when they misbehaved, rarely did he follow through. His parenting style was a complete contrast to Amy's. They tried his way, then her way, but they never developed an "our" way — a discipline approach they both felt comfortable with.

Soon the chaos became too much. Although John and Amy finally agreed to see a counselor, they had waited so long they found it impossible to move beyond their anger and fear. Because their therapist didn't have special training in how to work with stepfamilies, she couldn't help the couple resolve their differences. She didn't understand how they were a different kind of family and faced different challenges than other families. Within two years, John and Amy divorced.

Susan and Paul's story takes a little longer to tell. You'll soon understand why...

As they left their parenting class one Tuesday evening, Susan and Paul agreed that this investment in strengthening their stepfamily was turning out to be one of the best they could have made. During their courtship, they'd realized each of them had a very different approach to discipline. After much confusion, they decided to learn some child-rearing skills — something neither of them had ever done before. There were too many good things about their new family life to let conflicts between them continue.

Mostly, things felt right for Paul and Susan. After divorcing, both had taken time to redefine relationships with their former spouses. Susan's first husband had moved to the West Coast shortly after they finished with divorce counseling. Her children only saw their father on long visits twice a year, but he regularly kept in touch with them through email, postcards, tapes, short notes, and a weekly telephone call. Paul's former wife had remained in the local community. She and Paul shared custody of their children, who spent alternate weeks in each home. Before their remarriage, Susan and Paul had taken a stepfamily information class at a local college so they understood the importance of the children's continued contact with their other parents. The couple supported shared parenthood however they could.

As single parents, Paul and Susan had both dated a variety of people and consequently felt they knew what they wanted in a relationship. Paul had attended workshops for divorced and single adults and had read several books that helped him recognize and understand how he had behaved in his former marriage. He learned lessons he didn't want to repeat, and Paul was more in touch with his feelings. Susan had returned to college and earned her degree in management — a long-cherished dream. She liked the new job she had since taken on. During their courtship, Susan and Paul had discussed having more children. Paul was already supporting four and money loomed as a future problem area. Still, Susan looked forward to the day when she and Paul would have their own child. After seeing they could both manage careers and expenses with enough income left over to pay for child care and household help, he agreed that adding an "ours" child to their lives might be possible. But they agreed to wait until their children were more settled into stepfamily living and, as a couple, they were managing discipline better.

At first, they'd considered moving into Susan's roomy old house, which could easily accommodate their large stepfamily, but they decided making a fresh start would be wiser. They found a house that was new to everyone and let the children help make decisions about their rooms.

The first year or so of remarriage was challenging. Paul and Susan had very different ways of doing things and they argued about who was right. Paul missed daily contact with his children; sometimes he felt guilty and resentful. Susan struggled to keep up with her job and find enough time for Paul and her children. Realizing she felt indifferent toward Paul's children, Susan worried that something was wrong with her. She began to think it might be better not to have another child. Although Susan and Paul were able to talk with each other about their feelings, their concerns deepened when they couldn't resolve them. After months of continual arguments about discipline, the couple finally agreed to talk with a professional counselor who knew a lot about stepfamily dynamics.

The counselor listened as Paul and Susan shared their concerns. Both feared that their new family was failing and that pressure was creating more stress. Although they believed some confusion was normal, they didn't realize how much their differences were creating problems. Susan and Paul spent several sessions with the counselor, clarifying some expectations and learning more how stepfamilies worked. The counselor guided them to a local support group for stepfamilies and assured them that the troubles they were dealing with were the same ones most stepfamilies faced early on. After attending a few meetings, they began to realize that they weren't alone, and it felt great to talk with others sharing similar struggles. Their fears lessened. As Susan and Paul began to spend more time together, their relationship strengthened and many of the problems diminished. The couple began to renew faith in their love for each other and to trust the process of making a stepfamily. When they still couldn't agree on discipline, someone in the support group told them about a parenting class at the local elementary school.

Paul and Susan had been warned that stepfamily living held many challenges; now they knew how true this was! But they also knew their commitment to meeting those challenges would make the difference and that their stepfamily would be successful. And it was!

Two stepfamily scenarios. Two different ways of approaching the challenge of remarriage with children. And two very different results; one far more effective.

By not preparing for remarriage and by believing some myths about stepfamily living, like Amy and John, you might develop some very unrealistic expectations for your new life together. After a while, if your hopes and dreams remained unfulfilled, you'll start to feel disappointed and defeated. You might have different ideas than your partner about raising children. Worse, you may be unaware that discipline dilemmas will most likely cause the most problems in your new stepfamily. If you deny the problems or keep quiet and avoid discussing your feelings, everything can get out of control quickly, as they did for Amy and John. They remarried too soon. With too little helpful information, unresolved grief, and inadequate skills, Amy and John denied their ever-increasing family problems until it was too late. Sadly, they became another remarriage divorce statistic.

Paul and Susan did it differently — and more wisely. Before moving into their new relationship, each had worked on completing important growth tasks — including resolving former relationship issues. They improved interactions with their former spouses, even talking about what would happen if either of them were to remarry one day. During their courtship, Paul and Susan noticed some differences in their approaches to raising children, so they talked about taking a parenting class. The couple discussed the specifics of where they would live, how to manage their money, and even whether to add another child to their already complex family. They asked hard questions that many people avoid because they fear that such discussions might rock the boat. They saw a professional to help fine-tune their communication skills and to work through some new issues that had developed. Sometimes they laughed at how unromantic these hard talks were, but this wise couple knew that reality could kill their romance if they weren't well prepared. After their marriage, they shared their fears and feelings; when they couldn't resolve matters, they sought support to stay on track.

Do you identify with John and Amy? Or with Susan and Paul? Even if you approached stepfamily living like John and Amy, and family life has become challenging, it's not too late to get back on the track toward success. Or, like Susan and Paul, maybe you tried to learn something about the stepfamily by reading a book or attending a class in advance. Maybe you talked with others who live in stepfamilies. Perhaps your approach was, or is, somewhere in between.

Stepfamilies *can* work well. You can find pride and satisfaction and reap rich rewards, as many in healthy stepfamilies do. Some cynics say the idea of "family" is dying; reality reveals otherwise. While traditional families once existed to fill economic needs, today's families focus on fulfilling emotional needs as well. Whatever form a family takes, a happy family life still remains the goal of most people. Isn't that yours?

These days, families take many forms. You've probably already lived in several kinds. You were born into your *family of origin*, your biological family. Later, if you married, you created a nuclear family that may have produced children. Often, this family form is called *traditional*. When that family ended, through divorce or the death of your partner, you may have become part of a single-parent family, either rearing your children alone or sharing parenthood with your former partner. Maybe you had a child and never married. You may have a gay or lesbian relationship. One biological parent may be absent from your children's lives. There are many kinds of families, but whatever form it takes, each is a *real* family! Every family needs to provide an environment in which children can be reared successfully, and where a sense of love, unity, and happiness can be achieved. And now, upon remarriage, or by virtue of blending two families, you are creating a *stepfamily*.

To outsiders, a healthy stepfamily can look just like any other family. But the stepfamilies that are truly successful know they are different from the start and accept and respect those differences! They don't pretend to be traditional families! A successful stepfamily comes in many sizes and shapes. It may be large or relatively small. Depending upon legal custody and shared parenting arrangements, it may be a full-time or a part-time stepfamily. Sometimes adults with children live together but haven't legally married; they too comprise a kind of stepfamily. For our definition purposes, *a stepfamily is a family in which at least one of the adult partners has children from a prior relationship.*

Do you wonder how the stepfamily got its name? The term is rooted in the Anglo-Saxon word *steöpchild,* meaning bereaved or orphaned child. Cinderella was such a child, and stories like hers have helped give the word *stepfamily* a generally negative image. At one time, most stepfamilies formed after the death of a parent. Today most begin following a divorce and single-parent family living. Some people have tried to create a new name for the stepfamily to avoid the negative image. Adjectives like *blended, re-coupled, remarried, binuclear, combined, prefabricated, reconstituted,* and even *synergistic* have all been used to describe this special family form. New labels, however, are merely new masks. All of them cover up an important reality: the stepfamily is a different kind of family with special obstacles and opportunities, special strengths and stresses. Changing the name of your family helps little; learning how it works and accepting those realities is what will make a difference and head you toward success.

Whether you are considering remarriage, are living together, or have lived in a stepfamily for some time, you can learn to build a healthy family life, making your stepfamily strengths work for you. To make your stepfamily successful, to build from your differences rather than deny them, you need to understand the inherent challenges you face. By focusing on specific relationships within the stepfamily, *Strengthening Your Stepfamily* will help you come to understand both the problems and the potential of your stepfamily.

Chapter 1, *A Different Kind of Family,* examines what makes your stepfamily different from the start. Understanding the structural and developmental differences that make each stepfamily unique will help you reduce your struggles.

Chapter 2, *Clearing the Path to Stepfamily Success,* explains common myths and realistic expectations that can invite trouble.

Chapter 3, *Letting Go of the Past,* explains the importance of completing your "emotional divorce" and other grief work before continuing on your stepfamily journey. You'll learn how the tools of divorce counseling, divorce mediation, and personal therapy can help you prepare for remarriage and building a healthy stepfamily.

Chapter 4, *Your Stepfamily Journey,* describes the normal developmental process of making a stepfamily and stresses the importance of taking time to move through those predictable stages.

Chapter 5, *Creating a Comfortable Stepfamily,* provides encouragement guidelines of attention, acceptance, appreciation and affection. Nurturing the "four A's" will allow you to merge two separate ways of doing things into one way as you build a new family history.

Chapters 6, 7, & 8, *Strengthening Your Couple Relationship,* focus on your new couple relationship — the key to stepfamily stability. You'll identify strengths and weaknesses and learn the importance of sharing and communicating. This exploration my identify some unfinished premarital tasks you've left undone and encourages you to revisit and resolve these issues.

Chapter 9, *Recreating Roles and Relationships,* addresses what it means to become a truly effective stepparent — the roles you'll play and the talents you'll need to develop.

Chapter 10, *Overcoming Stepfamily Obstacles,* examines stepfamily configurations and special challenges that create confusion for new and unaware stepparents.

Chapter 11, *Dealing with Stepfamily Discipline,* explores the number one issue that new stepfamilies face and explains why it's so difficult.

Chapter 12, *Why Do Children Misbehave?* examines behavior from a motivational view and guides you how to change your child's misbehaviors into effective ones.

Chapters 13, 14, & 15, *Your Stepchild's Challenges,* discuss specific issues your children face, and allow you to see stepfamily life from their perspective. As you learn what to expect and to understand some of your children's actions, you'll be better prepared to help them deal with the challenges of *emotional healing, differences,* and *stepfamily relationships.*

Chapter 16, *Hope! The Heart of Your Stepfamily,* examines much powerful strength to remember when the journey gets challenging. Stepfamily strengths offer gifts to family members that help you heal and grow.

Included at key points throughout the book are unique "Stepfamily Workshop" sections, that offer you opportunities to extend and apply what you've learned in the preceding chapters, and to check out how you're doing in *Strengthening Your Stepfamily.*

There are many special, rich rewards to gain from stepfamily living. Challenges that at first seem troublesome, or even overwhelming, can lead to growth and expanded horizons for all family members. *Strengthening Your Stepfamily* will help you gain information and skills that can lead your family to success. Your commitment is the only other tool required.

1

A Different Kind of Family

It took me a long time to realize that divorce didn't end my family — it simply changed it. Now, remarriage has changed my family again. Jane and her kids haven't replaced anybody or anything in my life: better than that, they've added to it. Our stepfamily is a very special kind of family and we're working at making it better and better! But it's definitely a different kind of family!

The stepfamily *is* a different kind of family. And it's a very special kind of family. The variety of backgrounds, past experiences, and values that go into making it offer the potential for a family life that's as enriching as it is challenging. Meeting the challenge of stepfamily living requires patience and perseverance, knowledge and skills. The more awareness you gain early on, the smoother and steadier your progress will be.

This journey to success is a process; it takes time. Depending on the amount of preparation done by both partners before such a marriage, it can take up to several years for a stepfamily to stabilize — for everyone to be truly comfortable with one another. While this may seem like a long time, just recall how much you and your children have been through until now.

If you have not married or been a parent before and are now a stepparent, it's important that you understand all the changes your partner and his or her children have experienced, so your expectations will be realistic. With realistic expectations, acceptance will be easier for you.

This chapter provides a foundation of basic information upon which your stepfamily can build. As you start out, of course, your stepfamily will be affected by stress. By understanding what is happening, you'll be able to cope better. Above all, your entire family needs to recognize a basic reality: *your stepfamily is a different kind of family.* Some of those differences make it impossible to function like your first families and, the more you accept this reality, the easier the journey will be. Much of the material in this chapter will explore why this is so.

Stepfamily: A New Shape and Structure

"We're a special kind of family with a different kind of structure." When you and your family members can make this positive statement about living in a stepfamily, you'll be on your way to reaching your potential. A stepfamily is not worse than, better than, or a substitute for other families in which you have lived; it is simply different.

Too often, stepfamilies deny this reality. Consciously or unconsciously, they try to be like the traditional families they just came from — only better. This causes stress and leads many stepfamilies down the path to trouble. But understanding and accepting that your stepfamily is *different* provides a strong foundation for success. It allows family members to build on those special qualities and strengths that make your stepfamily one of a kind.

Let's take a look at some of the differences that make each stepfamily unique.

Stepfamily Difference #1: Born of Loss

A newly formed stepfamily often presents a paradox: along with joy and hope lingers sadness. You may feel depressed and your children may seem sad — just when you'd hoped everyone would be happy. If the future looks so rosy, why are you feeling blue? As changes continue to take place, everyone in your stepfamily is confronting loss in some specific way.

Two people entering marriage for the first time usually haven't experienced the major losses of death or divorce that the members of a new stepfamily have known. These losses affect the very stability of your stepfamily in many ways. But as you begin to identify, mourn, and let go of this sadness, your stepfamily can move to a higher level of awareness and satisfaction.

Kids have lost control, contact, and continuity. No one in the stepfamily has experienced more loss than your children. They had no choice or control in parental decisions, yet their lives have been changed forever. There's a good chance they've lost daily contact with one parent. They may have had to move and, if so, they lost major touchstones: school, teachers, home, neighborhood friends and familiar activities, maybe having their own room. Financial changes may have created losses as well. If, for example, their mother began working outside the home, or changed from a part-time to a full-time job, the children probably lost some of the attention they were accustomed to when she had more time for them.

Before the remarriage, everyone pulled together to make things work, and the kids probably adjusted to life in a single-parent family. Many children recall that they liked the special family closeness and personal attention they experienced during that time. But for many kids, remarriage threatens this closeness and represents yet another of the many changes your family has undergone. The hardest thing children in stepfamilies must learn is to share a parent, not only with stepsiblings, but with another adult. Many children harbor the fantasy that one day their parents will work things out and get back together — that their family will be restored. Remarriage forces children to confront the loss of this dream. Depending upon age and psychological maturity, children may respond to remarriage much as they did to divorce or parental death. Chapter 13, *Your Stepchild's Challenges I,* explores these losses further.

The biological parent has lost status and stability. Between marriages you experienced losses and changes, some of which you may not have recognized. These changes began with the loss of your marriage partner — through death, divorce, or ending a long-term live-in relationship — and the structure, status, and stability your relationship provided. When it ended, your self-esteem might have slipped and your courage might have disappeared as you faced the future alone in a challenging new role. You might have blamed yourself for the divorce, wondering, "What's the matter with me?" And, like many divorced people, you might also have suffered financial loss, forcing you to make radical changes in your lifestyle. It is important that you become aware of these losses, some subtle and intangible, and acknowledge them.

One of the most difficult things many divorced parents face is the loss of daily contact with their children. In the past, it was usually men who coped with this; today, as fathers take a greater role in their children's lives, many women experience this loss as well.

Absentee mothers say they never dreamed that not being with their children would be so painful. The stigma attached to non-custodial parents — especially mothers — and the lack of support and sympathy from today's society compounds their loss.

Upon remarriage, the parents whose children live elsewhere often find themselves sharing responsibility for their new spouse's children. While seemingly pleasant on the surface, this daily interaction with stepchildren may actually intensify the pain of stepparents who don't see their own children often. Parents cut off from their biological children often feel guilty: to compensate, they may respond by avoiding a serious commitment to their stepchildren. This holding back — often unconscious — does little to build respect and trust within the stepfamily. Yet because stepchildren have already lost much of their faith in adults and themselves, building trust is essential to stepfamily success.

For some new stepparents, a long-held marriage dream is shattered. People not previously married who choose divorced or widowed partners may become stepparents before ever having been biological parents. They too face a loss: the loss of privacy and intimacy they had imagined would be part of their newlywed bliss. Fresh from the ceremony, these stepparents face the "instant family" they've acquired — perhaps far different from their dream family. Visions of romantic dinners and cozy times alone with their new spouse become realities of hot dogs and miniature-golf games with the kids. A hoped-for lazy Sunday may turn into a mad dash to an early soccer game. And, when a dream is shattered, there will inevitably be resentment and hostility.

In chapter 3 you'll learn how to deal with these losses that are a normal part of a stepfamily's early development.

Stepfamily Difference #2: Nonresidential Parent

One of the most important differences between the stepfamily and the traditional nuclear family is the "presence" of the nonresidential parent. While this biological parent may be *physically* absent from the daily scene in the stepfamily home, he or she is *psychologically* present to everyone living there. As a custodial parent or a stepparent, you might wish you could change this fact. But although the role your child's other parent once played in *your* life has changed, one reality will never change: your former partner will always be your child's parent. Depending upon how old your children were when your marriage ended, they had probably already developed an identity and sense of well-being that came, in part, from the other parent. Whatever contact and closeness this parent can continue to provide will be essential to your child's psychological well-being.

A different kind of family creates a different kind of honeymoon.

Your children's ability to continue a healthy relationship with their other parent is largely up to you. Under the strain of the separation and divorce, you may have said some harsh things about this person, fostering a negative image of the parent in your children's eyes. If your relationship with your former spouse *remains* a negative one, continued unresolved feelings may be played out through the children. Your adult hostility and unresolved feelings creates loyalty conflicts for them, one of the greatest challenges kids of divorce face. This hurts your children and damages your relationship with them. When your relationship with their other parent is neutral or — better yet — positive, the children can be free of loyalty conflicts. They can grow up knowing they are valued and loved by both parents. Your children will reap the rewards if you transform your relationship with their other parent from partner to co-parent. Ultimately, so will you. When you and your former spouse can respect one another, you'll feel good about

Your children will reap the rewards if you transform your relationship with their other parent from partner to co-parent. Ultimately, so will you. When you and your former spouse can respect one another, you'll feel good about yourselves and reduce loyalty conflicts for your children.

yourselves and reduce loyalty conflicts for your children. Further, the more positive your attitude toward your former partner, the greater the chance that your children will adjust to their new stepparent more easily. They'll feel no need to defend their absent parent and can reap the benefit of having two caring adults of the same sex to guide them — a father and a stepfather, or a mother and a stepmother.

If you are a stepparent, your acceptance of the other biological parent as part of the stepfamily reality is a loving gift to your spouse and stepchildren. Remember, you're an addition to their lives, not a replacement.

Stepfamily Difference #3: Children Move Between Two Homes

Regardless of legal custody arrangements, your children will most likely spend time at both Mom's house and Dad's house. Whether they spend every weekend or a single month each summer in the other home, your children need to feel that they belong to, can learn life's lessons from, and are expected to contribute to — and be responsible in — *both families*.

Moving between two homes is not easy: transitions rarely are. Parting from loved family members is difficult for children *and* adults. Children have to learn to cope with friends and possessions being in two places. They face two sets of rules and routines. Too many children are treated as visitors or guests in the nonresidential parent's home, sleeping on sofas and living out of suitcases. Try to avoid this so that your children don't feel that they are intruders rather than family members — even when they come for a short time.

When your children travel between two homes, they can feel supported and wanted by others. You can provide a permanent space for each child — a room, corner, cupboard, or drawer — depending on your available space. You can display their artwork year-round, whether your children are there or not. Include them in your family plans with a letter or telephone call if your child isn't scheduled to be with you when something special is happening. Spontaneity is challenging when two households are involved but it's part of creating joy in your stepfamily. Belonging, learning, contributing: this trio fosters psychological and emotional well-being for your children.

In spite of the two household challenges, many long-term benefits can result. When your children move between two homes, they are offered new learning opportunities. The physical reality of living with two families in two places broadens children's horizons. It allows them to see different lifestyles and family systems. Step-children may gain travel experience; and two geographies provide new friends, different customs, and activities.

If you are a stepparent, your acceptance of the other biological parent as a stepfamily reality is a loving gift to your spouse and stepchildren. Remember! You're an addition to, not a replacement in, their lives.

Psychological strength can be another benefit. As children develop relationships with two families, they learn to view life from different perspectives. Parents and stepparents may offer new skills, values, or ways to cope. Step-siblings may introduce new and different interests and hobbies. When faced with making decisions, children exposed to these varied approaches will have two sets of experience to draw from.

Stepfamily couples, too, can benefit from children's coming and going. The nonresidential couple can find a child's time in their home enjoyable and enriching. For many, it can open new vistas in their marriage: if young people aren't part of the usual daily scene, interacting with visiting children might bring a refreshing new dimension to the couple's relationship. For the couple in a custodial home, the time the children spend with their other family gives the adults special alone time together to work on their relationship — or to play together!

Stepfamily Difference #4: Previous Parent-Child Relationships

Because your children existed before your stepfamily formed, previous relationships and understandings did too. This is yet another important stepfamily difference.

As a biological parent, you have shared many years of memories and alliances with your children. When conflict arises, it's natural to align yourself with your children — after all, it seems as though you're really defending your own identity and child-rearing methods. If you're a stepparent, you need to accept this strong biological parent-child bond and try to avoid feeling rejected or unfairly treated when your partner aligns with his children. Stepparents must get this important difference or you will create much suffering for yourselves and conflict in your new marriage.

The relationship between biological parents and their children is long-standing! Further, the longer your new partner and her children lived in a single-parent family before the remarriage, the stronger their child-parent bond has grown. As a new stepparent your relationship with your partner and her children may be relatively recent. When you come to understand this powerful pre-existing bond — biological, legal, and emotional — you can focus on building friendship with your stepchildren. As rules and roles are explored, this growing friendship allows stepfamily members to function in a relatively neutral family territory, reducing the pressure some of you to love each other overnight. Indeed, "instant love" is one of several destructive myths; the important goal is to build respect and trust. The chapters that follow provide guidelines for building various new stepfamily relationships.

Stepfamily Difference #5: Different Family Backgrounds

In traditional families, people share a common background. Rituals and routines are understood; unspoken rules are often quite clear. Everyone knows how and where holidays and traditions will be celebrated. Religious practices are generally shared by most family members.

In stepfamilies, however, people come together with diverse histories and expectations. Maybe a Jew and a Gentile have married. Perhaps a white and black American couple created a stepfamily. A man from England might marry a Greek woman. At first, these different backgrounds and cultures may create great confusion; later, as family members learn more about each other's histories, negotiate new traditions, and make new memories together, these differences can enrich family life. As you learn alternative ways of thinking and behaving, and learn to understand another's belief system, children and adults in stepfamilies gain a broader view of life and teach each other helpful living skills. Acceptance helps merge your two families into one. But it takes time.

Stepfamily Difference #6: Lack of Legal Relationships

In traditional families, everyone is legally related. These legalities provide family members with rights to insurance, inheritance, medical attention, access to school records, and other important benefits; above all, this legal relationship represents a commitment between adults and children. In the stepfamily, while marriage creates a legal bond exists between the husband and wife, it does not

Since stepfamily members share no common history, traditions may at first collide.

Stepfamily traditions can be built around sharing so many things! Here's just a few possibilities:

- The stepfamily's anniversary
- Tuesday-night spaghetti suppers
- The first day of spring or autumn
- The first snowfall of the year
- A monthly game night
- A stepfamily journal or scrapbook
- Sunday-night suppers that kids plan and prepare
- Any number of other dates, events, or activities meaningful to your stepfamily.

between stepparents and stepchildren. In most states and provinces the law does not recognize this adult-child relationship. Stepfamily issues such as custody, visitation, and child support may be decided by the court, but the court's decisions are subject to individual circumstances, state or local statutes, and different interpretations.

Should I adopt my stepchildren? You or your partner might talk about considering adoption but be very careful before moving on the idea. Examine your reasons closely and be sure they aren't about trying to push out the other biological parent or some other control issue. Remember, for adoption to occur, you need the permission and release from the other biological parent to proceed; few parents will do that. Nor should they because, to have a successful stepfamily, your goal is to integrate the other parents in as a healthy a way as possible — not push them out of your children's lives. That could ultimately cause far more trouble down the road. While there might be some specific instances where stepfamily adoption is appropriate, talk it over with a professional who can help you examine your motives. Rather than focusing on legal measures, work hard at building strong, healthy relationships. The law cannot legislate love and, indeed, can make things worse.

If a remarriage ends, stepparents have no legal right to a continued relationship with children to whom they may have developed strong personal ties. While stepparents have, in some instances, been granted visitation rights or custody, a ruling of this sort is still unusual. Each case is determined by such factors as the length of the relationship, the motive for seeking visitation or custody, the role the stepparent plays in your child's life, and the quality of your child's relationship with the her biological parent.

The law, with regard to the stepfamily, remains filled with inconsistencies. Family mediation, child custody and support, visitation rights, inheritance, insurance, tuition, medical expenses, and adoption are all areas that need to be addressed in an effort to clarify and improve the legal aspects of stepfamily living. It will take expanded social awareness to instigate the necessary legislative and judicial changes. Adults in stepfamilies need to advocate for thorough examination of current laws and practices before changes will come about.

Many obstacles remain in the stepfamily's search for satisfaction and success. Unrealistic, undisclosed, and unexamined expectations are one. Unexplored myths are another. Both these troublemakers are caused by a lack of information.

2

Clearing the Path to Stepfamily Success

E xpectations, myths, assumptions, beliefs... All these very human — but
often hazardous — ideas can be real obstacles to success in creating a
family. And, as you've already learned, stepfamilies are subject to even bigger
hurdles because they are very different from traditional first families.

Examine Your Expectations — Communication is the Key!

For the stepfamily, unrealistic expectations, positive or negative,
can cause extra pressure or become self-fulfilling prophecies that
create negative outcomes.

Often our reactions to life are based on our expectations. We all
carry hidden agendas — unspoken plans or wishes for what we
want and hope will happen. And we have certain expectations
we hope can be met, but many adults are afraid to discuss these
expectations before the remarriage because it doesn't feel romantic
or, worse, it might shake things up too much.

Many adults hope to make up to their children for the past. With
a new marriage, you anticipate another chance to succeed. Your
expectations are positive and you are optimistic about the future.
For your children, it may be very different. Children, especially
teenagers, who take a more negative view of their parent's
remarriage, may feel anxious. With fairy tales providing a poor
stepfamily image, some children may actually feel dread and
apprehension, fearing the worst. Children who have lived in a
single-parent family for a long time, or sense that there will be less
contact with their other biological parent, may view the remarriage
with a sense of loss.

The reality is that the most critical skill needed in any marriage is
communication! Talking about issues and sharing your feelings

about specific issues brings into the open expectations of adults and children. It's essential for you to talk about your hopes and needs, and it's helpful for you to encourage your children to do so also. If you are forming a new stepfamily, or living in a stepfamily in which you think the expectations may be different, unclear, or unmet, now is the time for you and your partner to start communicating about these issues. Here are some topics for discussion:

Roles. How will each of you relate to your stepchildren? What are your rights and obligations where they're concerned? Who will discipline whom?

Rules and responsibilities. Who will take care of which household chores? How are rules to be enforced? Who'll feed the dog? Take the children to the dentist?

Your relationship with your partner. When will you spend time alone together? How often will you go away without the children? How will you communicate your fears? Resolve differences? Grow together? Will you be willing to see a family therapist if things get difficult?

Your relationship with the other parent. What issues with the other parent(s) still need to be resolved? What level of involvement do you expect from the other parent? Can you co-parent with your former mate without causing your new partner to feel threatened?

Possible custody changes. Can you handle having your partner's children come to live with you? How would you feel if your child should ask to live with your former spouse? What will you do if this happens?

Work and money. Will both of you work outside the home? How will the two of you manage child-care duties? Who'll pay for what? Will you be a "one-pot" family or keep separate accounts?

Love and remarriage. Have both of you mourned the losses of former relationships? Let go of failure feelings about divorce? Do each of you truly have an "emotional divorce?" What do you expect from your couple relationship?

Children and stepchildren. Do you have certain expectations about how two sets of children should get along? How children are to relate to the adults? Do you understand the value of family meetings? How do you plan to help the process work smoothly? What pressures are you feeling about accepting or loving each other's children? What pressures are the children feeling in this marriage? Have children completed mourning earlier losses?

If you don't discuss these issues, how can either of you possibly know what is expected or whether it's possible to meet those expectations? Can you identify other areas of stepfamily living where you may have unclear expectations?

"Should we move to a new home?"

"Should we have a baby?"

"Should we all observe the same holidays, regardless of our religious beliefs?"

"Where will the kids spend the holidays and vacations?"

Debunking the Myths

Myths are based on misperceptions and stereotypes, and in no way represent the real world. Myths are closely linked to expectations, and when these expectations aren't met, the stepfamily may experience feelings of disappointment, inadequacy, and profound discouragement. Our beliefs and expectations guide our attitude and affect our behavior; when we start with misperceptions or myths, we set ourselves up for disappointment, and perhaps disaster! Some common stepfamily myths are far removed from reality:

Myth: **Stepfamilies should work just like traditional families.** *Reality:* **The stepfamily is a different kind of family; it does not function in the standard traditional way.**

We've already examined several major differences in your family's structure that make it difficult or impossible to function like you did in your former, more traditional, family. They were:

- Your new family is born from loss
- In many areas, no legal relationships exist between stepparents & stepchildren
- The "other" biological parent remains important to your stepfamily
- A powerful biological parent-child bond predates your new couple bond
- Your children move between two households

Chart 1

MOVING FROM UNREALISTIC TO REALISTIC EXPECTATIONS

In your stepfamily, it's important for partners to recognize unrealistic expectations and replace them with realistic ones that can support your family, rather than sabotage it. This chart points out the positive effects such clarity and changes in your thinking can have on your feelings and the outlook of all stepfamily members.

Unrealistic Expectation	*Underlying Hope*	*Resulting Feelings*
"We will all love one another."	To be a happy, harmonious family.	Guilt when love doesn't occur quickly.
"Life in our former families won't matter."	To forget the past and make a fresh start.	Isolation from each other; fragmentation of parts of ourselves.
"We'll do it better this time around."	To make up for past sadness and loss.	Disappointment in our new family when everything doesn't go smoothly.
"We will and *must* function smoothly as a family."	To present a picture of family unity to friends, families, outsiders.	Discouragement about all the differences to be resolved; defensiveness about how outsiders see us.
"Everything will fall quickly into place."	To find immediate success and happiness as a stepfamily.	Fear that new marriage is failing and that this family might end.
"Our children will feel as happy about the remarriage as we do."	To give children security and stability.	Resentment toward children for not being happier and blaming our partners.
"Our stepchildren will respond readily to our efforts at discipline. Discipline won't present difficulties for us as a couple."	To have a positive effect on children's lives.	Anger resulting from division about rules, responsibilities, acceptable behavior, and discipline techniques.

Realistic Expectation	Resulting Feelings
"Love may or may not develop later; what's important is accepting and respecting each other."	Satisfaction and comfort among stepfamily members.
"Differences in our backgrounds will remain part of our daily lives. We all need to deal with these differences, and we can all grow because of them."	Connection to, and pride in, the past; optimism about enriching one another's lives in the future.
"This new family will be neither better nor worse — it simply is different."	Excitement at the prospect of building this special family together.
"All stepfamilies have difficulties and differences to work through. Presenting a polished picture to outsiders isn't what's really important."	Relief to know others face similar challenges; greater ease in working to build understanding and closeness.
"Becoming a stepfamily takes time; satisfaction comes from working together to build our family."	Confidence that we can build a strong stepfamily and satisfaction in our gradual progress. Less discouragement when obstacles and setbacks occur.
"Children will feel confused — both happy and angry — about our remarriage; they had no choice either in the ending of their first family or in the forming of this new one."	Empathy and responsiveness in dealing with the children in our stepfamily.
"Many children, teenagers especially, will be unwilling to accept authority from stepparents. Just as in all families, adults won't automatically agree about how to discipline."	Less resentment or sense of threat. More patience and willingness to compromise. Interested more in building relationships than in wielding authority, in cooperating, rather than competing with partner to do this.

Myth: **Stepparents are cruel and insensitive.**
Reality: **Stepparents share the same human qualities as other adults.**

Fiction and fairy tales have given bad press to stepparents — especially to stepmothers, who may consequently spend too much of their energy over-compensating for this negative image. Early on, the stepparent's role is challenging and, like all parents trying to do their best, stepparents make mistakes. Unfortunately, your mistakes — the same ones that any parent — step or not might make — become magnified by other people, and by stepparents themselves.

Myth: **A stepfamily is created instantly.**
Reality: **While marriage vows, or physically moving two families together into a single household create stability, becoming a happy, loving and functional stepfamily is a gradual, long-term process.**

All stepfamilies seem to go through certain stages — some quite difficult and chaotic — before they begin to stabilize and make a commitment to work together. But there is a clear and predictable trail map to guide you during your stepfamily journey. We'll examine the stages of stepfamily development in chapter 4.

Myth: **All stepfamily members should and will love one another.**
Reality: **It takes time to build caring relationships.**

There is no such thing as "instant love." Because everyone has suffered loss and experienced change, time and patience are needed to build stepfamily relationships. Trust levels are low and fears are high. No one *has* to love anyone else, but when people concentrate on respect and acceptance, warmth and friendship may, in time, come naturally. Sometimes love, too, will grow.

Myth: **Stepfamilies formed after a death have fewer problems than those formed after a divorce.**
Reality: **All stepfamilies face challenges and painful feelings.**

Unresolved grief, whether the result of death *or* divorce, can get in the way of building new relationships. People have to say good-bye to *any* departed partner or parent before moving on, and mourning takes time. To have a successful remarriage, it's crucial to let go of anger and guilt in a healthy way and make sure you have achieved an "emotional divorce."

Myth: **Part-time stepfamilies have it easier than full-time step-families.**
Reality: **When children live between two homes, *both* families experience stress.**

As they seek a sense of belonging, adults and children alike will experience the stress that the challenges of transition create. It takes time for your children to learn to live with and adjust to two sets of rules and expectations.

There are probably as many myths as there are stepfamilies; no doubt you can identify others. Accepting stepfamily myths — whether consciously or unconsciously — allows the unrealistic notions and misperceptions about stepfamily living to grow stronger, causing sadness, disappointment, and problems. The resulting disappointment can lead to defeat, and possibly to another divorce.

Other ideas and beliefs that you hold about stepfamily living may be getting in the way. Take this "What I Believe About Stepfamily Living" true-or-false quiz to see how you can change misperceptions into accurate beliefs, and create realistic expectations. You'll find the answers on page 33.

"What I Believe About Stepfamily Living"

Mark these statements true or false, according to your beliefs:

___ 1. A stepfamily is like any other family only there are more people.

___ 2. Most people have dealt with past losses before they remarry.

___ 3. An ideal way to show a serious commitment to your stepchildren is to adopt them.

___ 4. Stepfamilies formed after a death sometimes have fewer problems than after a divorce.

___ 5. It takes from six months to a year for a stepfamily to become fully stabilized.

___ 6. Stepfathers should immediately start disciplining their stepchildren.

___ 7. For the sake of the children, adults should avoid contact with their former partners.

___ 8. If a stepparent is doing a fine job, children probably don't need to see much of their other biological parent.

___ 9. Stepparents must try to get close to their stepchildren right away; once too much time passes, close relationships cannot form.

___ 10. Adults who discipline sternly with their own children are especially effective with their stepchildren.

___ 11. It's wise for remarried couples to deal with their stepfamily problems privately and avoid sharing what's happening with relatives and friends.

___ 12. Talking about sexual feelings among stepfamily members often helps reduce such feelings.

___ 13. One of the children's greatest difficulties involves loyalty conflicts.

___ 14. The most effective stepparents start out by being a friend or another parent figure in stepchildren's lives.

___ 15. Children who have lived in an effective single-parent family a long time welcome their parent's remarriage.

___ 16. If you're already remarried and your former partner won't let go emotionally, there's little you can do to change the pattern between you.

___ 17. Problems you never resolved with your own parents can affect your relationship with your new partner and stepchildren.

___ 18. If you're remarried, and you and your former partner continue to have conflict, the two of you could benefit from some counseling — if you're both willing.

___ 19. Children adjust better to stepfamily living if you encourage them to suppress strong negative feelings and avoid talking about them.

___ 20. Stepfamilies move through predictable stages.

___ 21. While it takes time for love to develop between stepparents and stepchildren, this must happen or the family won't succeed.

___ 22. Professional counseling can help you reduce stepfamily confusion and conflict.

___ 23. Stepparents who feel sexually attracted to a teenage stepchild probably lack a secure couple relationship.

___ 24. Biological parents should discourage children from expressing negative feelings about their stepparent.

___ 25. Part-time stepfamilies have it easier than fulltime stepfamilies.

___ 26. Anger toward a former partner generally reflects a lack of an "emotional divorce."

___ 27. All of a child's parents-biological and stepparent-should always attend parent-teacher conferences and other school events.

___ 28. An effective stepparent helps children confront feelings of sadness, grief, and fear.

Reaching for Reality

As you read this book, you'll learn how to debunk stepfamily myths and replace misinformation with an understanding of reality. When you know what's normal *and* possible, you can adjust your expectations and begin to build a successful stepfamily. If you have been stuck at a difficult stage, awareness and education are the keys to help you change a cycle of defeat into one of success. If you have the courage to talk about your wants and needs, they can be met — and the challenges of living in a stepfamily can be dealt with creatively and effectively.

Getting the Help You Need

Agencies and professionals whose job it is to help families have, in recent years, generally become much more sensitive to the special needs of stepfamilies. Clergy, counselors and social workers, schools, legal and judicial professionals — even some publishers and media organizations — are better prepared than ever before to recognize and respond to the special qualities that make stepfamilies different.

The *church or synagogue* is in a powerful position to help. It provides for many the rite of passage that creates the stepfamily in the first place — the marriage ceremony. It also leaves its mark in other ways, by offering great hope to the stepfamily through education, as in pre-remarital counseling, where clergy and laypersons can teach the importance of commitment and communication for all marriage partners. You may be reading and discussing *Strengthening Your Stepfamily* as part of a family-education program sponsored by a synagogue or church, where you will gain the skills to move from stress to survival to strength.

Many *counselors, therapists, and social workers* have contributed greatly toward strengthening stepfamilies. No longer is the stepfamily viewed as an oddity or exception, or one that can be treated as a traditional nuclear family. They've learned what makes the stepfamily complicated and special — and how to turn stressors into strengths. By validating feelings, creating an awareness of what is happening and what can be expected, and teaching skills for helping the stepfamily deal with problems that may be occurring, these professionals are helping stepfamilies see themselves as normal. Millions of stepfamily members are learning that their feelings aren't unusual, that they aren't alone, and that there are actions they can take to strengthen their family.

School can be a steady, unchanging part of children's lives. When their families are in transition, children may see teachers as stable, important people to whom they can turn for help. Often, educators are the first to learn of a child's family crisis of death, divorce, or remarriage. They are in an ideal position to help — if they know how.

Those in the *legal profession* can help the stepfamily by becoming sensitized to its complex relationships and shortage of resources. Whatever the legal issue involved — adoption, custody, child support — the law cannot legislate love. Family mediation can allow couples to arrive at their own decisions about finances and custody arrangements. Legal professionals are learning that mutual agreements made by a divorcing couple will more likely be carried through than orders dictated by the courts.

Family law is state law. As for all families, the legal scenario for stepfamilies varies from state to state, so legal issues can get complicated. Some issues, such as access to school records or consent for medical care, may be determined by local policy, rather than state law. Each situation is unique, and required careful research and specific legal advice.

Since legal professionals are only beginning to recognize the complexities of stepfamily relationships, don't assume that any and all will be informed and empathetic about your family's needs. Exercise caution in selecting legal counsel, and consider those who have certifications in the specialty areas of divorce, stepfamilies, mediation and/or collaborative law. The recommendation of a trusted friend or local social service agency might be a good starting point.

Military families present another special situation. Clarifying legal issues is very important for military families as they anticipate deployment and need to provide stepparents with authority to safeguard their children in the absence of the biological parent. On virtually every military base, the Office of Family Advocacy staff is available to help with all kinds of family matters, and these specialists assist in pre-deployment preparation. Most of their family life educators and chaplains have had training in working with stepfamilies and are sensitized to the special issues involved. (The *Strengthening Stepfamilies* workshop is also offered on many bases.)

All of these agencies and professionals can affect your stepfamily in a positive way. But their potential to help begins with you — by reaching out to teachers, clergy, friends, and relatives to tell them what kind of support would benefit your family, and to local counseling agencies to seek guidance for yourself and your family.

A good place to start, if you have online access, might be a Google search on stepfamilies. You'll discover thousands of hits! A good site with many referrals to start is that of the Stepfamily Association of America: www.SAAfamilies.org.

It's clear that your stepfamily is a different kind of a family. Your exciting journey toward success begins by understanding these differences, clarifying your expectations, and debunking some of the stepfamily myths. It also involves assessing what "emotional baggage" you might have brought into your stepfamily and working that through. Chapter 3 guides you through that important process of letting go. All of these conscious choices can lead you toward strengthening your stepfamily.

Reach out now for the help you need. Changes are possible, but they must start with you!

The Stepfamily Workshop
Session One

Questions for Review

Chapter 1

1. Name six factors that make stepfamilies different from traditional nuclear families. Can you think of other differences?_____

2. Of all the factors making the stepfamily a different kind of family, which do you believe is the most important? Why?

3. What are some of the benefits of living in a stepfamily? List ideas both from reading Chapters 1 and 2, and from your own experience or thinking._____

Chapter 2

4. In what ways do unrealistic expectations affect your stepfamily? Specific individuals in your stepfamily? Your couple relationship?

5. What expectations do you, your partner, and the children have concerning your present or future stepfamily? How will you express your expectations and explore them?_____

6. What myths about stepfamilies have affected you? How can believing myths affect the welfare of a stepfamily?_____

7. What specific things can you expect from your school, church, synagogue, or community to help your stepfamily? What might be some steps you could take to help such institutions play a more effective and positive role? _____

_____

_____

Challenge to Conquer

Not too many months after they married, Sarah started talking to her new husband about adopting her two children. Ian was reluctant. He knew that Sarah and her former husband had a pretty unpleasant divorce, and that her feelings toward him remained extremely negative. Sarah made it difficult for the children on the rare times their father did try to visit them. She thought that if Ian adopted them, her children would have a more stable situation by being legally related to her new husband and his children. Ian worried that adoption might backfire and make things worse.

1. What might be some of Sarah's motivations behind her wish for Ian to adopt her children?_____

_____

_____

2. What would be the best thing for this stepfamily to do? Who has the major responsibility to make some changes? What changes need to be made and how can they be achieved?_____

_____

_____

3. How do you think adoption — or even the discussion of it — might affect Sarah's children? Should they have contact with their father even if he may not be the most effective father in the world? _____

_____

_____

Stepfamily Activity

This week, take time with your stepfamily to begin to create a new history. Gather around the kitchen table, or in a circle on the floor. Make a batch of popcorn or brownies. Talk about some things you'd like to have happen for your family. Together, set some goals. Have the children brainstorm ideas of trips they might want your stepfamily to take together. What activities do they like?

What are their wishes and dreams? What are yours? As everyone shares possibilities, let the children make a big chart and list the ideas with magic markers.

Discuss the idea of starting a scrapbook or photo album or journal (or a combination) that everyone can contribute to. Come up with a family mission statement and let everyone have input and describe what they want the family to be like. Last but not least, remember to have fun; you're creating your family history!

In the "Stepfamily Workshop" sessions throughout the book, we'll remind you to add items and to maintain the evolving record of your stepfamily history. Be creative and have fun with this project!

Answers to Chapter Two Quiz

1. F	8. F	15. F	22. T
2. F	9. F	16. F	23. F
3. F	10. F	17. T	24. F
4. T	11. F	18. T	25. F
5. F	12. T	19. F	26. T
6. F	13. T	20. T	27. F
7. F	14. T	21. F	28. T

Points to Ponder

- The stepfamily is a different kind of family. It is a real family and offers great possibilities for a rich family life.

- Making a stepfamily takes time — a long time. Be patient, because stability takes time to achieve.

- Acceptance is necessary to begin the process of building trust, a must for merging two separate families into one.

- The biological parent who doesn't live in your stepfamily remains very important to your children or stepchildren. Encourage continued contact.

- Children should be able to move comfortably between mom's house and dad's house. Understand that their transitions are stressful, and help them feel a sense of belonging in both homes.

- Unrealistic expectations and myths are the great destroyers of stepfamily potential. Clarify your agendas and expectations.

- Living in a stepfamily can offer day-to-day benefits, as well as many long-term rewards for adults and children.

3

Letting Go of the Past

Before you can begin a successful "stepfamily journey," you'll need to have examined your part in your ended relationship so that you can use those lessons in your remarriage. Good grieving, for yourself, and your children, can make an incredible difference for everyone.

Are you looking for a guarantee that your new stepfamily will succeed? Do you know how to heighten that probability? This chapter provides you with information to help you create the successful stepfamily you desire. Even if you're already remarried, if you have left the important work of grieving undone, you still can back up and clean up some of your emotional roadblocks. That's why information on the divorce process and your healing process is being included in this revised edition. We know from our work with families and from lots of feedback from readers that many of the challenges remarried families face are clearly connected to the leftover "emotional baggage" from former relationships. Unresolved feelings of grief, anger, and resentment can burden your new stepfamily in ways you may not even realize. As you read this, you'll become aware of what you have or have not done, and you'll learn how to start taking smart steps that will move you forward in creating your successful stepfamily.

Take Care of Yourself First

One great predictor of stepfamily success is how well your family members have healed from former losses. As you deal with the immense grief associated with the death or divorce of a partner, you'll need to work through many issues before starting a new relationship. As you struggle with ending your family as it once was, your best investment now is to be there for your children. You can improve your relationships with them during this transition, reassure them that they are loved, and help them with their feelings of sadness or anger. Parents may stop loving one another and living together but, through your children, you remain tied together.

As you complete your important emotional work of mourning the lost relationship, you'll be in a better position to help your children, who also need to grieve their changed family.

As you complete your important emotional work of mourning the lost relationship, you'll be in a better position to help your children, who also need to grieve their changed family. That means taking care of yourself first. Do you think that sounds selfish? It's not! Think about when you fly in a commercial airplane: the attendants advise that, should the oxygen masks drop during the flight, you put on your mask first. *Only then* do you proceed to put one on your child. Likewise, as your family moves through loss and change, when you take care of your own emotional distress — following the suggestions in this chapter and get yourself to a stronger place, then you can better guide your children through their grief and all the changes they face.

Taking care of yourself may be a foreign concept to you. Or maybe it got lost in the stress of your current reality. But how do you know you need something beyond a hot tub or a pound of chocolate? Serious self-care is about the critical need to find *you* in the midst of all that's going on during this time of transition. To discover what you want for the rest of your life. To start to follow dreams that might have become side-tracked during a youthful marriage. To become all you can be while staying on top of your most import role — as a parent. To get de-stressed. To avoid falling apart yourself when everything around you seems to be coming apart.

Symptoms for a major meltdown are many: overwhelmed, scattered, irritable, powerless. Are you paralyzed and plagued by uncertainty about everything? Fear, anger and guilt are probably causing your "stuckness" and you'll need to uncover the source of your fear. Do you feel scattered? Unable to focus? You're irritable and can't finish what you start. Quite likely you're on "information overload" as you're trying to juggle so much in the midst of great change. Rather than trying to master multi-tasking — at which you're probably already an expert — start by making lists, doing one thing at a time. Develop energizing habits: exercise, good nutrition, plenty of sleep. Hit the bookstore for ideas on how to make this happen, or get advice from a "roadrunner" friend.

Do you feel unworthy, powerless, overwhelmed? Are you allowing someone to chip away at your self-esteem? It's time to move away from people who put you down and find a new network where you feel supported and validated. Find a support group or a group of folks who share an interest you enjoy. Join a musical ensemble, hiking club, or health spa. If you're singing or exercising, you'll feel good about yourself and regain your power. Try dealing with your emotional stress in ways you've never considered before: massage, meditation, support groups. Journal away your anger and fear. Seriously consider working with a therapist who can help you say goodbye to your sorrow and stress.

While chocolate bars and hot tubs are great "quick fixes," serious commitment to taking care of you is more about refreshing and reviving yourself on a deep level. It's a spiritual journey toward wholeness. It's about remembering who you really are and coming home to yourself. Or perhaps finding your real self for the first time. Taking care of you and the changes it brings is a critical part of healing, for it will influence your choice of — and relationship with — a partner who would become a stepparent to your children.

Unresolved loss affects your stepfamily in various ways, and can handicap new relationships. A good barometer is to check in with how your children are feeling. When they are happy, you can feel successful as parents and stepparents. When your children are unhappy, or have problems, you may feel inadequate, or somehow at fault, as though you caused them to feel this way. In some ways, this may be true, because the changes they are experiencing resulted from adult decisions. As you face that reality, you may feel guilty. But if you continue to harbor guilt, anger, and sadness about the death or divorce that changed your family, your children will be affected, and their behavior may reflect those negative feelings. It's time to take some positive steps!

It's a Healthy Thing to Grieve

We all must mourn our losses. Grief is a normal and healthy process. Yet, many times we get negative messages about grief — that it's inappropriate or selfish; that it's weak or immature to show emotions. It's common for men to adopt this cultural belief and harbor their pain, often by hiding in work. Outwardly, they are stoic; inside they ache from holding in difficult feelings. If you feel embarrassed about the feelings you have, you may deny or suppress your sadness. You can actually make yourself physically sick from keeping things inside and, without a doubt, your suppressed feelings will carry over into new relationships.

Denied feelings are destructive to yourself and to your new stepfamily. Ultimately, your feelings will come out, but often that'll happen in unproductive or even harmful ways. In adults, suppressed feelings may be a contributing factor to alcohol abuse, depression, infidelity, illness, family violence, or hypochondria. Children may experience school problems, illness, delinquency, or phobias. Once you remarry, you might unknowingly project unresolved feelings onto new partners and stepchildren, delaying the bonding process that's necessary for successful stepfamily living.

Good grieving invites change, and change invites a challenge to transform your life and live up to your full potential. You owe it to yourself, and your new family, to choose happiness!

We'll offer more thoughts about grieving later in this chapter when we discuss the idea of "emotional divorce."

Say Good-bye to Your Old Life — Say Hello to Your New Stepfamily

Your role with your former partner changes; your role as parent continues. This challenging task involves ridding yourself of feelings that keep you tied to the past.

Quality beginnings start with successful endings. In order to get your new family life off to a great start, you'll need to take time to say good-bye to parts of your old life. When your first family ended, your role with your former partner changed, but your role as a parent continues. It's a real challenge for parents who now live apart to remain concerned about, supportive of, and involved with their children. This challenging task involves ridding yourself of feelings that keep you tied to the past.

If you can, for example, move from conflict and competition with your former spouse to clear communication and cooperation, your children will be the winners. Your efforts will make the transitions easier for them, while continued conflict will hurt your children in many ways. Some of your negative behaviors will be obvious; others more subtle. If you continue to have difficulty communicating with their other parent, your behavior will make it harder for them to accept stepfamily living and bond with their new stepparent.

Letting go of a marriage that is no longer healthy can be an exhausting and challenging process. Your "day in court" should mark the end of one period and the start of another. But divorce is rarely that simple. While the law provides the piece of paper that legally severs your relationship, the real work — freeing yourself emotionally from your former partner — must be done by you.

The late Dr. Bruce Fisher, in his popular divorce recovery guide *Rebuilding*, calls this process "disentanglement." He details the process of *accepting* that the old relationship is over and *getting on* with your new life.

Make a Plan

Wise divorcing adults create a "lesson plan." They learn all they can from the past, then use what they learn to make a better future. Usually, the process of change only begins its unpredictable course when you and your former partner can no longer bear the pain that old patterns produce, or when you begin to realize how much your negative interactions are hurting your children. Since most people do eventually remarry, it's wise to create a parenting plan at the time of the divorce that will continue to work later within a new family's structure, or that can be tweaked without having to resort to using the legal system. Such a plan needs to be clear and well-defined, yet flexible enough to work after remarriage of one or both partners

Problems may continue to surface well into your stepfamily life. Often, the challenges involve the children moving between mom's house and dad's house. Finances, discipline, and house rules can present additional issues from an unresolved divorce.

No Regrets

Leftover feelings of regret and resentment just might be the culprits keeping you from claiming an "emotional divorce."

Leftover feelings of *regret* and *resentment* just might be the culprits that have kept you from claiming the "emotional divorce" necessary to complete your work of forgiveness. *Resentments* are the feelings you retain about emotional injuries, affronts, or unmet needs and expectations. Resentments reflect angry feelings. *Regrets* are rooted in your feelings about disappointments and dissatisfaction in your former relationship; they involve sadness and loss. Regrets often involve guilt. Generally, resentments involve feelings toward others, in this case your former partner; regrets usually involve only yourself.

Are you still too angry to consider forgiveness? Does your heart still hurt from the shock and sadness of the loss? You might be thinking revenge and that you'll never forgive him. But forgiveness is less about the other person and more a gift to you from yourself! In a way, it's a selfish act so that you can be free and feel good again. Once you forgive yourself and your former spouse for all that has

Regrets & Resentments

Part of the process of moving ahead into successful stepfamily living is to release remaining negative feelings about your former relationship. Take time to identify as many regrets and resentments as you can that you still hold about your former relationship. Whenever another one surfaces, add it to your list. Often, just being aware of the specific regrets and resentments can help diffuse the intensity. Taking time to ponder just what part you played in creating each of these will help you take responsibility for your share of the problem. This process can also help you avoid repeating the same scenarios in your new relationship. At the very least, this examination can help you take ownership of those feelings so you can correct the problem more quickly when it surfaces in your new relationship.

REGRETS	RESENTMENTS

Over time, as you examine these leftover emotions and work with them, they'll begin to diminish. Time also helps heal wounds, but beware of that old adage. It is the commitment to your *process* of healing that matters! Ideally, you can go through this process with your former partner and share the regrets and resentments with one another by talking through each painful leftover. If your relationship remains too raw, it's best to work with a professional who can guide you through this and other coming-apart experiences — perhaps helping you plan a "good-bye ritual" of your own creation.

happened, you are free. Ideally, you've reached this point long before you start thinking about remarriage but, if you're already there, it's never too late to backtrack and do this important work. Saying good-bye to your past is an excellent investment for your new stepfamily.

The rest of this chapter offers positive ways to begin to end your former relationshp effectively — emotionally and legally.

Saying Good-bye

Before you can truly do an effective job of building a new family life together, you must spend time and energy saying good-bye to parts of the old life that could keep you stuck in the past. Saying good-bye legally is one thing, but the important good-bye is the emotional one, and it involves achieving an "emotional divorce." While this important task is best done during the time you are single and between marriages, it's never too late to complete unfinished emotional work. But be advised: working two different processes — saying good-bye to one relationship at the same time you are trying to build bonds in your new stepfamily — is much more challenging.

Achieving an Emotional Divorce

An emotional divorce takes time — more than most people think. The mere passage of time is not enough; getting divorced emotionally requires resolving feelings and letting go. No magic formula exists. Your ability to reach an emotional divorce depends on many factors: the length of your marriage; how many children you have and their ages; how much anger and guilt you harbor; the amount of self-confidence you feel; the support you seek and receive from family, friends, and other outside sources. If it was your decision to divorce, it may take less time to resolve your feelings because you may already have worked through many of the issues before deciding to end your marriage. But many people who make the decision to divorce never think through the deep emotional issues and feelings involved, and may experience the same problems in a new marriage.

If your marriage ended through a divorce you did not choose or want, or through the death of a mate, you need to move through the steps of the grieving process with great care. Your first reaction to your loss was probably *denial:* "This really isn't happening." Then, as you gradually accepted the reality that your marriage was ending, you probably began to feel *anger* — first holding it in, next directing it toward others. Then, reluctant to let go, you may have started *bargaining* with your mate or yourself: "I'll do anything if you'll just come back." The final letting go, like the darkness before a storm, was black and *depressing*. From it, though, you moved toward *accepting* your ended marriage and began to feel free from the emotional pain that tied you to the past. Only then did you begin to move toward personal freedom and independence.

To complete an emotional divorce, it is essential to work through the five stages of grief first described by Dr. Elisabeth Kubler-Ross in her classic book, *On Death and Dying*: denial, anger, bargaining, depression, and acceptance. It's especially helpful to do as much of this grief work as possible before remarriage, because unresolved mourning will eventually be played out in your stepfamily. Don't, however, avoid doing the work just because you're already well entrenched in stepfamily living. The future of everyone in your stepfamily depends on making a clean break with the past.

Too Close, Too Soon

Though it seems strange to use the same term, an "emotional divorce" is equally important for someone whose marriage ended through the death of a partner.

Many people get stuck in one of the stages of grief. Whether divorced or widowed, many remarry too quickly, before they've resolved their feelings about their loss. After all, grief work isn't exactly fun; meeting someone new and moving on feels much better. Some people may wish to avoid further pain; they may hope that a new marriage will make things better, soothe the loneliness, and help them forget. They don't realize that the grief gets carried to the new stepfamily. Haste to remarry, for whatever reason, is one of the prime causes of the high remarriage divorce rate.

If you suspect that you remarried too soon, without having worked through some important feelings, don't despair. Stop and take the time to do that work now — before past unfinished business damages your present relationship. Begin by recognizing the feelings that link you to your former mate — especially the negative ones. Often, there is anger, a tie that can bind two people as tightly as their wedding vows once did. Then, through the process of letting go, as described in the next few pages, work toward acceptance and the achievement of an emotional divorce.

As you work through this process, some of your efforts might upset your new marriage. If you recognize you're in this situation, it's wise to alert your spouse to what you are experiencing so he or she won't feel threatened. Explain what you know and ask your partner for support and understanding. Your healing process may unearth buried feelings that you may unconsciously project onto your partner. If that person understands what you are going through, it's a bit easier to be patient and supportive. To complete the process of letting go of old feelings, you may need help from a professional family counselor. Don't hesitate to seek one out. And don't forget that your children need to grieve too, and include them in family therapy counseling sessions. The process may take a year or two — and requires conscious effort, not just time. Again, you'll find Bruce Fisher's *Rebuilding* helpful if you'd like to read more about how to let go in an effective way.

Unresolved grief carries two leftover feelings: anger and guilt. These emotions can negatively affect stepfamily relationships, and although these emotional leftovers didn't originate in the stepfamily, their presence impedes its progress.

Anger. Anger often comes from the perception that you've been treated unfairly. The anger that comes with divorce reflects the rage you feel when your love relationship ends, especially when ending it wasn't your idea. Unresolved anger is an emotion with little positive payoff. Continuing to hold it in neither changes the past nor helps you create a better future. Anger can be expressed in negative ways, such as revenge and vindictiveness; unexpressed anger can result in depression or psychosomatic problems, including tension, headaches, back problems, ulcers, and even more serious physical problems. Anger toward your former spouse can be a sign that you've not completed an emotional divorce.

Unresolved anger can dominate your thoughts and waste precious moments as you try to build your stepfamily. Until you are able to let go of these unproductive feelings, you will have trouble co-parenting with your former spouse. Rather than looking after the best interests of your children, you may continue to fight with one another. Your unresolved relationship with a former spouse may cause problems for other members of your stepfamily as well. Your new partner may feel insecure or jealous. Your children will sense the strain, and the loyalty conflicts that arise may make moving back and forth between two homes difficult for them — and may affect their ability to bond with new stepfamily members.

Since anger feeds on blame and resentment, the best way to get rid of it is to identify the events that caused those feelings, realize the events were growth experiences, and put to rest the blame or resentment you've been harboring.

Guilt. Guilt reflects the other remnant of unresolved grief, and is the feeling that you've done wrong. If you perceive that you've let yourself or someone else down, you may feel bad or worthless. Perhaps you feel you did something that caused your former partner to leave. Maybe you left your marriage even though your mate didn't want it to end. You may feel guilty for disrupting your children's lives. Guilt tends to damage self-concept and self-esteem and, again, can create loyalty conflicts. If you still harbor guilt about your former relationship, it'll be harder to channel all your energies into your new one.

Guilt is self-disappointment and anguish over having failed your ideals. It is often the common denominator among stepfamily members. Stepparents may feel guilty if they left their own children behind, and suffer even greater guilt when they find they cannot love their new spouse's children as their own. Biological parents feel guilty for sharing time and resources with their new spouse's children, shortchanging their own kids. Stepchildren who blamed themselves for their parents' break-up, or for having any negative thoughts at the time of a parent's death, often feel guilty. And, although everyone may be feeling guilty, *no one talks about it*.

To rid yourself of guilt, give yourself permission to be an imperfect person who makes mistakes like everybody else. It's wise to discard your high demands for personal perfection and to love yourself as you are! Both anger and guilt keep you stuck in the past. Isn't it time for you to move on?

Steps to Letting Go

If you confront guilt, anger, and other strong feelings openly, you'll be free to let go of your emotional leftovers. Use these six steps as a guide:

1. ***Recognize the feeling.*** When a feeling emerges, don't push it away. Instead, stay with it, taking time to identify it. Close your eyes and experience it. Locate the feeling in your body. Can you attach a color or an image to it? Give the feeling a name: for example, *sadness*.

2. ***Express the feeling.*** Say aloud, to yourself or to another person, "I am feeling sad about my marriage ending."

3. ***Clarify the feeling.*** Examine the feeling further to see what's behind it. In the case of sadness, you're probably mourning the ending of something that began with joy and hope. But you may find you are also angry at your partner for leaving or dying, thus destroying your dream of marriage. Then you feel guilty about being angry at a dead person. You may feel guilty for having left or for being the one left alive. Clarify what the feeling really is all about and its many complex components: "I'm sad, mad, afraid. And I feel guilty, too."

4. ***Explain the feeling.*** As you go deeper into the feeling, you may find another reason at the core of it. Sadness about your ended marriage may have concealed anger about your mate leaving. In turn, this recognition may have exposed deeply rooted fears of abandonment or rejection from your past. When you can identify and explain the feeling's source, you can begin to respond with new behavior. At this point, you may even want to rename the feeling. Beneath what you once labeled sadness, for example, may be a deep fear that can be traced to your childhood: "I felt the same way when I was a child and watched Dad and Mom fight."

5. ***Accept the feeling.*** Feelings are neither good nor bad; they just are. You're not a "good" or "bad" person because you have these feelings. None of us has constant control over what we feel from minute to minute. Realize that you're human, like everyone else in the world! When you stop labeling feelings as "good" or "bad," you can learn to accept them. Having accepted your own, you'll find it easier to accept the feelings of others as well.

6. ***Get help if you need it.*** Books, online resources, workshops, support groups, clergy and professional therapists are readily available to almost everyone. Check out what's offered in your community for dealing with anger, guilt, and grief. Note the books on these subjects in our list of References at the end of this book (e.g., Fisher and Alberti, Kranitz, Kubler-Ross, McKay and Maybell). If your self-help efforts are not enough, don't hesitate to contact a reputable and experienced divorce therapist for professional guidance.

To check your progress on letting go of your old relationship, take the brief version of Bruce Fisher's "emotional divorce" quiz in The Stepfamily Workshop — Session Two, on page 51, or ask your therapist to provide you with the *Fisher Divorce Adjustment Scale* (see the References).

Help Comes in Many Forms

As you move through this difficult time, there are other good "tools" to help you break free in a healthy way. Three possible ways to help you divide up the "material stuff" of a household and sort through some of the "emotional baggage" and painful feelings are *divorce counseling, divorce mediation,* and *collaborative law.* These non-adversarial processes involve a neutral third person trained to guide the two of you as you make some difficult decisions that will affect the future of you and your children — and, ultimately, life in your new stepfamily.

Divorce Counseling — From Conflict to Cooperation

Divorce counseling is used after the decision to end your marriage is made. This process isn't about reconciliation, although sometimes that happens. Rather the goal is to help adults coming apart to find healthy ways to resolve emotional leftovers so that the relationship with your former partner can shift from one that's adversarial, to one of mutual respect and trust — from disappointed, angry or sad *partners* to effective *parents.*

Divorce Mediation — Getting Apart Together

Divorce mediation helps couples move ahead with some very concrete decisions — again from conflict to cooperation. Resolution is the goal. The premise is that marital partners are not competitors fighting over a hypothetical pie; rather, both are adults who can draw on their inner strength to solve problems and make rational decisions. Mediation is not the arena in which to decide to separate or divorce. That is the function of effective divorce counseling which, ideally, you and your former spouse used to come apart in a positive way.

In some states mediation is mandated and the service is free. Several states offer court-related mediation. The yellow pages of the phone book offer listings of people who provide this service, but finding the right person for this complicated process is important. Choose this person wisely, because a successful mediation can make a vast difference in achieving positive divorce results. Seek a referral by someone who has completed a successful mediation. Inquire about the person's professional training. If this highly structured process fails, as it can, people are left with even more negative feelings — about themselves and each other.

Mediators guide couples through working out specific areas of agreement: *parenting issues, custody agreements, financial decisions,* and *property division*. It involves lots of paper and pencil work, preparing budgets, and planning for the long term. The process can become very emotional; if it does, your mediator should refer you back to your therapists until you can work through your feelings and proceed more calmly. After the concrete issues become clear and are worked through between you and your partner, your mediator draws up an agreement that has been mutually agreed upon. Each of you will sign it and take the document to your individual attorney to complete the legal transaction. One advantage of mediation is that the structured process can help reduce the adversarial relationship that often develops during court proceedings. It can also cost significantly less than the attorney fees that mount as two hurting adults war against one another.

Custody is often a major issue in mediation, and studies show that more and more mediations result in joint custody. Generally, that is a positive step for children of divorce, but *joint custody is not for all couples*. If you cannot communicate effectively with one another, have totally different parenting styles, or if your bitterness cannot be contained for the sake of your children, joint custody probably won't work well. But when it does, joint custody and co-parenting is usually the best option for your children. Research reveals that when both parents have continued contact with their children in the most positive way possible, children of divorce can do well — emotionally, academically, and socially. Later, these positive relationships pay off greatly in your stepfamily because, ultimately, you reduce loyalty conflicts for your children.

If new challenges arrive after your remarriage, you can always return to mediation and work out a new plan that's in the best interest of your children.

A very useful self-help book, Martin Kranitz' *Getting Apart Together*, will guide you in working out the key issues in divorce mediation, and may save you substantial attorney fees.

Collaborative Law

Another way to come apart together successfully is by using *collaborative law* — the newest divorce dispute-resolution model. Similar — but not the same as — mediation, the hallmark of this legal process involves working towards a negotiated settlement rather than going to court. Both you and your lawyers commit to working together in a cooperative way to create the best solutions for you and your family. As with mediation, couples who use this process find that they have a much better chance at successful co-parenting and a civil relationship with one another than those who go to court. You can find information about a collaborative law practice group near you on the website of the International Academy of Collaborative Professionals: www.collabgroup.com.

What's the difference between these two similar processes? In mediation, one neutral professional helps you work things through; with collaborative lawyers, each of you has legal advice and advocacy built in at all times during the process. If you and your partner aren't on a level playing field with one another, or if one of you becomes unreasonable or stubborn, mediation could be challenging because a mediator cannot give you legal advice nor help advocate your position. Collaborative law was designed to deal with such problems, yet the process offers the same commitment as mediation to protect your family from being torn apart emotionally, and perhaps financially. Whichever of these creative processes you choose, you'll do better in your newly restructured families because the two of you have carved out the terms of your divorce, not a judge.

Both of these processes can motivate you to do what you thought you could not do during a difficult time. You'll also be asked to think of the time ahead, when you or your former partner might remarry, and plan for your children for when they become part of a stepfamily. Much of the bickering about money and kids in new stepfamilies is often linked to unresolved issues between former spouses; of course, a congenial relationship with your former partner reduces stress — and loyalty conflicts for your children. Since most single parents eventually remarry, such planning ahead alleviates many of the problems folks face during the early developmental stages of stepfamily living.

. . . And Now It's History

When you finally achieve for yourself an emotional divorce, you'll experience the free feeling of leaving the loss behind you. It takes time to arrive at this point. If you're already in a stepfamily, you'll see how taking the time to resolve losses and saying good-bye to parts of the past can change your attitude and behavior and positively affect your new relationships. Making the time for this important healing process can be one of the wisest investments you can make to strengthen your stepfamily.

The Stepfamily Workshop
Session Two

Questions for Review

1. What's one of the best ways to give your new stepfamily a chance to truly succeed? Why is this so important?_____

   _____

   _____

   _____

2. Why is taking care of yourself first an unselfish deed? Discuss this in length with examples from your own experience._____

   _____

   _____

   _____

3. How can regrets and resentments get in the way of your stepfamily's development? Which ones do you still harbor? What's the payoff for holding onto them?_____

   _____

   _____

   _____

4. What are some losses your children or stepchildren experienced before joining a stepfamily? Which loss has had or may have the greatest effect on your stepfamily? Discuss how it has affected your family._____

   _____

   _____

5. What has been the hardest good-bye you've had to say concerning your former family? Have you said good-bye completely? How did you or can you complete this process?_____

   _____

   _____

   _____

6. How can your unresolved feelings create loyalty conflicts for your children?_____

   _____

   _____

7. What are some advantages of using mediation or collaborative law to resolve your ended marriage? _____
    _____
    _____

8. What guilt and anger do you still feel? What steps can you take to let go of these feelings? _____
    _____
    _____

Challenge to Conquer

Nine months after his wife died, Rudy married Phyllis and she moved into the home he shared with his two children. Before the wedding, Phyllis seemed to have a warm relationship with the children, especially Rudy's 11-year-old daughter Monica. Lately, Monica has withdrawn. She spends lots of time alone in her room; sometimes Rudy and Phyllis hear her crying. Yesterday, when Phyllis asked her stepdaughter to clean up the mess she left in the family room, Monica screamed, "You're not my mother — leave me alone!"

1. What might Monica be thinking and feeling? _____
    _____
    _____

2. How might Phyllis be feeling about herself? _____
    _____
    _____

3. How can Phyllis and Rudy help Monica adjust? How can they help each other? _____
    _____
    _____

Stepfamily Activity

This week, take time out to get in touch with unresolved mourning issues within your family. Plan a time to be together just to talk about each person's losses. Listen intently to each other. Clarify and explain the feelings. Accept resentment and sadness as a real part of your stepfamily's beginnings. By all means, avoid anger and placing blame. Then, before you leave for other activities, have each person tell at least two things he or she likes, or might grow to like, about your stepfamily. This positive ending provides hope!

Understanding My Stepfamily

1. *Identifying losses.* In this chapter you learned how important it is to mourn the losses experienced by stepfamily members. Use the list below to identify the specific losses for each member of your family and to determine if the mourning is finished, or if further steps need to be taken.

   Name of Family Member
   Loss Experienced
   Mourning Completed?
   Ways to Help Finish Mourning

2. *Do you have an emotional divorce?* Check your progress on letting go of your old relationship by answering "yes" or "no" to the following statements:

   ___ I think of my former spouse only occasionally now.

   ___ I no longer become upset when I have to deal with my former spouse.

   ___ I have stopped trying to please my former spouse.

   ___ I no longer seek excuses to talk with my former spouse.

   ___ I rarely talk about my former spouse to my friends.

   ___ I have accepted that we are not getting back together.

   ___ My feelings of romantic love are gone.

   ___ My emotional commitment to my former spouse is over.

   ___ I can accept my former spouse having a love relationship with another person.

   ___ I am no longer angry at my former spouse.

The more "no's" your responses reveal, the more work you have ahead. These items were adapted, with permission, from *Rebuilding: When Your Relationship Ends.* A full version of this quiz appears on page 134 of that book (see References).

Points to Ponder

- Taking time to grieve the loss of your former family is critical.

- The more you complete your own emotional work, the better position you're in to help your children who also need to grieve their changed family.

- Even though you have remarried, you may not have achieved an emotional divorce from your former spouse. Recognize this reality and work on letting go.

- Wise adults learn from the past and practice those new lessons in their new relationships.

- Divorce counseling, divorce mediation, and collaborative law are effective tools to guide you through a positive divorce.

- Achieving an "emotional divorce" is more important than the legal divorce. It involves a great deal of time and work to achieve.

- Getting help to strengthen stepfamily living is a wise investment to making your stepfamily succeed.

4

Your Stepfamily Journey

For a safe journey on an unknown wilderness trail, smart hikers use an accurate trail map. Likewise, to move successfully through some predictable stages in your stepfamily journey, you'll need guidance about the pitfalls and possibilities that lay ahead as you build your new stepfamily. This stepfamily "trail map" will help you stay on a successful course!

Throughout this book, we emphasize two critical facts that you'll need to understand:

- Making a successful stepfamily is a process.
- Making a successful stepfamily takes time.

This chapter shows you the normal passages through which all stepfamilies travel — your "trail map." With this information, you can better identify where you are now and, as your stepfamily develops, where you're headed. In the next chapter, you'll explore ways to set a comfortable stepfamily atmosphere and build a sense of family unity.

Developmental Differences

Every person moves through certain predictable stages — cycles — in life. First, people struggle to meet their own needs in *individual developmental cycles*. Then, if they decide to pair up with a partner, they face the challenges of a *couple's cycle*, surviving relationship stresses in a series of stages — from romance, through differences and challenges, to commitment. If they have a family, another cycle begins. Both individuals, and ultimately their children, are involved in a *family life cycle*, consisting of predictable phases: leaving the family of origin, marrying, having children, coping with kids as they grow, having children leave the nest, becoming grandparents, dealing with aging.

The couple with children is involved in all three cycles simultaneously, juggling roles as individuals, partners, and parents. In any two-parent family, mastery of the phases in the family life cycle is linked directly to the stability of the couple's relationship which, in turn, is based on how comfortable each partner is in his or her own personal life cycle.

In the stepfamily, death or divorce and remarriage have disrupted the normal cycles, creating new complexities. People who remarry may be out of sync with each other in one or more of the developmental cycles. The ability to successfully adjust to stepfamily living and to the role of being a stepparent will vary, and is dependent on the developmental stage the person has reached. Each partner in a new stepfamily may be at a different stage in the cycle of being a parent. One may have teenagers, while the other one has toddlers. As a result, their parental experiences are greatly different. If someone who's never been a parent marries a person with children, the couple faces a different challenge. One may want to have children, the other may not. Partners who have vastly different parenting experiences — or none at all — will want to give serious thought to the pros and cons of having another child.

Although developmental differences can create conflict — especially when important transitional changes are taking place as the stepfamily tries to stabilize — change can also produce positive effects. As personal growth strengthens their self-esteem, stepparents can set examples of success and competence, and serve as role models for the children they are helping to raise. Rather than let growth threaten your couple relationship and, ultimately, your stepfamily, you can learn to accept the change that growth brings as one of the rewards of living in a stepfamily. In chapter 16 we'll go into more detail about the rewards and strengths of stepfamily living.

Stepfamily Life Cycle — Stepping Through the Stages

Keeping in mind the three cycles you're involved in as a step-parent — individual, couple, and family — let's explore the specific developmental stages stepfamilies move through. The model presented here was developed by Elizabeth Einstein, and is based on the research of Elizabeth A. Carter and Monica McGoldrick (1980), Patricia Papernow (1980), and Virginia Satir [1988] (see References). Elizabeth calls this model "The Stepfamily Journey," and it describes five identifiable stages that nearly all stepfamilies experience.

- Fantasy

- Confusion

Stress can result when partners are in different phases of the parenting cycle.

- Crazy Time
- Stability
- Commitment

In the next few chapters, you'll be introduced to many issues that will help you understand these five stages. You'll explore a variety of coping techniques as well. Transitions from one stage to another may not be smooth or steady; indeed, progress is sometimes downright rocky. If you discover you've left some work undone, backtracking may be necessary — just as you might have to do on a hike if you got off the trail. Some stages overlap, so it's often hard to tell if you've reached a new plateau. This *Stepfamily Journey* model is "cyclic" — rather than "linear" — each stage is not dependent on succeeding in the former stage. By knowing and understanding the stages, you'll gain a vital perspective on where your stepfamily is now, and where it is headed. This "trail map"

This Stepfamily Journey model can serve as your trail map to keep you safely on the path toward success.

keeps you on course and helps reduce your anxiety as you meet the normal challenges of stepfamily living.

Stage One: Fantasy — The Grand Illusion

Fantasy is important in our lives. Without dreams of "what could be," we might never be inspired to begin. The problem with fantasy is that it fails to provide the firm foundation stepfamilies need to build a successful life together.

Your remarriage began with romance. You and your partner shared a dream that you could make this family the special one you'd both hoped for the first time. By now you may have found that the glow of love has blinded you from seeing the realities your stepfamily faces. Romance, wonderful as it is, often clouds reality. And it tends to set up denial, a dangerous defense for stepfamilies.

We've already looked at some of the common myths about stepfamily living and the unrealistic expectations we might have. To maintain the storybook illusion, you may be denying that your new stepfamily will be different. Many adults expect remarriage to return them to square one — where they were before their former marriage began to deteriorate. Some might believe they just need the right partner to succeed. Often, they try to fit their stepfamily into a traditional nuclear family mold, and fail to accept the fact that the stepfamily, born of loss and built around complex biological relationships, is a different kind of family.

Another common remarriage fantasy is that a new stepparent can rescue children from the inadequacies of the absent biological parent — that the stepfamily will make up for the past. Yet, dealing with the former spouse on child-related issues can bring old wounds to the surface, and allow the past to intrude on the present. While it's tempting to try, a new stepparent can never replace a biological parent who's no longer in your child's life on a regular basis. Rather, by offering love and support, you can play an important, *different* role in your stepchild's life. As your children grow up, they may feel a need to reconnect with a missing parent, and you'll want to be supportive in that challenge. Trying to replace your stepchild's parent can create loyalty conflicts for children and anger from their other biological parent.

Children, too, get caught up in fantasy. Many children dream that their biological parents will magically get back together one day and restore their original family. As their dream of reuniting Dad and Mom crumbles, some children, hanging on doggedly, turn against the stepparent and act out their anger in obnoxious behavior, hoping to drive that stepparent away. Stepparents need to be strong in their sense of self in order to tolerate hurtful behaviors from stepchildren who are lashing out.

To avoid getting stuck in this fantasy stage, it's important to understand the notion of process, and to remember that making a stepfamily takes *time*. You must also be aware that a trio of troublemaking "uns" can get you into trouble fast. These are *unresolved grief, unrealistic expectations*, and *uninformed adults*. These culprits have already been addressed in earlier chapters so, if you remain unclear about this trio, go back and review the related material in chapters 1, 2, and 3. If you've avoided dealing with one or more of these troublesome "uns," you'll delay your chances for moving ahead in your stepfamily development.

The perfect stepfamily is an illusion. The perfect family never existed — except on idealistic magazine covers and T.V. shows. Yet many couples can and do build happy remarriages and harmonious family relationships. This kind of success is a challenge that requires lots of hard work. As leftover grief is resolved, expectations are clarified, and the notion of "instant love" is relinquished, stepfamily members move into a second stage: confusion.

Stage Two: Confusion — What Are We Doing in a Stepfamily?

During this stage of development, everyone starts to sense that something is wrong, but no one knows what it is, or what to do. Suppressed feelings of anger and disappointment begin to emerge. Fear of failure makes stepparents anxious; as you try to become part of an existing parent-child unit, you might feel left out and perplexed. Maybe you cannot figure out how to fit in. Unclear roles cause confusion and discomfort for new stepparents. In reaching out to your stepchildren, you might be met with indifference or outright rejection. And as the discipline issues come up, tensions rise.

Romance can start to lose its glow as you deal with the stressful tasks of coping with children and managing money shared by two homes. Your initial couple harmony may become dissonant. Sex may still satisfy, but it may be increasingly less frequent and the

The perfect stepfamily — like any perfect family — is an illusion.

The confusion stage requires clarifying and resolving issues so that you feel confident that two different families can begin to work together as an "our" family — a stepfamily.

intimacy may no longer linger beyond the bedroom door. As you're confronted with all the courtship tasks left undone, you begin to wonder about your decision to remarry. Your children begin to sense the growing tension. Their greatest fear is that this family won't work either. To protect themselves from more loss, children may either withdraw from, or stop building trust in, their new stepparent. And the confusion and stress can extend beyond the custodial home as well. Moving between two homes and managing loyalty conflicts can create inner turmoil. Further, if you don't help your children to understand that it's normal to feel unsettled, the turmoil can intensify.

Boundaries in your new stepfamily cause more perplexity. A child may worry, "Where do I really live?" Adults wonder, "Should we invite the former spouse?" Whether financial, legal, or emotional, the obligations and decisions that spill across family lines can leave everyone feeling confused. By having to share responsibility for the children, you may feel you're losing control, which is a very normal feeling.

Clarifying the issues that contribute to this confusion is essential to your stepfamily's ability to stabilize. Clarification, however, is a gradual process. To begin with, take stock of what you have together, and ask yourself the following questions:

- What was it that first attracted us to each other?
- What promise does our relationship hold?
- When will we have time for our relationship?
- Why is the discipline issue so difficult?
- Are we overdue for a parenting class?

Stepfamily relations can be baffling.

- Should we move into a different house so we have more space?

Although this may be an uncomfortable passage, the confusion stage forces you to take specific steps in order to turn your dream into reality. If you don't, things can worsen.

During the confusion stage, many conflicting needs and expectations emerge, but others may be left unexamined. As family members gradually recognize and begin to understand their differences, they may at first remain quiet about them. Fear of change can keep families mired in old ways because what has become familiar — painful as it may be — somehow seems more tolerable than the unknown.

Eventually, though, too much stress and too many uncommunicated feelings will force these issues into the open. When the "leftovers" pile up to the point where they can no longer be contained, family members begin to speak and act out, and a new time of chaos and conflict emerges: crazy time.

Stage Three: Crazy Time — The Pain and Disappointment of Crisis

At this stage, highly charged issues find the stepfamily divided into different teams. Suddenly everything seems to be out in the open, yet nothing gets resolved. Struggles between you and your partner combine with those between the other family members, snowballing into one big battle. Your stepfamily has reached a point of crisis.

In Greek, crisis means *decision* or *turning point*. The final result of crisis is a decision to either stay together or to separate. Crisis forces your family to begin to resolve differences, for if you don't, your stepfamily can't survive. The process starts with renegotiating, rebuilding, and creating a new set of rules for your stepfamily to live by. Roles, communication channels, discipline, and decision-making processes are tested. Goals are set. As your stepfamily moves through this difficult time, trust can begin to take root and grow.

Unresolved former relationships, unclarified expectations, lack of information about what's normal for stepfamilies, guilt, denial — these are only a few of the forces that can trigger crisis. Issues that emerge vary from family to family. Two areas that might provoke serious difficulties for many stepfamilies at this time center on adolescence and shifting custody.

Adolescence. In many families, adolescence is viewed as a stage of crisis, or at least a challenge. Your teenager's normal behavior — mood swings, rebellion, brooding, disobedience — can be maddening. As teenagers struggle toward independence, family clashes are common.

For the new stepfamily, the difficulties of adolescence are intensified because teens and pre-teens are struggling to move away from their family just when they are expected to come closer in order to form new stepfamily bonds. This dilemma creates a developmental Catch-22. Remarriage studies have often overlooked the fact that most children who become stepchildren are at or near this turning point in their lives. When a teenager's individual development is out of sync with

Appreciation is the fine art of focusing on what is right rather than what is wrong.

the stepfamily's stage of growing together, everyone is affected and crisis often erupts.

Shifting custody. Loyalty conflicts and competition — between the children, between the adults, and between the children *and* the adults — push many stepfamilies into crisis. To resolve competition, a change in custody might be considered. This is rarely done without pain and guilt. The way a change in custody is handled is as critical as the decision itself. If children feel unwanted, they may conclude they are unloved and therefore unlovable. This in turn can lead to low self-esteem. Custody changes arouse fear and feelings of loss in adults as well. A parent whose teenager decides to live with the former spouse may feel rejected and be hounded by guilt. That guilt could damage the couple relationship in the stepfamily.

Shifting custody for sound reasons and in a positive, structured way can be a wise move. If the decision is discussed thoroughly by everyone involved, and no one ends up feeling unloved or rejected, shifting custody can help your stepfamily stabilize and meet the needs of your child. A warning! As they confront conflict, children should not be permitted to move back and forth between their two houses as they please, or to manipulate parents with threats of leaving. Adults, too, must not let intense momentary emotions take control, resulting in a custody change that is made without rational thought.

Whatever crisis forces the stepfamily to action, the chaos and struggles that accompany it must be recognized for what they are: normal and inevitable.

Whatever crisis forces the stepfamily to action, the chaos and struggles that accompany it must be recognized for what they are: normal and inevitable. It's up to you and your partner to help everyone persevere, and work toward resolution and satisfaction of the family's diverse needs. For too many stepfamilies, crisis means danger. But crisis need not signal the end of your stepfamily. It really presents an opportunity to take the first step toward building unity and a sense of family. Crisis *does* force confrontation and change. But change and chaos are merely part of the overall process — they need not be signs of failure.

During this challenging time, stepfamilies are encouraged to seek help and support. Reading books about stepfamilies, taking a parent-education class, or enrolling in a stepparent support group are all positive steps adults can take. Many fine books are available (we've identified some we like in the References), and stepfamily support groups are forming all over the world. Many are under the umbrella of the Stepfamily Association of America, an organization dedicated to the support and education of stepparents. Check out the SSA website at www.saa.org.

If things seem out of control for your stepfamily, and you haven't already done so, seek the help of a specially trained counselor. Such a person can reassure you that you are not a "sick" family, nor are you failing. You are merely in crisis and you need information, guidance, and support. But be certain that this person understands family systems and stepfamilies. Two professional groups have a listing of such therapists. For a referral to someone in your community, you can check with the Stepfamily Association of America (SAA) at www.saa.org, or the American Association for Marriage and Family Therapists (AAMFT): www.aamft.org.

Crisis need not signal the end of your stepfamily. It really provides an opportunity to truly begin.

It is only by taking the plunge — by using crisis to force needed changes — that you and your stepfamily will propel yourselves toward stability. Serious change cracks open many difficult issues. You may find that to reach that hard-earned goal, you must first move through pain, disappointment, and discouragement. Most stepfamilies agree that it took a crisis to clarify feelings, roles, and boundaries, and to move family members to regroup and begin to build strong relationships. Have courage, because surviving the crazy times can actually strengthen your stepfamily, and move you toward the next stage: stability.

Stage Four: Stability — Coming Together

As your stepfamily begins to stabilize, a key attitude is mutuality, building a sense of "us," or "our family." Responsibility for making your stepfamily work is shared by all members: every family works as a system and each person's behavior affects the entire group. In your stepfamily, each of you has become aware not only of yourself, but of others in your family. All of you now understand that becoming a stepfamily is a process, and that your struggles are only a part of that process. As you move to this new plateau, you come closer to success. You are on the same team!

But stability does not mean remaining the same. On the contrary, a stable stepfamily is adaptable and open to change.

This stage requires perseverance. It's a time of practicing the lessons you learned as you resolved your crisis. Again, that takes time and the willingness to try new things. Confronting challenge after challenge is difficult, and resistance may be great. Now that you know you don't die from divorce, it might be tempting to bail out. Don't! Believe it or not, your stepfamily is starting to stabilize. Conflict can now be used as a chance for learning about yourselves, rather than competing. You and your partner are learning to accept one another — even those things you maybe thought you'd like to change. As a stepparent, you are learning to accept your stepchildren for their own unique selves, and your children now feel safe in their stable stepfamily. It is at this stage that your role as stepparent begins to emerge clear and solid. As you move toward acceptance of what can and cannot be, you can concentrate on creative solutions and remain aware of the changes you and your family have agreed upon.

By now you've seen, too, that feelings change. Anger over differences can become an appreciation of the diversity and richness offered by two perspectives. Fear can dissolve into understanding. Guilt can give way to inner freedom and family harmony. Anger can be released, self-respect reclaimed, energy redirected. What was once viewed as loss can be seen as gain. Acceptance and liking can lead to trust. And trust and respect can often, over time, become love.

This is a time for integrating the lessons you've learned during the crisis stage. You must practice them and try on new ways of doing things. During this time your stepfamily may have setbacks, but don't let that slow you down. A setback doesn't mean you're failing; it merely means that you have to work harder to continue your progress.

Take pride in what you and your family have already accomplished. Focus on your stepfamily's strengths and remain aware of what's good. Hold hope high! It requires courage to reveal feelings and express differences, and it takes work to resolve problems. Having done this, you and your stepfamily will recognize that you've reached a new level: commitment to one another and to continued growth as a stepfamily.

Stage Five: Commitment — Choosing to Connect and Create

This welcome calm allows time for insight and reflection. Commitment means making a choice, and taking continued responsibility for making sure your choice works. Commitment is characterized by a strong wish and dedication to improve and invest in your family. Once you and your family resolve to build a successful stepfamily, you stop playing games that hinder your progress. Committed stepfamilies move out of the win-lose business; they no longer waste energy trying to place blame for the past. They understand that the past happened; no matter what your family does today, it cannot erase yesterday's hurts. However, a committed stepfamily can integrate the past with the present, and learn and grow from yesterday's hurts.

Commitment continues to help your healing process, and so you accept what is and proceed forward. You're able to do that now because you have learned what is normal for your kind of family — you understand how family patterns of growth and change are related, how they influence one another. This understanding came from persevering, from working through earlier difficult passages together. Stepfamilies can transform earlier hurts and difficult experiences into a fresh perspective about family members and new ways of doing things. Overcoming differences offer chances to learn another way.

— — — — — — — — — — — — — —

Raymond learned that while he and his children preferred to eat dinner late — rather than early, as his wife and her children liked — the early dinner "they" preferred freed up long evenings for everyone to enjoy favorite activities. He appreciated the change.

— — — — — — — — — — — — — —

When her stepson screamed, "I hate you!" Carolyn discovered that he was really hurting because his biological mother had again forgotten his birthday. She stopped personalizing behaviors and developed compassion for him.

— — — — — — — — — — — — — —

Commitment means accepting the rhythms of change and the concept of balance — both between you and your marriage partner, and among family members. During your times together, there will be distance and closeness, sadness and joy, fear and trust. Denial will be a thing of the past, because you realize that it was from your courage to confront difficulties that your stepfamily finally connected.

Chart 2

STEPPING THROUGH THE STEPFAMILY STAGES

This chart depicts both general guidelines and specific tasks you'll need to complete as you move through the stages of the stepfamily journey. No time period is indicated for any stage because each stepfamily requires a different amount of time to work through the tasks. Trust the process, and anticipate good results!

General Guidelines	*Stage/Tasks Fantasy*	*Stage/Tasks Confusion*
• Seek information and outside support from books, lectures, communication and parenting programs, stepparent support groups or a family therapist. • Believe and accept that the process of working toward stability and commitment takes time. • Work slowly toward gaining your stepchildren's trust and respect. • Plan family enrichment activities to help build closeness. • Hold regularly scheduled family meetings to air annoyances and joys. • Work continually to enrich and strengthen your couple relationship — the foundation of your family. • Encourage open, nonjudgmental discussion of feelings among all stepfamily members. • Resolve stepfamily problems together openly and respectfully, seeking creative solutions. • Seek support from a professional trained in stepfamily dynamics.	• Complete as many tasks of this stage as possible during courtship. • Discuss the wisdom of adding an "ours" baby. • Decide where to live — or whether remodeling might be necessary. • Explore money and discipline issues early on. • Plan a marriage ceremony that includes your children in a meaningful way. • Begin to recognize and resolve leftover grief. • Help children deal with fears and let go of fantasies about their parents reuniting. • Learn as much realistic and practical information about stepfamily living as possible.	• Begin to resolve decisions you failed to negotiate during courtship. • Let go of notion your stepfamily can make up for the past. • Say final "good-byes" so new beginnings can happen. • Avoid taking all stepchildren's misbehavior personally. • Decide how to relate constructively to your former spouse. • Define and begin establishing your stepparent role. • Work to create a system of shared discipline. • Learn to share children and accept that they live between two households. • Explore any uncomfortable feelings about sexual attractions among family members. • Clarify relationships with the school. • Discuss feelings, especially fears.

Stage/Tasks Crazy Time	Stage/Tasks Stability	Stage/Tasks Commitment
• Examine needs and expectations of family members to see which aren't being met.	• Build a sense of family — "we" and "ours."	• Accept that commitment means a choice to succeed.
• Restructure and clarify boundaries between the two households.	• Become aware of the roles that finally have emerged.	• Recognize that your stepfamily feels solid and reliable. Celebrate it!
• Be honest about existing problems; don't deny them.	• Connect with family members in a meaningful way.	• Be aware of traditions and rituals that feel good, and create new ones.
• Reduce power struggles and competition.	• Share memories. Build traditions and goals.	• Take full responsibility for choices.
• Consider custody shifts if they seem in children's best interests.	• Continue to plan family activities and enrich your couple relationship.	• Let go of stepfamily games.
• Recognize crisis as a need for change. Confront it, stick through it and learn the lessons.		• Accept change as a non-threatening reality.
• Recognize which issues are not specifically *stepfamily* stresses (abuse, infidelity, low self-esteem, alcoholism, adolescence).		• Accept ambivalence and paradox: sadness and joy, closeness and distance coexist.
• Identify destructive stepfamily interactions, for example, teasing, playing games, pushing each other's "buttons."		• Reconnect and renew difficult relationships.
		• Begin to reap the rewards your stepfamily has worked for!

Elizabeth Einstein's Stepfamily Journey model is adapted from the research of Elizabeth A. Carter and Monica McGoldrick, The Family Life Cycle: A Framework for Family Therapy *(New York: Gardner Press, 1980), and Patricia Papernow, "A Phenomenological Study of the Developmental Stages of Becoming a Stepparent — A Gestalt and Family Systems Approach" (unpublished dissertation, Boston University, 1980), and integrated with Virginia Satir's "Process Model of Change" (Satir, et al., 1991).*

Your stepfamily now begins to feel solid. Relationships no longer require constant vigilance. You'll continue to face changes as you resolve differences and make decisions. All healthy families do. These continued changes will send shock waves through the family, causing more changes that ultimately result in still others. But because you've made it through earlier stages, you now know that confrontations need not be threatening. They are part of change. Under the umbrella of acceptance, respect, and trust that your commitment has created, your stepfamily members can feel secure. You can risk being yourselves and speaking up because you share confidence that neither anger nor conflict will break your connections. In fact, you've learned that facing and resolving conflict actually strengthens your stepfamily.

5

Creating a Comfortable Stepfamily

As your stepfamily moves ahead, you'll want to build an atmosphere that is cooperative, supportive, and flexible — where everyone's needs get met. In this environment, stepfamily members can establish the rules and routines by which you will all live. When mutual respect prevails, your stepfamily shares a strong sense of unity. Building a sense of family identity and working toward common goals begins with getting to know one another. Where do you begin?

The Four A's

Adults can create a relaxed stepfamily environment by using the processes of encouragement and enrichment. The focus is on giving positive *attention*, demonstrating *acceptance*, expressing *appreciation*, and showing *affection*. We call these techniques the *Four A's*. Learning to use them consistently takes time and effort, but you'll find them fun to use — especially when you see how your children respond!

Attention. We all like positive attention. Getting attention in the stepfamily isn't always easy because there are more people with whom time must be shared. But children in the stepfamily need attention from parent and stepparent alike. Attention provides a sense of security, importance, and belonging. You can make children feel special and significant by giving them attention in any of the following ways:

- Spend special time alone with them doing what they like.

- Share daily routines and activities providing chances for them to talk.

- Get involved in their activities — even when it's not your favorite thing.

- Learn to *listen* — *really* listen. Conversations in the car are good because they don't have to make eye contact with you.

- Use schoolwork or activities as a springboard to conversation — without prying.

- Find special tasks for children that earn them recognition and compliments.

- Plan special occasions that provide one-on-one time.

- Focus on a "Kid of the Week," highlighting the activities and achievements of one child.

Many of these simple techniques will help you get to know your stepchildren in depth — to understand not only their present concerns, but their personal history. This is the easiest way to build strong bonds.

Acceptance. The basis for all successful relationships is acceptance. One of the earliest challenges stepfamily members face is coming to understand and accept each other's differences. You can work toward acceptance by concentrating on the following:

- Treat all family members respectfully, setting a tone for mutual respect among stepfamily members.

- Focus on each child's assets. Ignore the liabilities as much as possible.

- Avoid comparing siblings and stepsiblings.

- Avoid judging differences and playing games like "Who's Right?"

- Encourage children to express feelings and to respond to others' expressions without judgment or scorn.

- Get to know each other well. Ask questions, pursue shared interests, do chores together, inquire about preferences, opinions, and feelings.

- Never try to change a child to fit your image of how you'd like that child to be.

- Don't confuse accepting children with accepting misbehavior. When children misbehave, separate the deed from the doer.

Remember, too, that acceptance doesn't keep you from helping a child who wants to change, or taking appropriate disciplinary action when a child has misbehaved. In chapters 11 and 12 we'll talk about dealing with discipline.

Appreciation. Appreciation is the fine art of focusing on what's right, rather than what's wrong. Letting other family members feel appreciated is especially important in the stepfamily because during the adjustment time, no one's certain what behavior is or isn't acceptable. It's easy to notice what's wrong, especially during the early stages of confusion, but when children hear they are appreciated, they feel good about themselves. It raises self-esteem. Some tips about showing appreciation include:

- Use verbal statements: "Andy, I appreciate you keeping your room so clean."

- Write appreciative notes: "Dear Madison, Thanks for being so interested in my new work project. It made me feel so good when you wanted to learn more about it. You're a super stepdaughter!" Whether notes are tucked in a back pack or under a pillow, children enjoy the surprise of being told they are appreciated. So do adults.

- Focus on small steps, not just final achievements. If a child has only begun to rake the lawn, tell the child you appreciate the nice job she or he is doing and how it contributes to the family. It makes the job more tolerable, and perhaps motivate the child as well.

Affection. We all want — and need — affection. But even though affection is a way to become closer to your stepchildren, it's important that you proceed slowly. Too much affection too soon may frighten them away. Children may have come from a family where people didn't touch one another frequently. If you start right in with lots of hugs and kisses, some children might be uncomfortable. Be patient! Early on, your stepchildren may not feel enough warmth for you yet to show physical affection. Even if they do, they may feel the tugs of loyalty; as though sharing affection with you somehow diminishes what they share with their parent. Respect their concerns.

What is important in showing affection is the comfort level. Begin with attention and appreciation, and as comfort levels and acceptance grow, more physical affection can be given. Some of the ways you can begin are:

- Start with verbal appreciation. After a while, begin to add a light touch on the shoulder or a squeeze of the hand. Be aware of the child's response and proceed accordingly.

- Use "I like you" statements: "I like the way you help your brother." "I like to hear you laugh like that." Make sure some of your statements are unconditional — not tied to any behavior: "I like living with you." "I'm glad you're my stepchild."

- Be patient about showing affection. Enjoy small successes, waiting for stepchildren to feel more comfortable before you proceed.

Laughing Matters

Throughout the trying times, and during the humdrum ones as well, a sense of humor helps you keep stepfamily living in perspective. Take things lightly. Learn to laugh at yourself, and give others the freedom to do so too! Humor is contagious; your own relaxed attitude can lead other family members to look for the funny side as well.

Stepfamily living offers countless opportunities to turn irritation or confusion into laughter. Complicated plans, mistaken meanings and assumptions, and daily struggles to juggle schedules all present situations that can be perceived with humor, if not sheer hilarity.

Establishing Traditions and Goals

One of the most important ways in which stepfamilies build bonds and form a solid identity is by establishing your own unique traditions and goals.

Traditions form family history. The celebrations and rituals that are repeated year after year create family continuity and happy memories. Since stepfamily members share no common history, traditions may at first collide. This is especially true around the holidays. One way to balance this is to create *new* traditions built around days that have special significance for the stepfamily. A natural is your stepfamily anniversary, the day all of you became a family. Since this is also your wedding anniversary, you might want two celebrations — one private for you and your partner; the other, possibly the day before or after, a family celebration with the kids. Both are important. Your list of special days could also include the day you moved into your home, took your first trip together, planted the first tree in the yard. It doesn't matter how significant or insignificant the event seems to others, as long as it has meaning for your family.

Diversities find two sets of traditions collide.

Certain days of the year also lend themselves to traditions. How about celebrations of the first winter snowfall or spring crocus? Talk about how friends celebrate family occasions. Share library books together about traditions around the world and plan activities around what you've discovered.

A difficult problem for many stepfamilies is deciding where children will spend holidays. No one solution fits all families. Some families alternate — for example, Thanksgiving with Mom this year, Dad the next. The parent who doesn't see the kids can still celebrate Thanksgiving with them on another calendar date. If both parents live in the same town, the families might split the day, having kids spend the morning in one home and the afternoon in the other. Adding an afternoon and evening before or after the actual holiday makes the time with each parent longer and more memorable. Talk to your children about what feels right for them and try to work around their wishes. Remember, those calendar dates are just that; instead, focus on the meaning of holidays — gratitude, spending time together, and love.

Holidays *are* emotionally charged, yet they can also be the time to begin a history unique to your stepfamily. Why not create a stepfamily Christmas banner that you'll use year after year? Hold an annual pre-Halloween party that includes a trip to the pumpkin farm and a jack-o-lantern carving contest? Celebrate national Stepfamily Day in September? Celebrate your family's heritage by holding an "international day," with costumes and food representing the cultural traditions in your family history. Children love traditions. They'll want to share the ones they know, and you'll see them eagerly join in to create new ones as well. The traditions and rituals you establish now will give meaning and permanence to your stepfamily. These new traditions will also help you let go of the past more and more as you walk more securely into the future.

Goals bring families together. Goals provide a sense of future. With a common set of aims and pursuits in mind, stepfamily members feel as though they are truly working together. Over time, your main goal is to develop family unity and identity.

To start, have family members share how they see themselves, as individuals and as part of the family, on a timeline:

What will people be doing next month? Next year? In five years? What does each person hope to accomplish? What hopes do people have for your stepfamily? How does each person see other family members fitting in? What challenges will have to be met individually? As a family?

Even your youngest children can share their wishes and what they'd like to contribute, though the "timeline" concept may be difficult for them to grasp. You may have to prompt them some: "Johnny, what do you want to get from our new stepfamily?" "Susie, what special things can you offer to our family? How about your sweet voice? Can you make up a song about our new family (or draw a picture, etc.)"

Look for and define the goals you can work toward together. Then take the next step by setting a plan to achieve them. Create a chart.

Identify what needs to be done when. Explore some of the problems that might get in the way. What support will you need?

This is a good time to begin to discuss designing a set of family principles — guidelines for living together in a positive way. What's the most important value family members share? Honesty? Sharing feelings? Living in the present moment? Sharing information? Get a large piece of paper and, after dinner some evening, begin to brainstorm what principles family members think to be important. Have one of the children write them with a magic marker. Work on this list over time. Tweak it. One day, negotiate and agree on three or four of the most important ones and print them out attractively. Display this "family code" in a prominent area of your house and review them at times. If a family member violates the family code, use this as a time for discussion about what happened. How could things have gone differently had the family code been taken into account?

Family meetings provide a comfortable setting in which your stepfamily can begin to establish traditions and goals. These important discussions together aren't just for airing gripes; it's also a time to celebrate the joys of stepfamily living and to plan for the future. The family meeting could end with a family activity. Making a stepfamily scrapbook, discussing holiday rituals, comparing notes about traditions in your former families, planning a picnic or trip are just a few activities stepfamilies might enjoy.

When stepfamily members share their dreams for the future, they give each other insight and enjoy one another's successes. *The Stepfamily Journey* is a process and it takes time to work through the various tasks of each stage — a long time. As we've discussed, if you hold the unrealistic expectation that within a year or so, everything will be working just right, you're headed for trouble and disappointment. But when you truly understand the concepts of process and time, and stay committed to the tasks which strengthen your family, your stepfamily journey will be successful and fulfilling.

Remember, when goals and dreams are reached, it's time for a celebration!

The Stepfamily Workshop
Session Three

Questions for Review

1. Are you and your partner in similar stages of your individual life cycles? As parents? In your professional lives? In your relationships with your own parents? What stresses can you identify that come from being out of sync? _____

_____

_____

_____

2. What can you gain by understanding the stages of stepfamily development? Can you identify the stage you are in? _____

_____

_____

_____

3. Identify the "trio of uns." Which of them has created the greatest challenge for your stepfamily? How did you resolve it? What remains to be done about this issue? _____

_____

_____

_____

4. Was the fantasy stage a short or long passage for your stepfamily? Are you through it yet? If so, what things did you do to move on? If not, what do you think needs to be done to propel your family into the next stage? _____

_____

_____

_____

5. Are you presently in the confusion stage? How can you, or how have you been able to, determine boundaries and roles? Clarify discipline issues? Expand communication? _____

_____

_____

_____

6. Can you identify the major crises in your stepfamily? Have you confronted them? How? If not, what steps do you need to take?

_____

_____

_____

_____

7. Choose one crisis you've weathered. What did you learn during this painful time? How are you applying that lesson to your stepfamily today? _____

_____

_____

_____

8. Can you think of when your stepfamily finally made a commitment to succeed? What caused that important decision? How do you celebrate it? _____

_____

_____

_____

9. What four factors contribute to a comfortable stepfamily atmosphere? How can you emphasize each one in your stepfamily?

_____

_____

_____

_____

Challenge to Conquer

Jan and her 17-year-old stepdaughter, Gina, are involved in a heated argument. For two weeks in a row Gina has not finished her weekly chores and, again, is gives excuses. When her stepmother says she can't use the car Saturday night, Gina blows up at her. "If it weren't for you, my parents would be back together! They'd understand me — and not make me do housework!" Jan holds her ground on the use of the car, so Gina stomps off to her father. He tells his wife she's being too hard on the girl. "Give her another chance," he suggests. "She says she'll do her chores on Sunday afternoon." But Jan feels he's taking Gina's side, and she's angry at Gina for involving him. Soon everyone is yelling at everyone else, and things feel out of control. When Gina finally storms out, Jan and her husband are left fighting.

1. What is happening in this stepfamily? How are people handling it? _____

    _____

    _____

    _____

2. What's the result for Gina? For her father? For Jan? _____

    _____

    _____

    _____

    _____

3. What stage would you say this family is stuck in? What do they need to do to move on? _____

    _____

    _____

    _____

4. What might each of the adults do to build better family cooperation and prevent triangles? _____

    _____

    _____

    _____

    _____

Stepfamily Activities

(1) If your stepfamily does not already hold family meetings, begin to do so by holding one this week. Follow the guidelines in chapter 15. Be sure to take time to plan future activities that you'll enjoy doing together and that will help all of you get to know each other better. Even people who have lived together for years can get better acquainted.

Before you finish your meeting, take time to do one more thing. Have an "Appreciation Session." Take a few minutes to go around with family members and tell each person one thing that you appreciate about them. Make it a simple but complete statement such as "Jane, I appreciate your constant cheerful attitude about things." "Jamahl, I appreciate how you share your ideas about music that leads this family to new musical opportunities." Then pass the baton (It could be a dinner knife or a pencil) to the next family member until everyone has received a gift of appreciation from one another.

(2) Continue recording the history of your stepfamily journey. This might be the time to add photos (or children's drawings) of your new house or events you're doing together to build a family identity in your stepfamily scrapbook. Or start one now. Are you creating new traditions?

Understanding My Stepfamily

"Who's Right?" is a game many stepfamilies play. In this game, one person tries to show that his or her way of doing things is the "right" way and everyone else's is "wrong." Yet in many situations there is no right or wrong way — each is just different. Ultimately, these differences can become strengths.

This activity helps you to recognize areas in your family life in which "Who's Right?" is being played. Below are some issues that often lead stepfamilies into this game. Check *yes* or *no*, depending upon whether your stepfamily plays "Who's Right?" over the issue. Then identify other "Who's Right?" issues in your stepfamily.

- Kids do/do not need to be dressed before   ___ Yes ___ No
  breakfast.

- The TV is/is not allowed on during meals.   ___ Yes ___ No

- Elbows are/are not allowed on the table.   ___ Yes ___ No

- The Chanukah latkes are always small/large.   ___ Yes ___ No

- Christmas presents are opened on Christmas   ___ Yes ___ No
  Eve/Christmas Day.

- Ketchup does/does not go with hot dogs.   ___ Yes ___ No

- Boys and girls have different/the same   ___ Yes ___ No
  curfews.

Create Your Own Stepfamily Cartoon

As you work at integrating two often very different ways of doing things, or trying to understand different ways of thinking about family issues, some funny things happen in your stepfamily. One example of that is the cartoon on page 73. Discuss some of your more amusing events that you've experienced as a family and then create a cartoon to illustrate it here. Don't forget the caption!

Points to Ponder

- Making a stepfamily is a process. It takes considerable time.

- Individuals, couples, and families move through separate, predictable cycles of development. The more harmony among these life cycles, the greater the chances for stepfamily success.

- The five stages of stepfamily development are fantasy, confusion, crazy time, stability, and commitment.

- Getting stuck in the fantasy stage can delay stepfamily development.

- Confusion and chaos are normal and *do not* mean your stepfamily is failing.

- Stepping through the stepfamily stages requires completing certain tasks.

- Stepfamilies can learn to use crisis to produce positive changes that will propel them toward stability.

- Trust and perseverance are essential in working toward stepfamily stability.

- Adults can use the *Four A 's* — attention, acceptance, appreciation, and affection — to create a comfortable family atmosphere.

- A sense of humor helps defuse intense times.

6

Strengthening Your Couple Relationship I:

Dealing With the Past

*"*We have a pact: When things get too crazy, we chuck it all, arrange for a sitter, and head out for a day in the country — sometimes for an overnight. We just get in the car and go. It's amazing what that time alone together — unstructured, unplanned — does for us as we remember what brought us together in the beginning! Then we go home relaxed and ready to be with our children again."*

In your stepfamily, as in any two-parent family, the strength of your couple relationship is the key to stability and success. Falling in love is a great experience, but building that love requires constant nurturing and care. Building a strong marriage is always a challenge; for two people establishing a stepfamily, that challenge can seem overwhelming. From the start, your task is learning to juggle three roles: parent, partner, and individual. You will each need to build new relationships with your partner's children, while still maintaining a strong commitment to your own. Your instant family gives you little time alone together. Balancing intimacy and romance in your couple relationship, along with family responsibility and personal needs, is your special, immediate challenge.

This chapter provides information about stresses that can intrude on your growing relationship as a couple. It explores past and present factors affecting stepfamily stability, and discusses how you can make your marriage thrive in this complex family environment.

Integrating the Past with the Present

The past may intrude on your new couple relationship, causing stress. Children and former spouses cannot, of course, be wished away, but you can change the meaning that the past — and the relationships it included — has on your new relationship.

Reality Reigns

Child support, alimony, shared parenthood, telephone calls, school conferences, Father's Day, Mother's Day — even the way a child looks (so like the *other* parent) — all are constant reminders that you or your spouse had a previous love relationship with someone else. Although you may find this reality unpleasant, you're going to need to accept it.

Ex means *former* and implies that something no longer exists. But an ex-spouse *does* exist, and even though the marriage may be legally over, a psychological attachment usually remains. Let's start making a cultural change — thinking and saying *former spouse*. This connection to the past needs to be accepted, so that neither partner is denying the history of a former marriage. Acceptance is important, whether a prior marriage ended through divorce or death. In either case, denial and resistance bring pain, and keep your stepfamily from moving forward.

How much you allow a former marriage to interfere in your new relationship depends on many things: the amount of time that's gone by; help you may have gotten after the marriage ended; your individual maturity; and the maturity level of your relationship. For you, individual maturity may have come through a commitment to personal growth between marriage and remarriage. Your divorce or the death of your spouse may have led you to make great strides in your own personal development. As you explored your share of responsibility for the ended marriage, you probably began to see what you could have done differently; what you want to avoid repeating. You learned that you can take charge of your own life. You might also have discovered that you can change your behavior with a new partner; that you can *choose* how to respond to your present spouse, your former one, and all the other people you interact with. Rather than dreaming of what might have been — if only this were your first marriage, if only there were no former spouse, no children, no support to be paid — you are coming to terms with what is. When you stop trying to change things and accept reality, you can let go of the idea that you can make up for the past, and begin to accept new family members and their histories. Then, and only then, a true commitment to making your stepfamily work becomes possible.

Coming to Terms with the Past

Once you accept the reality of former relationships — your own and your partner's — and bring concerns and long-denied feelings out into the open, you can move ahead in your stepfamily journey.

Express and explore fears. Unexamined fears breed uncertainty in relationships. Many possible sources of fear exist for stepfamily couples. If your own relationship started during a former marriage, you may have nagging fears of continuing infidelity. Too often in a situation like this, people may have ended one marriage and moved into another without identifying, examining, and leaving behind the guilt and anger such a triangle produces. While unfaithfulness is often the impetus for first marriages breaking up, rarely is it actually the underlying cause.

"Neither of us would have gotten involved with someone else if we'd been happy with our spouses to begin with."

Infidelity is less common in remarriages; still, the knowledge that you or your partner has had past affairs may cause feelings of insecurity.

When a former spouse has emotional or physical problems, these problems may intrude on the stepfamily. Out of guilt, you or your partner may feel the need to rescue a former mate. But, since time and money are often scarce in stepfamilies anyway, doing favors for your former partner, who's still emotionally hanging on to the marriage, may be costly to your remarriage. Likewise, being overly nice to stay on a former spouse's good side may cause your new partner to fear that you aren't emotionally free of the other person. There may be a kernel of truth in that. Do you truly have an "emotional divorce?" Your partner might also worry that your former spouse is trying to win you back.

Lifestyle patterns carried over from past relationships can affect new ones. If your tastes, values, political views, or hobbies were acquired during your former marriage, your new spouse may feel competitive, jealous, and resentful. As a couple, you'll need time to develop a shared lifestyle. In the meantime, an insecure mate may worry that he or she cannot measure up to your former spouse. This is especially true when a deceased wife or husband has been elevated to near sainthood by friends and family.

One of the greatest fears of people in stepfamilies is that of another failure. If this marriage seems to be a replay of your first one, your commitment to the stepfamily may be weak; your remarriage may be in danger. Because family members have already experienced a great loss, their fear of failure can become acute, leading to one of two responses: Some people, knowing they can survive the pain, might again consider divorce as the solution. Others may deny problems in their current relationship, allowing them to worsen.

In an effort to deny problems, couples sometimes focus instead on a child. This is called *scapegoating*. In an attempt to reduce their unspoken fears that this marriage is failing, partners instead direct their energy and attention toward changing a child's behavior or emotional state. You may take your defiant son to a counselor, hoping that if his problems are solved, your stepfamily will then be fine. Blaming a child appears less threatening to you than admitting your relationship has problems. But, in reality, scapegoating keeps you from facing fears, pinpointing sources of conflict, and getting the help you need to stabilize your marriage and your stepfamily.

To avoid facing their own problems, a couple may focus instead on changing a child.

Progress can only be made when you accept the reality of former relationships — your own and your partner's — and bring concerns and long-denied feelings out into the open.

Unexamined fears can create unnecessary worries. Sometimes stepparents personalize the misbehavior of their stepchildren, believing the children dislike them. Some question themselves:

"What if I devote myself to raising them and they reject me?"

"Can I ever be important in their lives?"

"Is it too late to make any difference?"

Often, stepparents — especially stepmothers — take their roles too seriously, fearing the worst and putting pressure on themselves; but most do a better job than they give themselves credit for. While some stepparents fear they are failing their stepchildren, others worry about their relationship with their own children. Or, with so much energy being directed toward child-related issues, they may fear that their couple relationship is losing its edge of excitement. When you don't take the time to examine them, these common fears can lead to guilt or produce needless pressure on a relationship.

To check how much your current marriage is influenced by a past one, explore how your choice of a new partner reflects your personal growth. Are you repeating patterns? Did you take time before this marriage to really discover what you want from life and in a life partner? Was your mate selection from choice, rather than need? Did you give yourself a year or two to work through the divorce process before you committed to your new love relationship? See Bruce Fisher and Robert Alberti, *Rebuilding: When Your Relationship Ends* — an excellent self-help book on putting your life back together after divorce.

If, as you answer these questions, you realize you left much undone that might have helped make things easier, don't despair. Recognize what your tasks are and start to address them. Do you have unresolved issues with your former spouse? Is your emotional divorce as complete as you believe it to be? Are you fulfilled in your work? Comfortable with your parenting? Are you holding in unspoken fears about aspects of your remarriage? Talk with your partner about your discoveries so she or he is not threatened as you work to clear up the past. Seek your partner's patience and support, explaining that this will ultimately strengthen your relationship.

It's never too late! Whether you're about to remarry, recently remarried, or already several months or years into stepfamily living, take the time now to talk with your partner about hidden fears. Eliminating fears won't be a simple process; you'll both need to be willing to be vulnerable and reveal feelings to each other, to be honest about them and discuss them openly. In the process, you'll be building trust on which your relationship can grow. To do this, many couples need the help of a marriage counselor or support group. Remember, all your efforts are for the benefit of strengthening your marriage and stepfamily. There's no better cause! It's a healthy family that seeks support.

Examine and resolve relations with your family of origin. Ideally, the important psychological task of becoming independent from your parents will have been completed before your marriage or remarriage. If this isn't the case, you may find that many of your current approaches and responses are a result of your relationship with your first family, the one into which you were born. Problems you blamed on your former spouse may be recurring in your new marriage; you may now begin to see that you are repeating behavior based on early ties and unresolved struggles with your parents.

We are who we are, whether in harmony with our parents or in reaction to them. Childhood memories, conflicts, and feelings continue to affect all our relationships. Two negative reactions commonly carried into adulthood are the need for parental approval and the desire to get rid of unpleasant traits that we associate with our parents. Once you begin to see that old fears, ways of thinking, or insecurities are repeating themselves in your life, you may decide to release this emotional backlog through counseling or self-help books. Two excellent books on this subject are *Making Peace with Your Parents*, by Harold H. Bloomfield and Leonard Fender, and *Cutting Loose: An Adult Guide to Coming to Terms with Your Parents*, by Howard Marvin Halpern. (See "References" at the end of the book.) A marriage and family therapist can also help you come to terms with your past. The approach you take matters less than the reality that you choose to leave negative parental influences behind you. Resolving old conflicts with parents helps reduce struggles in current relationships, and may in fact be the most important investment you make for the future of your stepfamily.

It's important to understand that coming to terms with your parents may result in radical changes within you. As you leave negative feelings behind, you may disturb or confuse your mate by responding differently in familiar situations. This, in turn, could alter and possibly disrupt your marriage relationship. If your couple commitment is strong, however, personal growth work that helps you become a healthier person also strengthens your marriage.

A warning! Once you realize that personal "unfinished business" — either with your parents or your former partner — is getting in the way, it's time to share this awareness with your new partner. Discuss specific situations you believe are being affected. Talk about your plan to resolve them and how the changes could affect your relationship as you work to strengthen it. Discuss expectations of how much you want to share from therapy sessions and how much privacy you need.

You might invite your partner into couple therapy — especially if it involves a model in which you each do individual work within the context of couple counseling. An example of this is Harville Hendrix's "Imago Therapy." Read his *Getting the Love You Want*, showing you how these unresolved parental issues affect your intimate adult relationships. During therapy, this approach provides an understanding of what brought you together in the beginning, and how you can help each other grow up. It's powerful healing work that can enhance your stepfamily spiritual journey. Another good resource is "The Couple's Spiritual Journey," from the *Stepfamily Living Audiocassette Series*, by Elizabeth Einstein. (See ordering information in the back of this book.)

When a former mate won't let go, change your own response. In chapter 3 we explored ways to achieve an emotional divorce. But what if you have done so and your former mate has not? Much as you try to devote energy toward making your new family work, you may often find yourself listening to your former spouse's attacks or demands. As you deal with ongoing letters, emails, and phone calls, you are caught between two people who feel they have an emotional claim on you. This can cause unhappiness and stress for you and your current partner, and wreak havoc in your remarriage.

Not surprisingly, it is often — but not always — the spouse who chose to end the marriage who is first able to let go and heal. If infidelity ended the marriage, the pain is heightened for the person left behind. It is not unusual, however, for the "dumper" (to use Bruce Fisher's term) to carry considerable guilt, which can make the healing process more difficult. Because infidelity *is* traumatic, the rage, resentment, and wish for revenge that accompany it can

As you leave negative feelings behind, your mate may find you responding to familiar situations in unfamiliar ways.

last for years, and result in antagonistic behavior by the former spouse.

Hostile feelings can link two people together as strongly as their wedding vows once did. But it's vital to break that link. If your former spouse has chosen to cling to you through anger, has done little to let go of the marriage, and continues to try to push your buttons, there is nothing you can do to change that. You cannot change that person, no matter how hard you try. What you *can* do is *change the way you respond to your former spouse* until, eventually, the relationship is transformed. *You can learn to respond to old patterns in a new way.* Relationships are like wind chimes: blow on one piece and everything moves. Completing an emotional divorce can change your behavior and responses; eventually your former mate will react differently too.

Think for a moment about the "games" you continue to play with your former spouse.

In the past when Consuela's former husband Martin criticized her, she would feel defensive. His put-downs reminded her of when she was a little girl and her father scolded her. To get even, Consuela would attack Martin; their battle would escalate. Now remarried, Consuela needs to learn a new response so she will no longer be affected when Martin displays this behavior. To Martin's, "With all the money I give you, the kids' clothes sure look shabby," she might respond calmly, "I'm sorry you feel that way," and finish communicating about the business at hand. Should Martin continue with the game, Consuela might simply say, "I have to go now. I hope we can settle this issue at another time. How about 4:30 tomorrow?" After a while, when Martin sees that Consuela is no longer upset, the game will cease to be rewarding to him.

Psychological games of competition require two opponents. If you simply refuse to take part in a game with your former spouse, it cannot continue. In the long run, not playing will be easier on everyone. Changing your way of responding isn't simple. It takes genuine effort and practice. But it's worth the effort! Instead of wasting time with this dead relationship, put your energy into learning skills that can change your response. Once free of emotional entanglements with your former spouse, you can redirect the energy you were using when you became angry and use it creatively to build the relationship with your new spouse.

When you form a stepfamily, you face three major tasks: coping with family and children, building the marriage relationship, and continuing to grow as an individual. Each is a challenge in itself, yet the trio of tasks must be met simultaneously. You must become a master juggler.

7

Strengthening Your Couple Relationship II:

Making Practical Decisions Together

Certain decisions affect your entire stepfamily. Both partners need to agree on such basic issues as how to handle money, where to live, how to discipline. Ideally, you'll have discussed these critical issues before the wedding!

Living in the Present, Looking to the Future

Family Matters — Making Major Decisions

Maybe you didn't have those discussions before you created an instant stepfamily. If not, it's important now to identify problem areas and learn to either accept the present situation or begin to change it. These potential conflicts require swift resolution so they'll not interfere with overall stepfamily stability. If you have serious disagreements or problems that don't seem easily reconciled, seek the support of a counselor. The success of your stepfamily is worth the investment!

Money Matters — One Pot or More?

For better or worse, marriage creates an economic enterprise, so it's important to clarify money issues as soon as possible. Beyond dealing with discipline in your stepfamily, money is your next greatest challenge. Money can divide or unite a stepfamily — especially when it gets linked to commitment and love. The emotional commitment promised in your marriage ceremony is only a first step toward building financial commitment. Economic commitment to a new spouse may come slowly. A stepparent's commitment of resources and assets to stepchildren may come even more slowly, if at all.

Money in the stepfamily can be managed in different ways. Although variations exist, stepfamilies tend to handle finances using either a "two-pot" or a "common-pot" approach. For many couples, when responsibilities include children and former spouses, it seems fair to keep two sets of books. This two-pot system resembles a business partnership. Sometimes lawyers are consulted and documents drawn up to protect interests. Arrangements are made based on past financial histories, divorce settlements, and child support. In growing numbers of dual-career stepfamilies, each partner takes the financial responsibility for his or her own children.

Having individual control over money may reassure people that they are protected, particularly those who suffered economic hardship when their former marriage ended. This approach works less well, however, when one partner has considerably more money than the other, or when a former spouse indulges one set of children. Under these circumstances, the stepfamily can become two subfamilies — one richer, one poorer — and bad feelings may result.

With the common-pot approach, couples pool resources and distribute them according to need, not blood ties. Adults avoid distinguishing between *yours* and *mine,* and do away with extra bookkeeping. This method reflects a high level of trust and commitment to the stepfamily. Remarried adults who manage money in this way report strong family unity and a positive attitude about the future of their stepfamily. But the common-pot approach works only when money matters really *are* managed for the good of all.

Some stepfamilies use a creative but complicated "three-pot" approach: "yours," "mine," and "ours." This provides for continued independence of some monies, but requires a great deal of work up front to come up with the numbers for all monthly household expenses. You also have to decide if the contributed portions will be equal or pro-rated in some fashion, perhaps dependent upon income, or number of children. Since money is a power issue for couples, you may have some heated discussions as you work this through, but it's necessary. Then each partner contributes his or her share and all the major family expenses get paid from this common pot. The "yours" and "mine" pots reflect personal money that remains free of family responsibilities — unless a need arises and a decision is made to share some of it. Many stepfamilies start out with the three-pot approach and, after they feel strong and committed, move to the one pot model.

There's no right way. If what you are doing works well, leave it alone. Regardless of what approach you choose, you must be willing to talk over all the issues and emotions relating to money, and arrive at a specific agreement about how money matters will be handled. Of course, this is best done before you say "I do."

Living Arrangements — Your Place or Mine?

A house is not a home, you may say. It's only a residence, a place to live. As long as we can all be together, what's the big deal about which place we choose? Don't kid yourself. Space — its allocation and adornment — defines one's identity. Someone's home reveals a lot about that person — hobbies, sports, interests, achievements, social relationships, economic status. Deciding where to set up your stepfamily household is a *major* decision.

Couples who respect this reality resolve the issue before the wedding. It might seem simpler to move into one home or the other, and your thinking may be rational. Your decision might be based on one home's proximity to school or work, in addition to the condition or value of the property. Your deciding factor might be cost. But as you think about where to live, practicality is only one consideration; emotional cost is another, and it's important. You and your partner may each already have a house or an apartment; living in either one can create problems. As the newcomers move in, some stepfamily members feel intruded upon; the rest feel like intruders, outsiders. In addition, "emotional ghosts" — unpleasant reminders of the previous spouse — aren't easily evicted. The situation can become a Catch-22: changing things can upset grieving children, while leaving them alone can upset your new partner.

A fresh beginning can spare a stepfamily "space wars," while giving everyone a head start on building a positive stepfamily atmosphere. Yet sometimes a neutral move simply isn't possible. When this is the case, altering the appearance and use of the space with paint, wallpaper, and some different furnishings can make a vast difference. Maybe a renovation can provide some needed space, such as an additional bedroom for a teenager. Including children in decisions that affect their space can help ease their resentment and increase their sense of belonging.

Yours, Mine — and Ours?

To add or not to add a new baby to your stepfamily affects all family members. Couples may hold vastly different expectations about having another child, especially if your partner hasn't yet had children. Hopefully you've discussed this at great length before your remarriage; delaying this discussion can cause couple conflict. If you postponed this serious decision, or have a hidden agenda, you may need a counselor to help you unearth the reasons behind your avoidance of talking this through. This is a subject that needs to be brought into the open!

A new baby can link the two sets of family members and strengthen your stepfamily. Biologically related to everyone, this child can bring the family together. Be aware, though, that the new arrival can elicit both good and bad family feelings. Children from former marriages may feel excited about another child, or jealous and resentful, or both. And in a stepfamily — as in any family — having a baby in order to hold together a shaky relationship can be a big mistake.

The Discipline Dilemma

Until your children and stepchildren leave home, one of your main challenges will be dealing with discipline.

The skills needed to guide children's behavior are the same for all families, but the stepfamily faces some special challenges. In stepfamilies, parents must deal with an instant family; you haven't usually had time to develop a child-rearing plan. In biological families, children and parents have usually developed close bonds over time, so children more readily accept the parents' right to set limits and boundaries. In the stepfamily, stepchildren often tend to reject any discipline attempts by a new stepparent.

Until stepchildren and the new adults in their lives have developed rapport, you'll find it best for each biological parent to handle primary discipline issues with their own children. It can be made clear, however, that the stepparent has the right to discipline in the biological parent's absence. To achieve this interchangeable authority, the adults must share a similar approach to discipline. While a totally united front is unnecessary (all parents do not always agree on all issues), it's important that partners support each other.

To develop this support, talk with each other, and share your views and expectations about discipline and responsibility. Then, when one of you enforces the rules with your children, the other will understand the thinking behind the behavior and be able to be supportive. Stepchildren will test you — at times to your limits! Part of that testing is to check out your new adult relationship. Children need to sense that a spirit of cooperation and respect exists between their parent and stepparent. As time goes on and a friendly, caring relationship with your stepchildren is built, you can begin to share in their discipline. But, remember, achieving such a relationship takes time.

Because we know that discipline is the biggest challenge stepfamilies face, we've devoted two entire chapters to this topic later in the book. Chapters 11 and 12, "Dealing with Stepfamily Discipline" and "Why Do Children Misbehave?" explore discipline in depth, and offer helpful guidelines for dealing with this critical issue in your stepfamily.

8

Strengthening Your Couple Relationship III:

Building Intimacy and Communication

*K*eeping a marriage exciting is hard work. In your stepfamily, it can be even more difficult. Life in a stepfamily is complicated; sheer numbers — of people and interpersonal problems — can overwhelm even the most well-meaning couple. And, as any marriage partner knows, dreams of happiness aren't magically fulfilled.

As you attempt to build your marriage, you and your partner face several obstacles. Unrealistic or undefined expectations, poor communication, and unsatisfactory conflict resolution are three common sources of relationship difficulties that need to be overcome.

Expectations

Many people expect marriage to meet most of their needs: economic, emotional, sexual, and social. Expectations about marriage arise from beliefs about your inner needs. Few people, however, understand all their own expectations, let alone their mate's. The resulting dilemma: How can you meet the needs of your partner if you don't fully understand what those needs are?

Sometimes people remarry with unspoken contracts — hidden agendas — about unhealthy needs, such as, "You help me rear my kids, I'll help you with yours." Once your children have grown, what do you have left to share as a couple?

In the stepfamily, as in any two-parent family, the strength of the couple's relationship is the key to stability.

Sometimes, too, partners are too dependent on each other. Such a relationship may create a sense of helplessness in your children. How can your child compete with an adult for parental attention? In defense, the children may band together against the couple — or withdraw from them. In either case, your new partner will be viewed as an intruder and stepfamily unity will be low.

Similarly, too much separateness can create a feeling of distance. If you and your partner function too independently, going your own ways and relating only to your own children, separate parent-child divisions become established. Instead of goodwill and close relations, two competitive camps form within the stepfamily. With boundaries drawn and defenses up, cooperation among stepsiblings will also be poor. Family cohesiveness cannot grow, the couple relationship deteriorates, and the stepfamily begins to falter.

Your first step, then, is for each of you to discover for yourself what needs and expectations you've brought to your marriage. Do you need physical affection? Daily time alone? Help managing the budget? A partner to merely listen, not fix the problem. The next step is to share your discoveries with each other.

Are your expectations realistic? Whenever a marriage is made to fill dependency needs, problems will eventually arise. Certainly, it's fair to want support and understanding. But if you expect your mate to make you happy, you're asking the impossible. While marriage can bring satisfaction and pleasure, it won't make an unhappy person happy. That's up to you. If you're depressed or chronically discouraged, seek professional help. Your partner can support and encourage your efforts to strengthen yourself.

In order to build an intimate marital relationship within your busy stepfamily, you must work hard, understand and clarify expectations, and learn to cope with intrusions. Two people with healthy individual identities will find it comfortable to nurture and be nurtured by one another. Building this kind of interdependence takes time. A strong commitment coupled with effective communication can make it happen.

Communication

Good communication is the most important skill for all good relationships. Clear communication — verbal and nonverbal — involves creating understanding. How you and your partner share your thoughts and feelings depends on many factors. Each of you has skills that evolved from your family backgrounds; one or both of you also practiced certain patterns of communication in a former marriage. Now, as you develop a style of communicating as a couple, you may be weeding out the old, destructive patterns. Or, you may find yourselves repeating those negative patterns in your remarriage.

Some people communicate with ease. For others, expressing themselves is a struggle. Couples may need to learn skills to become better at talking with each other. Techniques such as "I-messages" can help people express feelings without judging or blaming:

- "When I'm left to clean up alone, *I feel* used. It seems as if you and your children think of me as a servant."

- "*I feel* scared when I hear so much complaining — I'm afraid if you're unhappy we might not make it together and our stepfamily will end."

I-messages are a concept developed by Dr. Thomas Gordon, and first appeared in his book, *Parent Effectiveness Training* (see References).

Remarried couples who communicate well give their children a great gift. By example, and through encouraging conversation among family members, they teach their children and stepchildren skills that might never have been learned in their former families.

Many barriers inhibit stepfamily communication. Remarrieds may have a harder time taking risks and sharing feelings that reflect sadness and disappointment from former losses. If a person's history includes broken trust, lack of acceptance, abandonment or little respect, then rebuilding and learning to feel safe in a new relationship will take time. But work at it, because conflict avoidance is one of the most deadly communication styles in a marriage. Rebuilding of trust begins with clarifying needs and expectations within yourself, then sharing them with your partner. Talking through your fears and feelings releases harbored negative emotions and energy that can be redirected in positive ways in your stepfamily.

For example, you might feel disgusted with your stepchild's table manners, yet feel inhibited about speaking out about it. After feeling resentment for some time, finally you decide to have a discussion with her mother about changing the situation. As you talk and learn more about your stepchild, you begin to realize that you don't really dislike the child, just some of her behaviors — especially how she eats at the dinner table. As you learn more, you see that she was never taught proper manners. Once you discover this, you can treat the child more positively and begin to accept her, since you know the irritating behavior can be changed. It's best to have her mother's support to carry out the changes, of course; you can encourage her efforts and be the good guy. A nice cycle occurs. As you accept the child, her resistance to you will lessen, and helping her change her behavior gets easier. And as that happens, your bond with her strengthens. Through communication, you've broken through the barrier that was rooted in your fears of stating your personal concerns about table etiquette. Communication is the key!

Learning to recognize nonverbal messages helps you gather more information. A wink or a squeeze on the shoulder communicates affection; silence can be interpreted as lack of interest, hostility, or pain. Again, it depends on one's history and style. Children may attach a certain meaning to a non-verbal cue. When one mother raised her eyebrow, her son knew he needed to listen and shape up; the same raised eyebrow by his stepparent may indicate a feeling of amusement.

When both partners are willing to work on learning to communicate, progress is faster. Remarried couples who communicate well give their children a great gift. By example, and through encouraging conversation among family members, they teach their children and stepchildren skills that might never have been learned in their former families.

Conflict Resolution

The most important skill in the communication process is learning to resolve conflict. Conflict arises when one partner's behavior clashes with the expectations of the other. Poor communication sustains it. Avoiding conflict is dangerous, however, because nothing gets resolved and, over time, the issues don't disappear but can turn into a relationship crisis.

Conflict between remarrieds often revolves around the children. It can also stem from unrealistic expectations and a shortage of resources in the stepfamily: stretching time and money across more than one family calls for tolerance and creativity. Other sources of difficulty might include sex, work, in-laws — current and former — religion, friends, alcohol use, and choices about leisure time. Most married couples cope with conflict in these areas, but remarried couples are especially at risk because of the greater number of people involved.

Chart 3

SPOUSE SUPPORT FOR THE STEPPARENT

In times of anger, frustration, or discouragement, a stepparent needs the support of an understanding spouse. Simply listening and offering a kind, constructive response can make all the difference in the world.

Stepparent's Comment	Nonsupportive Response	Supportive Response
I've tried, but I just don't love your kids. I wish I could. I feel so guilty, letting you down.	You knew I had them when you married me. Love me, love my kids. So I guess if you don't love *them*. . .	It's much too soon to worry about loving them — you barely know them. I know you're trying to accept and respect them, and I'll help any way I can.
Today your son screamed at me, "I hate you! You're not my mother and I don't have to do what you tell me!"	Now don't get upset. He didn't mean it.	You must have been hurt when he was so insensitive. Apparently he's terribly upset about something. Let's try to figure out what it is.
Your kids always come back from their father's house loaded with stuff. It's not fair — how can I compete with that?	Make them take that stuff back. We don't have room for it here.	He probably feels guilty because he doesn't see the kids much. He gives them presents to make up for it. The time you spend with them means a lot more to all of us than "things."
Your ex-wife still runs your life. Whenever she calls, you jump.	Why are you so hyper? I'm married to *you*, aren't I?	I see you're upset. Can you tell me exactly what bothers you and what you'd like me to do differently?
Your daughter got into Christine's stuff again and they're fighting.	Christine does the same thing to her — she's just getting even.	Looks like we've got a case of sibling rivalry on our hands. If we're patient, they'll learn to get along — sooner or later! What can I do to help you bear with the fighting till it settles down?
I don't like it when your daughter runs around here in that bikini underwear.	You're getting upset about nothing — quit acting like a prude. We're her family, for Pete's sake!	I hear your discomfort. We got used to being casual when we lived alone. I'll ask her to wear a robe.
I'm not going to let Dane invite your ex-husband's parents to his graduation. He hasn't seen them in months and he doesn't need to see them now. *My* parents really like Dane — and make an effort to see him. They're expecting to come.	They're not ex-grandparents and they're coming. Stop being so selfish. Your folks should understand how it is.	I know you're uncomfortable around them, but please try to understand how important they are to Dane. They're still his grandparents. He wants them *and* your parents to come. And I'm glad your parents care enough to want to come also.
What do you mean you want to take your kids camping for a week? We haven't been anywhere alone since we got married.	You knew before we ever got married that my kids and I do a lot of camping.	Sounds like we need to spend more time alone together — thanks for the reminder. How about one of those hotel get-away weekends just for the two of us?

How you resolve conflict in your couple relationship affects your entire stepfamily. When conflict occurs, you have three choices:

- You can choose to fight. Fighting doesn't resolve conflict, however. Instead, it polarizes the partners, dividing you with "right-and-wrong" arguments and blame games that serve to intensify rather than diminish the conflict.

Sometimes couple conflict revolves around choice of friends.

- You can deny or avoid the problem. Avoiding the issue, however, virtually guarantees it will come up again — and again.

- You can choose to work together to solve the problem. Solving it clears the air. Learning to work through conflict brings you intimacy rather than emotional distance.

Solving conflict requires that couples take specific steps toward resolution. In their book, *Time for a Better Marriage,* Don Dinkmeyer and Jon Carlson suggest a four-step process:

- Show mutual respect.

- Pinpoint the real issue.

- Seek areas of agreement.

- Mutually participate in decisions.

Consider Maggie and Will. They argue repeatedly about Will's son Brian. No matter what Maggie says or does, Brian refuses to clean his room. When Maggie appeals to her husband, he says, "Don't expect so much from the kid — he's had a lot to adjust to." "Well, so have I," replies Maggie. "And, I might add, without a lot of help from you!" "Now, wait a minute," Will responds, "*I'm* just trying to keep the two of you from getting into a knock-down, drag-out fight!"

You can imagine how this frequent argument between Will and Maggie progresses. To begin to resolve their conflict, Maggie and Will can follow the four-step process:

1. ***They can show mutual respect.*** Will and Maggie seem to be working to prove each other wrong. This attitude may be at the heart of their conflict, and it certainly makes things worse. By showing mutual respect — and using I-messages to avoid placing blame — they can open the way to seeing each other's point of view. Their new approach might start off like this:

   > Maggie: "When you don't back me up and require that Brian clean his room, I feel resentful. I see you taking sides against me when I'm trying to build good habits in your son."

   > Will: "I worry that you're expecting too much from Brian too soon."

2. ***They can pinpoint the real issue.*** This could be any of a number of things: Will may feel threatened by Maggie's firm stand with Brian. He may fear that he's letting her be in charge, or worry that Brian will someday learn to respect his wife's stricter approach. For her part, Maggie may feel that she needs to assert some authority, and is hurt that her husband is discounting this. She may feel unfairly treated because she's expected to discipline Brian, but isn't allowed to follow her own judgment.

As Maggie and Will speak and listen to one another respectfully, they can begin to discover what the underlying issues are. Here,

Taking the time to build a strong bond with your partner doesn't mean you are depriving your children; building that bond is as important for your children's well-being as it is for yours.

the problem goes deeper than whether Brian should clean his room:

> Maggie: "I think I hear you saying you don't want to give up control over your son."

> Will: "I guess I don't — and it seems you feel I have no faith in your judgment."

3. ***They can seek areas of agreement.*** Will and Maggie can look closely at what each is really willing to do to begin to resolve this conflict. To find a solution, of course, both need to agree to a mutual change of behavior. But the wish to change and the decision to do so are the responsibility of each individual. Once they've agreed to cooperate rather than argue, they'll be able to search for what each can do to ease, and ultimately resolve, their conflict.

4. ***They can mutually participate in decisions.*** Here Maggie and Will can brainstorm all kinds of ideas, and begin to practice give-and-take:

> Maggie: "I could agree not to nag Brian so often or expect so much if you'll be willing to sit down with me and make a list of what we can expect of him."

> Will: "I think a list is too formal and threatening. But I'm willing to talk it through with you. Once we agree on something, we can all three sit down together and talk about it."

> Maggie: "But how will we get Brian to stick to an agreement?"

> Will: "Maybe we could ask Brian how he thinks that could be handled. He might have a few ideas of his own."

> Maggie: "I'm still worried that he'll want to find the easy way out and that, when he does, you'll be too lenient."

> Will: "Then let's try to agree ahead of time how to handle that, too."

Of course, resolving a marriage conflict isn't as easy as one-two-three-four! But these steps provide a framework you can follow. As you and your partner work to find solutions, keep the four steps in mind. If you get stuck, refer back to them.

Love alone doesn't conquer all; marriage takes work. Anger is normal in any marriage, so when conflict arises in yours, don't panic and fear that your stepfamily is failing. Conflict is one of the many challenges you and your mate will face. How you resolve it depends on how much you're both willing to restore harmony to your relationship. This willingness reflects your commitment to one another.

To work on improving communication and problem-solving skills, you might want to join a couples' group that focuses on these issues. (Look for a group led by a qualified and experienced professional therapist.)

Among the many self-help books on couple's communication and marital relationships are several that we suggest for your consideration (see also the References): Albert Ellis and Ted Crawford: *Making Intimate Connections;* Jon Carlson and Don Dinkmeyer, Sr.: *Time for a Better Marriage;* John Gottman: *The Relationship Cure;* Arnold Lazarus: *Marital Myths Revisited;* Markman, Stanley, & Blumberg: *Fighting for Your Marriage.*

If all your energy is directed toward children and their needs, your marriage won't have a chance to take root and grow.

Taking Time to Grow

One of the most rewarding challenges you face as a couple is creating a new home with a warm, happy atmosphere that brings everyone together. In the beginning, life in the stepfamily seems like a three-ring circus. As you balance your time between building a family, caring for your personal needs, and creating a solid marriage, you become masters at juggling resources and relationships. Too often, your couple relationship gets shortchanged. Your instinct and need may tell you to take time for each other; your guilt about the children or concern about money may keep you from doing so. The balance is tricky. You must constantly choose between family activities and time alone as a couple.

It's critical that you understand the importance of making your couple relationship a priority. If you don't nourish your marriage, you may not be able to stay together. There is a very high divorce rate among remarried families and, while not all of these are stepfamilies, too many are. People tend to remarry too soon and that "trio of uns" — *unresolved grief, unrealistic expectations, uninformed adults* — sabotages their chances for success. A major reason for divorce among remarried couples is that partners fail to spend enough quality time working to build their relationship. With the focus immediately and constantly on the children and their needs, the marriage never gets a chance to take root and grow. Many needlessly quit too soon, and then *everyone* suffers. Even if your remarriage doesn't end, your stepfamily cannot stabilize until your couple relationship is secure. Until children sense that your relationship is solid, they may remain distant from stepparents, afraid to trust. They'll continue to test you with misbehaviors. Taking the time to build a strong bond with your partner doesn't mean you are depriving your children; indeed, building that bond is as important for your children's well-being as it is for yours.

Personal Growth — Taking Time for Yourself

Just as stepfamily success requires that partners work on their couple relationship, a good partnership can only exist between two people who feel complete, who have had the opportunity to grow and to realize their individual potential — and continue to do so. A successful remarriage takes two happy, healthy people who are content with themselves.

Sometimes partners reach an impasse in building a stepfamily because they are at different places in their lives. One may be ready to spend more time outside the couple relationship, while the other wants more togetherness. Or one may require a relationship of harmony by avoiding conflict, while the other prefers to express and air disagreements. If couples can see individual growth and differences as enriching, rather than threatening, to the relationship, they can be compatible and share goals.

Continued personal growth after remarriage is essential. A balance of family, couple, and independent time is important for both partners because it provides satisfaction, good feelings, and a sense of competence. These sources of self-esteem are especially vital to stepparents, who may find helping rear someone else's children difficult, and not immediately rewarding.

Chaos and confusion, complex relationships, complicated schedules as children move between two homes, the never-ending challenge of juggling past and present relationships and carrying out your many roles, all this can make you wonder how you'll ever meet your own needs. Where will you find solitude to regain your perspective and calm your frazzled nerves? Do you feel selfish when you want time alone? Try to reframe your thinking and realize that, rather than alone time being a selfish act, it's intelligent self-interest. Everyone needs the luxury of time alone to think, sort through ideas, and dream. And, beyond this, if you're caught up in a difficult situation with a stepchild, you need time alone to resolve your feelings and figure out what to do. Just as you find time for household chores, errands, or the evening news, you can find the time from your busy family routine for yourself.

One day, when you can view your remarriage as a success, it'll be easy to say, "How could I have doubted?" But now, while you're trying to cope with so much, you have to give yourself the time and space you need. For it will be in that circle of quiet and centeredness that you'll begin to gain confidence, to accept your stepchildren and yourself, to remind yourself of the possibilities that you know you can change into realities. It is from that calm place that you'll begin, once again, to trust yourself.

What's Special About Your Relationship?

Like any marriage, a successful remarriage isn't a matter of chance. At times, as you struggle, you may even regret you were unable to keep your former marriage together: "If I only knew then...." To succeed now, you know you need skills in communication and conflict resolution. Marriage isn't a place to hide. The more you share your deepest dreams and fears, the happier your relationship will become. But it takes practice and time. Above all, as a couple you must have a deep commitment to building and enriching your marriage. Without this strong commitment, no marriage can thrive; with it, you have the power to make choices and control what happens in your stepfamily. When you commit yourselves to seeing how your differences add to, rather than subtract from, your marital satisfaction, you can begin to build a positive foundation for your stepfamily.

As you work at your marriage, focus on its strengths, and the qualities that attracted you to each other in the first place. Your strengths are a beacon of hope, lighting the way for you to create a positive environment for building the future. It is essential to keep your hope alive throughout your process of becoming a stepfamily.

The Stepfamily Workshop
Session Four

Questions for Review

1. What are some ways fears from the past can jeopardize your couple and stepfamily relationships? _____ _____ _____ _____

2. What steps remain for you to complete coming to terms with the past? _____ _____ _____

3. What is *scapegoating* really about in the stepfamily? How does it happen and where does the real problem usually lie? Do you see ways it happens in your stepfamily? _____ _____ _____ _____

4. How does resolving issues with your parents affect your role as spouse or stepparent? _____ _____ _____ _____

5. What loyalty conflicts do adults in your stepfamily face? Which is most difficult for you? Why? _____ _____ _____ _____

6. What major family decisions must you resolve as a stepfamily? _____ _____ _____ _____

7. What do you think is the best way for you to handle finances in your stepfamily? Why? _____
_____
_____
_____

8. Is adding an "ours" baby to the stepfamily wise? What have you decided and why? Please discuss. _____
_____
_____
_____

9. What reasons might a couple have for not revealing hidden agendas or clarifying expectations about remarriage before the wedding? Based on your reading of this chapter, how would you counter those reasons? _____
_____
_____

10. How can communication be a major source of stress? How can partners improve communication and reduce this stress?
_____
_____
_____

11. What are some areas of conflict most stepfamily couples face? Which is the greatest challenge for your stepfamily? How can you work to resolve conflict in your marriage?
_____
_____
_____

12. What three relationship tasks must adults in the stepfamily manage simultaneously? Which task needs to take priority? Why? _____
_____
_____

13. Do you believe it is selfish to take time for yourself, away from your spouse and stepfamily? Explain your answer. _____
_____
_____
_____

Challenge to Conquer

When Gail was 33, she married Jonathan, 14 years her senior. At that time, she believed she had found the man of her dreams. He had three children, but they lived with their mother most of the time. She liked them. When his children came to their house every other weekend, Gail thought it was fun to be with them and planned family activities. Her life revolved around her high-powered career that involved travel to exciting places, so having children was the last thing on her mind. She felt like she had the best of both worlds. Jonathan indicated that he was ready to be done with the "parenting project" as he called it and travel more himself. But they never seriously discussed whether they would have a child. Now, after four years of marriage and at 37, Gail began to think that her life wouldn't be complete without children. When she told Jonathan that she wanted to get off the pill and plan a family, he was very upset. "You knew I didn't want more children when you married me," he shouted. "But we never talked about it," Gail replied in tears.

1. What might Jonathan be thinking and feeling? Why is he angry? _____
   _____
   _____
   _____

2. What might Gail be thinking and feeling? What kept her from talking about children before the remarriage? _____
   _____
   _____
   _____

3. Can Gail change Jonathan's mind about adding more children? Should she? What can this couple do? _____
   _____
   _____
   _____

Stepfamily Activity

Take two sheets of paper, one for you and one for your partner. Each of you is to write the numbers 1-20 down the side of your own sheet. Then, as quickly as you can, without censoring and in no special order, list 20 things you love to do with your partner.

After both lists of 20 are completed, code your responses, using the following symbols. Place the symbols to the left, just before the activity numbers.

- Place a dollar sign (**$**) by each activity that costs money.

- Place a double dollar sign (**$$**) by those that cost more than $25.

- Place a **P** by each activity that, for you, is more fun with other people in addition to your partner.

- Place an **A** by those activities you prefer to enjoy alone as a couple.

- Place an asterisk (*****) in front of each of your five favorite activities.

- Place a plus sign (**+**) next to those activities you think your partner loves best.

Share your completed lists with one another, discussing the similarities and differences between them. Together, create one master list, representing a composite of both your preferences. Spend some time discussing your discoveries and present feelings, and agree to make a greater effort to enjoy time together doing the activities you've identified.

Now take out your calendars and set up three future dates for you and your partner as indicated here:

- Set a date for a three-hour time out together this week

- Establish a date for an overnight trip, and agree on who makes reservations and who's in charge of arranging child care.

- Start to plan a one-week vacation together and schedule it sometime within the coming year. Create a folder and start to collect ideas and information. Build enthusiasm by sending away for brochures, picking up guide books, and perusing websites.

Movies are not allowed for the first two dates, because you can't talk to each other. And, except to share positive things about your children, avoid talking about them. This time is for enriching your couple relationship by focusing on your shared needs, dreams, and goals. (Adapted from Sidney B. Simon, Leland W. Howe, and Howard Kirschenbaum "Twenty Things I Love to Do," from *Values Clarification*. Waltham, MA: Warner Books, 1995)

Understanding My Stepfamily

For you and your partner to gain the most benefit from this activity, first complete it individually, then share your responses with one another. Together, identify and discuss the similarities and differences in your answers.

How much is my current marriage influenced by my past one?
Answer the following questions as objectively as you can.

1. When something — positive or negative — brings to mind my former spouse, do I overreact? Does my new partner? If so, in what ways?_____

_____

_____

_____

2. How is my new partner different from or similar to my former one?_____

_____

_____

_____

3. What did I learn from my former relationship? What am I still repeating?_____

_____

_____

_____

4. Does my present behavior duplicate any past behavior toward my former spouse? How? When I behave in this way, what response do I want from my new partner?_____

_____

_____

_____

_____

Clarifying expectations. Your couple relationship is strengthened when each of you knows the expectations of the other and you negotiate differences to reach a compromise. Use the following list of stepfamily issues as a springboard for such discussions with your mate. Check the items you feel haven't been sufficiently discussed and clarified. Then write down your expectations about each of these items. Further discuss and negotiate solutions.

1. **Career commitments and priorities.** Can both of us keep our jobs and manage the extra child care duties? If both of us work outside the home, how will child care be handled? What about household responsibilities? _____

   _____

   _____

   _____

2. **Money.** Who pays for what? Will the family finances be treated as a common pot venture or will separate accounts be kept? How will we handle child support? _____

   _____

   _____

   _____

3. **Love.** How will we continue to strengthen our love and enrich our relationship? How will we communicate our feelings? How often will we spend time together without the children? What are our emotional and sexual expectations? _____

   _____

   _____

   _____

4. **Children.** How will we relate to our stepchildren? Who will discipline whom? What are each of our rights and duties toward them? Should we have an "ours" baby? _____

   _____

   _____

   _____

What's special about our relationship? Sit back, close your eyes, and think of all the happy events you and your new partner have shared. What special skills do we each bring to the remarriage? What special traditions or rituals are we creating together? What difficult situations have we overcome successfully? After you have cleared your mind to let the joys and successes flow in, jot them all down, no matter how insignificant they may seem. Share this list with your spouse.

Points to Ponder

- Your couple relationship sets the tone and is the foundation for your stepfamily.

- Clearing up unfinished emotional business with your parents and former spouse enriches and strengthens your remarriage.

- Decisions about financial problems can affect stepfamily unity; you might need to find creative solutions.

- Setting up your household in a new, neutral environment avoids many problems.

- An "ours" baby can either link your two families or cause children to feel threatened. Prepare them by talking about it in advance.

- Three critical tasks you face as a stepfamily couple are coping with family and children, building your marriage relationship, and continuing to grow as individuals.

- A strong couple relationship requires that you clarify expectations, build communication and conflict-resolution skills, and maintain a deep commitment to making your marriage work.

9

Recreating Roles and Relationships

*B*ecoming a stepparent was the hardest thing I'd ever done! I had to
learn to listen — with my ears, eyes, mind, and heart — to what my
partner and stepchildren were saying without taking things personally —
even when it felt personal. But I knew enough about stepfamilies to give it
time and know that they would tell me where and how I'd fit into their lives.

Becoming a stepparent is NOT for wimps! The most important and
challenging role you've ever played is that of a parent — the one
we're often unprepared to fill. This is doubly true for a stepparent,
as you take on a mostly undefined role that's filled with inherent
challenges. The rewards of being a stepparent are long-term and,
too often, being a successful partner conflicts with being a
successful stepparent. Little wonder that you feel apprehension
about your decision to help raise another person's children. Yet,
like you, each year hundreds of thousands of people agree to
become stepparents.

This chapter explores the challenging task of becoming a stepparent
and examines ways you might define your role to begin building
trust. Success depends on taking time to develop relationships
slowly so that new bonds can be formed and strengthened.

Effective Stepparents

Although each stepfamily has a unique structure, all can be guided
by the same basic principles that produce well-adjusted children
and effective parents in any family. Like all successful parents,
effective stepparents possess certain specific characteristics:

An effective stepparent can empathize. When you can perceive
life as another sees it, you're exercising *empathy*. Empathy differs
from pity or sympathy. And having been in a similar situation

doesn't automatically make you able to empathize. To do this, you need to look at things from the other person's point of view, as though you're seeing the world through their eyes.

Can you enter your stepson's world of feelings and experience them in the same or a similar way? Can you feel the tug of your stepdaughter's loyalty conflict? Can you sense the sadness and loss that might overwhelm your stepchildren? Can you imagine any reasons why they might be hostile or indifferent to you?

You're practicing empathy when you can honestly say, "If I were in your shoes, I'd feel the same way." The more you're able to feel empathy toward your stepchildren, the more you'll understand them and the better your chances of becoming a successful stepparent.

An effective stepparent isn't defensive. Blaming, taking sides, and showing favoritism reflect reactions to a perceived threat. All these responses are defensive. Without a doubt, your stepchildren will test the limits and boundaries of your new relationship with them, compare you with their absentee parent, and maybe even blame you for their loss of that parent. Can you keep from reacting defensively?

Most of these comparisons or attacks aren't really directed at you, rather they represent your stepchildren's need to defend their biological parent, which is a natural response. While it's hard not to personalize these attacks and defend yourself, that's exactly what you must try to do. Their actions may be reflecting loss and sadness from their changed family life.

When an angry stepchild screams, "I hate you — you're not my mother!" an unthreatened stepparent empathizes with the child and explores the feelings behind the behavior. The child may really be worrying, "If I learn to care about you, will you leave me too?" or, "Will you take my mom away from me?"

The basis for remaining non-defensive is respect. When you can respect your stepchild's feelings, without defending yourself or attacking back, you both benefit. You might say, "I don't expect you to agree with the way I do everything, but I do ask that you respect my point of view and feelings. And I'll respect yours."

An effective stepparent avoids being judgmental. We're all guilty of judging at times, even when we don't mean to do so. Often judging may be subtle. You might tell your spouse, "My kids never do that," implying that your way is right and your partner's way is wrong. To your stepchild, you might say, "If you'd just use your head!" implying that the child is either stupid or wrong. When you resist evaluating your stepchild negatively, you'll be on your way to building a positive relationship with that child.

An effective stepparent shows acceptance. The cornerstone of good relationships with stepchildren is acceptance. Again, respect is the key. As an accepting stepparent, you respect children regardless of their behavior. Relate to your stepchildren as equals without setting conditions or insisting on changes to fit your way of doing things. Respect your stepchildren's ability to conduct their own lives, to make decisions, and to take responsibility for themselves. It's also important to respect the history of their former families and their need and right to continue an ongoing relationship with their biological parents.

An effective stepparent is open to change. The stepfamily is a reorganization of the traditional family system. These changes and transitions call nearly everything into question. Beliefs and behaviors are scrutinized, values are examined, skills are tested, and requests are resisted. While change can bring about a crisis, it's your response to the crisis that counts. Will you manage the crisis by reacting or responding in a calm and thoughtful manner? Keep in mind that remaining rigid or resistant to trying new and different things will only create more opposition.

Effective stepparents see change as a challenge, a chance for growth. If you don't fear that growth, your entire stepfamily can relax. When met with enthusiasm and expectancy, change can enrich your stepfamily.

An effective stepparent has a strong sense of personal identity. Since stepparents routinely encounter stressful situations, a successful stepparent needs a strong, positive self-image, and a powerful sense of personal value. Self-confidence and self-respect, the main components of self-esteem, contribute to a sense of personal worth. Hopefully, you've taken time to strengthen your sense of identity and develop a strong sense of self-acceptance before you've taken on the role of stepparent. A sense of humor helps too!

Do you have the courage to be imperfect, to accept yourself with all your faults and limitations? As you try to carve out a role with your

A positive outlook can ease everyone's adjustment.

stepchildren, you'll make mistakes and meet setbacks. To withstand the pressures brought on by these setbacks, it's important that you feel positive about yourself. Once you recognize yourself as a separate, strong person, sure of your identity, you'll be able to see others in your stepfamily as individuals too.

An effective stepparent believes in children's abilities and allows them to be responsible for themselves. You are responsible *to* your stepchildren, not *for* them. Why would you take responsibility for your stepchildren's habits or attitudes that were developed long before you became involved in their lives? You don't have to overcompensate for the pain they've experienced, or feel you must make up for lost time. Remember, rather than sympathize, you can empathize. Like you, your stepchildren are in the process of developing their new role. Choose to meet them where they are, and discover how you can fit into their lives in a positive way.

Redefining Roles

Can you view your role as a stepparent realistically? Most people about to remarry don't, and believe they'll work into it. The problem with this notion is there's no transition between becoming a spouse and becoming a stepparent. As you share your marriage vows your simultaneous roles as partner, parent and stepparent can begin to conflict immediately.

To cope with your anxiety, you may have taken on the role of either a Super Stepparent or a Reluctant Stepparent. Super Stepparents rush headlong into making their relationships work, often pressuring children who need time to deal with all the changes they've been through.

This approach can cause the natural bond between the biological parent and children to tilt the family into a power struggle. Reluctant Stepparents hold back and avoid building relationships with the stepchildren, creating feelings within the children that they are disliked.

As an effective stepparent, you'll realize that neither approach creates unity for your stepfamily or fosters close relationships. To succeed, you need more than crossed fingers and good intentions; you'll need information and clear guidelines.

How do you plan to relate to your stepchildren? You probably have your own ideas about what you're willing, or unwilling, to be to these children. And stepchildren will have their own ideas about your role too. It's important that somewhere along the line you and your stepchildren clarify your separate expectations and get on the same page.

Stepparents who approach their role at first as a friend are usually the most satisfied and successful.

Stepparent as friend. Building a friendship from the arranged relationship between a stepparent and a stepchild isn't always easy. Yet, stepparents who approach their role as that of a friend are usually the most satisfied and successful.

Remember this important fact: Your stepchildren already have a father and a mother; this remains true even if one of those parents died, is an absentee parent, or has never been known to the child. When they have continued contact with their biological parents, children usually don't need stepparents for general psychological survival. Yet in your role of friend, you can provide additional caring and concern.

Chart 4

STEPPARENTING ROLES

The contrast between a misguided and an effective approach to stepparenting provides you a key to success in the stepfamily. The effective stepparent works with accurate information and chooses specific behaviors to build positive relationships.

Misguided Stepparent

Tries to replace the absent parent
- Feels insecure about stepparent role
- Wants to own children and their affections
- Attempts to cut ties with noncustodial parent
- Assumes children cannot love several adults
- Creates loyalty conflicts for children

Demands love and acceptance
- Expects to care about stepchildren immediately
- Expects children to express affection right away
- Feels guilty when children express affection they don't really feel

Insists feelings for stepchildren and biological children are the same
- Tries to deny rather than accept differences in feelings
- Feels guilty for loving own biological children more
- Overcompensates with stepchildren by giving gifts, spending extra time, expressing phony feelings

Manages everyone else's relationships
- Takes on problems for all family members
- Interferes in communication efforts of siblings, kids, biological parents
- Keeps family members from forming direct relationships with one another
- Insists on being included in activities
- Deprives parents and children of needed private time and space together

Assumes peacemaker role
- Fears another family loss
- Believes difficulties imply failure
- Denies problems exist
- Shuts out negative emotions
- Reacts defensively when stated feelings and real feelings clash

Strives to be perfect to counteract "wicked stepparent" myth
- Allows no imperfection in self as parent figure
- Avoids mistakes at all costs
- Suppresses negative emotions
- Refuses to state any opinions that might create conflict

Feels sorry for children of loss
- Tries to make up for children's parental loss
- Pities children and delays necessary grieving process
- Indulges and pampers, therefore preventing stepchildren from learning to understand life as it really is with its pain and adversities

Insists on family unity
- Views goal as happiness and harmony at all costs. Uses family "togetherness" to show outsiders "how great we're doing"
- Dictates activities and denies free choice among family members
- Diverts family members from preferred activities

Effective Stepparent

Recognizes importance of other biological parent
- Respects children's need and right to love both parents
- Helps stepchildren nurture relationship by encouraging them to write, phone, visit their parent
- Allows pictures, mementos of biological parent without creating conflict
- Invites other biological parent to important milestone ceremonies and events
- Strives to be added parent figure and friend, rather than substitute parent

Acknowledges existing bond between new spouse and children
- Realizes it's natural to feel closer to biological children
- Reduces jealousy and competition for time and attention
- Controls resentment when child and parent need time alone

Allows time for relationships to develop
- Focuses on process of developing as a family unit
- Values each small success as evidence of relationship growth
- Minimizes worrying or trying to force progress
- Respects and accepts others as new family forms

Manages own relationships with each child
- Avoids interfering in other people's problems unless invited
- Encourages family members to care for own needs and relationships

Understands family life cannot always be happy
- Accepts that problems exist
- Understands that unhappy experiences teach children coping skills
- Allows full expression of emotions, whether negative or positive, pleasant or unpleasant

Possesses the courage to be imperfect
- Rejects fairy-tale myths and unrealistic media portrayals of stepfamilies
- Understands every mistake doesn't reflect cruel stepparent image
- Realizes that people learn by making mistakes, thinking about them, and trying again
- Shares own mistakes to give children permission to be imperfect and human

Accepts grief and loss as part of life's experience
- Encourages children to face the reality of death or divorce that preceded the stepfamily
- Feels empathy, not sympathy, with children of loss. Helps kids confront and express feelings that grief elicits
- Provides strength and encouragement so children can move into the future

Lets go
- Permits children to belong to two households with a minimum of fuss
- Allows children to spend time with peers, activities, other parent, without fearing stability of stepfamily is threatened. Plans family activities without forced participation. Uses time away from children to enhance relationship with spouse

Adapted from Elizabeth Einstein and Linda Albert, "Pitfalls and Possibilities," one of four booklets in The Stepfamily Living Series *(Ithaca, NY), p. 14–16. See References for more information.*

Becoming a friend to a stepchild isn't the same as being a buddy, and it doesn't mean that you have to get along perfectly all the time. You can be a friend who supports and empathizes with a stepchild's complex feelings. Offering friendship is far less threatening than coming in to take over. As you build your role from the basis of friendship, be sure to give children time to come to know and respect you.

Stepparent as confidant. A stepparent provides children with another adult sounding board. This is especially important for teenagers, who sometimes feel alienated from their parents and uncomfortable seeking their advice.

The normal assertiveness and anxiety of adolescence often cause stressful relationships between parents and their teenage children. Offering additional options and opinions, a supportive stepparent can soften the sharp edges of a child's relationship with their parent of the same sex. You must be careful as a stepparent, of course, not to develop an alliance with the child against the other parent, or to use the child to hurt the other parent.

Your role as confidant allows you to become an adviser. As you express values and beliefs to your stepchildren, you can feel good about yourself. When all the adults in a stepfamily are doing this for each other's children, everyone's life is enriched.

Stepparent as another parent figure. If your stepchildren are very young, or have little contact with their non-custodial parent, you might be considered as a primary parent, another parent. The key here is to understand that *another* means *in addition to* rather than *a replacement for.*

It's important to treat your children and your stepchildren alike; that is, to have similar expectations of and respect for them. But be careful! Being another parent doesn't mean you must *feel* the same about them as their biological parent does. Stepparents who serve as another parent figure in the lives of their stepchildren too often get their own needs mixed up with those of the children they are parenting. This can create tricky situations. If you become too emotionally attached to these children as a primary parent, denying that they have another parent somewhere, you could potentially be opening yourself up to a great deal of grief. Be clear about your role!

Stepparent as mentor. A mentor's role is teaching, consulting, and sharing expertise and information that may help prepare someone for life. Beyond their parents, children need special people in their lives to pass on skills, knowledge, and wisdom. Such a person might be a teacher, a scout leader, or perhaps a next-door neighbor.

Many stepchildren say their stepparent played an important role as their teacher or mentor. A mentor, however, is not a meddler. Before you step in, be sure your stepchildren want your help.

Stepparent as role model. The stepparent as mentor teaches a specific skill, and the child learns consciously and willingly. The stepparent as role model teaches by setting an example; here the child learns unconsciously and copies the behavior of the stepparent. An additional adult in the family provides another close-up model for stepchildren, giving them a new way of trying on life and viewing the world. Thus, what starts out as a challenge in the stepfamily — too many differences — becomes an opportunity!

As a stepparent, you may already find yourself in one or more of these roles. Depending everyone's needs, you might shift from one to another. What is critical is that you and your partner make a conscious choice about your stepparent role early on, allowing specific goals to be set. Who do you turn to for advice about which role to play? Ask the children for their thoughts by saying something like, "You know, I've never been a stepparent before so I don't quite know how to be with you. How would you like our relationship to look?" And, while input from the children is important, couples must discuss and make the final decision about which stepparent roles you'll play.

The Shape of Your Stepfamily

As a stepparent, your perspective and possible problems will depend on your basic stepfamily configuration. Are the children with you full-time or part-time? To whom do they belong? Have you and your new partner each brought children into the new stepfamily?

The Stepfamily with Children from One Partner Only

Being a biological parent is challenge enough; starting parenthood as a stepparent is even harder. Not only are you adjusting to your partner, but at the same time you're learning to be a parent to someone else's children who may not welcome you, or who may be harboring hurts from their other parent and all their losses.

Of all the stepparent roles, that of the stepmother with no children of her own is often the hardest. (See Cassell in References.) Having no experience raising children, you receive no validation as a parent — from your partner, your stepchildren's other parent, or society. Male or female, stepparents thrust into the role of a primary caregiver must often cope both with the unrealistic expectations of other adults and your stepchildren, who can be unappreciative and unpleasant as they try to adjust to yet another change in their lives. Little wonder that many stepparents feel like failures in their first efforts at being parents. "If this is what it's like to be a parent," some may reason, "I don't want children of my own."

Being a stepparent before you are a parent provides for an especially rigorous training ground — but it might even make you a *better* parent if you decide to have children. Many people in this position report that once they have their own child they feel really good about their parenting skills. And with the pressure lowered and a renewed confidence in themselves, they become even better stepparents.

If you're in this situation, your major challenge is figuring out how to belong — how to become a significant part of an existing family.

Many stepparents are welcomed with open arms — by their spouse who is glad to have a partner in parenting, and by stepchildren

Instant parenthood brings unexpected challenges

who are comforted to see their parent happy and pleased to have another adult around. Stepparents who've never had families of their own may come to the role with enthusiasm about sharing skills and special times with their stepchildren. Is this you? Then befriend the children slowly, keep your expectations low, and acknowledge the relationship the children have with their other parent. You can play a significant role in the lives of your stepchildren!

A warning! Sometimes stepparents face resentment and resistance from stepchildren and defensiveness from their new partner. The children may resent you taking up their parent's time; they may resist your early efforts at discipline. As a new stepparent, you may respond to your partner's request to help with discipline and take action where you feel it is needed; then your partner might turn around and defend the children! Such parent-child-stepparent triangles can create big challenges. This tends to be most common in the early stages of the stepfamily process.

A stepparent can easily feel like an intruder.

How long was your partner a single parent? Fitting into your new family can become more difficult for you if strong bonds were formed between your partner and his children during single-parent living. To survive and work together well, this family unit developed tight bonds. But after remarriage, your partner now needs to relax these bonds, relinquish some control, and let you — the stepparent — become part of the unit. If the connection between the biological parent and children remains too strong, and you fail to negotiate major issues as a couple, the building of new and necessary stepfamily ties will be inhibited.

Stepparents walk a tightrope between respecting the existing family relationships and trying to become part of them. Here are three common outcomes:

1. Stepparents take on the routines and rituals of the existing single-parent family and become integrated into the family.

2. Stepparents take control and risk alienating family members, especially teenagers.

3. The process of change creates a new family status: the needs, wants, and wishes of all stepfamily members are taken into account as the family evolves to a new, stable place.

An unfortunate fourth possibility is that the stepparent might be driven away, branded as unsatisfactory, and unable to meet anyone's expectations. Most often these unmet expectations were unrealistic or rooted in hidden agendas about what role the stepparent is to play.

How can you reduce your chances of being perceived as an intruder? Talk with your partner and, as a couple, explore these issues to the extent that they're known. Only when the biological parent lets you know what place he or she hopes you'll play in the children's lives, can you truly become an effective part of the family.

Most stepparents do a better job than they think

Most stepparents do a better job than they think. Researchers Paul Bohannan and Rosemary Erickson compared children growing up with biological fathers to those reared by stepfathers and found that the stepchildren were just as happy and well-adjusted as the children in traditional families. (See References.) The children said so; their mothers said so: yet the stepfathers rated their stepchildren as less happy and themselves as less effective than the biological fathers did. Overly conscious of their role, many stepparents tend to be critical of themselves.

In any stepfamily where only one spouse brings children to the marriage, no balance exists, no trade-offs. One chose and married a partner; the other gained a whole family. With no way to reciprocate for what the stepparent does for the children, the biological parent may feel guilty. Worse, she may have difficulty understanding why the stepparent is having trouble, and fail to support her partner in that role. Research shows that, above all, what stepparents need to succeed is strong support from the biological parent — your new partner. If your partner can empathize and show appreciation, your self-esteem will be enhanced and you'll feel more confident. A domino effect occurs! Encouraged, you'll feel good about being a stepparent, happier about your role, and become more successful as a partner *and* a stepparent.

Do you live in a stepfamily where only one of you has children? If you're the only biological parent, you may have an easier time adjusting. You don't have to get used to someone else's children or become an "instant parent." But if you have children and your partner doesn't, your important task is to be sensitive to integrating your new spouse into your existing family, to help that person avoid painful feelings of being an outsider or intruder. By understanding with empathy that the stepparent's role is not an easy one, you can offer support and encouragement. It's important to express your appreciation, provide helpful feedback, and listen to what your partner is saying about feelings relating to your children.

The Stepfamily in Which Both Adults Are Parents

When both adults bring children to the remarriage, similarities may smooth the merger. You're in the same situation: each of you is a parent. In most cases each of you had a former spouse with whom — in the case of divorce — it remains necessary to interact for the sake of the children. Each of you must learn to relate to the other's children. These common denominators often make it easier to offer empathy and support.

But children can also become dividers. Many — especially teen-agers — will do anything they can to get their way. If you're in the dual role of biological parent and stepparent, you may feel like a juggler, developing new relationships with your partner's children while nurturing existing ones with your own. If you're not on the same page with your expectations and aren't tending to your marriage, your children can come between you. Two armed camps

---

Guidelines for Easing the Adjustment to Stepfamily Living

For stepparents:

- Seek support — from your spouse, friends, clergyperson, other stepparents, a support group.

- Be there for your stepchildren, but allow them time to learn to trust and respect you.

- Respect the strong biological bond and the history that exists between your spouse and the children. Allow them plenty of time together. Avoid interfering where issues aren't your concern.

For biological parents:

- Include your new spouse in your existing family unit, but let relationships develop at their own pace — especially around discipline issues.

- Be supportive, ready to listen, and discuss difficulties.

- Encourage a cooperative spirit between your spouse and your children's other biological parent.

For both of you:

- Examine your parenting styles. Take classes together or join a support group to develop problem-solving and discipline skills.

- Work out ways for your stepfamily to communicate: family meetings, bulletin boards, complaint and compliment pots, and regularly planned activities.

- Talk about feelings. Airing them aloud diminishes their power.

- Be patient. Allow plenty of time for family members to work through many differences.

- Make your couple relationship a priority. Remember, when parents have a happy marriage, children feel more secure.

---

can develop. When this happens, everyone loses. As parents rush to the defense of their respective children, your couple relationship deteriorates. As your children sense your marriage coming apart, they'll react fearfully and begin to misbehave. Growing ties between stepsiblings loosen. Small rifts widen. Everyone gets edgy. Fear reigns.

Guilt becomes a common bond in the stepfamily. Parents who live with their biological children only part-time feel guilty about time spent with their stepchildren. The more they enjoy the stepchildren, the guiltier they feel about raising someone else's kids rather than their own.

When children spend only summers or weekends with a parent, that parent's guilt may provoke certain behavior. "Disneyland Dads" — and Moms — overcompensate with gifts and money, trying to make up for not being with the children more often. These indulgences don't make children feel better and, as relationships become strained, guilt increases. Time with their children may become so painful that some parents choose to see less and less of them.

Remarried people who receive little financial support from former spouses may feel grateful for the help their new spouse gives them, but also guilty about it. And children who still blame themselves for their parents' divorce may feel guilty when they hear their parent and stepparent fighting. Are they to blame again? They wonder — and worry.

As you've seen, there are many complex differences in the roles and relationships within and around the stepfamily. Each family member faces significant challenges in learning to adapt and succeed in her or his new role as part of a stepfamily. With patience, and effort, and acceptance of the fact that their stepfamily offers a new and different system of family roles and relationships, parents and children in the stepfamily can create a vital intimate environment for the nurturance and growth of every member.

10

Overcoming Stepfamily Obstacles

On the way to the wedding, Harry and Sally are understandably excited about the possibilities of marital and family joy. But there is more than romance and a celebration event this time around. They're juggling loose ends from former relationships, children and their confusion and uncertainties, and other distractions. The happy couple has failed to prepare for marriage in a meaningful way. Having heard that there are likely to be some challenges, they've read a book, crossed their fingers, and hoped for the best. In their rush to find happiness, however, they may have ignored neon-light warnings, or dismissed them as pre-wedding jitters.

The stepfamily's journey is not without hurdles and obstacles. Your stepfamily success can be sidetracked by a wide variety of issues and stresses. Challenges occur when expectations clash with reality, creating confusion for couples and children alike. In this chapter we'll take a look at some of the difficulties stepfamilies struggle with, and how to deal effectively with them.

Don't Expect to Be Noticed

Most stepparents today are well-intentioned people trying to counteract negative social images by becoming Wonder Woman or Superman. Many single parents juggling the demands of job and family have little idea what's in store for them when they marry someone with children. You may think you know but, once the wedding is over, reality hits! Struggling to cope as partner, parent, and stepparent, many people find themselves longing to have their efforts recognized.

Stepparents seek recognition from their stepchildren. Even the most enlightened stepparent, knowing better than to expect instant love or gratitude from stepchildren, needs to be appreciated. Many stepparents feel taken for granted and used. The feeling of being exploited becomes aggravated when children, who are simply trying to be loyal to their biological parent, make criticisms or comparisons like "Dad puts *lots* more butter on the popcorn" or "I like the way my Mom reads that story better."

Stepparents want recognition from their stepchildren's parent in the other household. Most stepmothers want to have their parenting efforts acknowledged in some way by their stepchildren's mother; most stepfathers want this from the father. Of course, these are the sources from which you are least likely to get recognition. Thus, a standoff: as a stepparent, you resent the same-sex biological parent for not appreciating all you do for her children; the biological parent resents you, the stepparent. She may see your parenting efforts as an attempt to replace her.

A stepparent needs a spouse's emotional support. If you're a stepparent who gives a great deal of time and energy to caring for and supporting your spouse's children, you need to feel that you're appreciated. You'd like your efforts validated. While lack of recognition generally results in deep dissatisfaction, you can take steps to improve the situation. Acknowledge it's unrealistic to expect recognition and gratitude — especially at first. Then, you can begin to ask for what you need in this realm, especially from your partner. You might feel uncomfortable asking to have your efforts noticed. But with practice your discomfort will lessen, especially once you realize that if you don't ask for what you need, you'll never get it. You can also learn to give yourself the occasional pat on the back for your efforts and successes.

Stepparents must learn to pat themselves on the back for their efforts and successes.

Competition — Creator of Conflict

As more people vie for the family's limited resources — especially money and time — competition in your stepfamily grows. Too often, resources get translated as love; their shortage can create conflict.

Your new husband's responsibility to a former spouse and his children usually means fewer resources for his new family. He may continue to care for his ex-wife's needs because she cares for his children. If this logic is hard for you to understand or accept, it may result in competition between you and the other biological parent.

Competition with the same-sex parent may be played out by pretending the former spouse doesn't exist, or by trying to outdo that person. The prize in this competition is the children's affections.

Competition with the same-sex parent might be displayed by outdoing.

Stepparents also compete with stepchildren for the spouse's attention and affection. For example, a boy who looks like his father is a constant reminder to the stepfather that his new wife once loved another man. This physical resemblance may heighten the competition.

In all families, girls compete with their mother for their father's attention; boys compete with their father for their mother's. This natural sparring is one way young people validate their emerging sexuality. While biological parents find this competition annoying, stepparents find it maddening — especially young stepparents who've never been a parent.

Such unresolved competition can sabotage the formation of strong family bonds. It can also breed jealousy. When unresolved issues from former marriages filter into the stepfamily, competition and jealousy can reach all-time highs. Jealousy destroys relationships and, ultimately, can undo your stepfamily.

Too many stepfamilies deal with negative feelings by denying them: "Jealous of my wife's former husband? Never." "Resentful of my spouse's child support? Heck no — I knew about it." "Guilty because

I don't love his children? Not me!" "Afraid our stepfamily's in trouble? Of course not — we're just having 'adjustment problems.'"

Although denial is a common way of dealing with resentment, guilt, anger, and fear, this defense is dangerous for stepfamilies. Denial only dulls the hurt and delays resolution; it doesn't erase the feelings. Continued denial pushes the pain deeper, increases feelings of doubt and jealousy, and creates more and more conflict.

The responsibility for reducing competition and jealousy in the stepfamily belongs to both marriage partners. If competition is a problem in your stepfamily, use the skills and guidelines introduced earlier to begin working toward reducing it.

Personal Responsibility

In most stepfamilies, time, space, and money are all in short supply. How much time should you spend with your stepchildren? You need time alone with your own children too. It's likely that you and your partner understand the importance of this, however you'd probably both prefer to spend more time alone — just the two of you. If children live in your new family only part-time, what are your expectations when they come for the summer, or across town for the weekend? To catch up on time with my own children, can I plan a camping trip *without* my spouse and stepchildren? Will they feel left out? How can I explain that I need some time alone with my kids? If that idea creates resentment, how can parents spend quality time with their biological children, so dearly loved and rarely seen?

Time issues need to be talked about so resentment doesn't fester. Discussing different kinds of love is important, too, so children and stepchildren understand the parent's need for special time alone with each of them. Otherwise they fear being left out.

Money is the resource everyone seems to be short of. Stepparents often feel overwhelmed by the great financial responsibility they've taken on. Many continue to assist their first families to some degree, and worry about how to stretch the paycheck between two households. It's difficult for some stepparents to accept such financial realities without resentment. Because money is such a big issue in stepfamilies, it's critical to clarify exactly what each of you feels responsible for.

Resentment is a tricky emotion. While you can understand the situation, even recognize your need to help support your stepchildren, you may still wish circumstances were different and resent the reality. When neither your biological family nor your stepfamily seems to appreciate your efforts as a stepparent, your resentment is further fueled. Some stepparents may soon begin to resent all the changes that have happened.

"Why must I help support another person's children? Where, in this sea of responsibilities and confusion, can I find a spot to be alone?"

Once Again — The Law Is Not On Your Side

What about inheritance? What is your responsibility in this area as a stepparent? Most stepparents believe their primary responsibility is to their current spouse and their biological children, regardless of living arrangements. In terms of child support, the law upholds this, and in most states in the United States, stepparents aren't legally responsible for the financial support of their stepchildren.

But what happens to those children if their biological parent dies? Must a parent entrust his or her estate to a former spouse? Since claims by former spouses should have been settled by the divorce, that person shouldn't have legal rights to the estate. If you're uncomfortable giving your former spouse access to your estate in order to care for your children, you could establish a trust fund from which monthly checks will be released. Ultimately, whatever arrangements you make, parents and stepparents should discuss them, so that your new partner doesn't feel that your financial loyalty to your biological children discounts your responsibility to your new partner.

With a stepparent's resources spread between two families, stepchildren might only receive money indirectly later, through the estate of their biological parent. If you want to leave part of your estate to your stepchildren, you must be precise and specific in the wording of your will. Most states don't recognize stepchildren as having legal rights to a stepparent's estate, so stating "all my children" in your will as an attempt to include them might leave your intent open to interpretation.

With regard to the stepfamily, the law remains filled with inconsistencies, so many people consider adoption as a solution to legal issues. Adoption offers the only way to create a legal connection between unrelated children and adults in the stepfamily.

Stepfamily adoptions, however, need to be approached cautiously. Some stepparents say adoption symbolizes their commitment. But this permanent legal change in status cannot guarantee a sense of belonging nor tighten bonds. While it might seem that adoption will solve problems concerning future inheritance, last names, or access to medical and school records, it can also put in motion a set of deeper, more far-reaching problems. If you consider adopting your stepchildren, it's very important to sort out your "logical" reasons and clearly examine your motivation for such a major event in the children's lives. Is there another legal document that can create the result you want without this drastic step? Remember, a legal resolution doesn't resolve emotional issues.

First and foremost, adoption requires the legal severing of a child's crucial relationship with their biological parent. Adults may initiate the adoption process, not with the child's best interest in mind, but because of their own need to push their former spouse out of the picture. Of course, formal adoption cannot ever erase the physical and emotional ties between a biological parent and child. Further, should the remarried couple later divorce, the legal adoptive relationship between stepparent and stepchild will *not* end. Adoptive stepparents hold the same lifetime responsibilities for their adopted stepchild that they do for their biological offspring.

Social workers and legal professionals who don't understand the complexities of stepfamily living may be insensitive to these crucial concerns. Although most adoptive parents are screened and counseled before they take on this serious legal commitment, stepparents who adopt often don't go through the same intensive process. Authorities may assume that because the people involved have lived together as a family, adoption is an appropriate solution. Too often, this simply isn't the case. Instead, what is done with good intentions may trigger a series of complicated psychological processes, actually damaging a once-healthy stepparent stepchild relationship. Proceed with the possibility of stepfamily adoption with great care and counseling!

"Instant Love" Is a Myth

One of the greatest stumbling blocks for stepparents is the myth of "instant love." When the belief that you can immediately love and be loved by your stepchildren proves unfounded, you'll be left feeling guilty and disappointed. As a stepparent, you can reduce guilt about not loving your stepchildren by wisely giving yourself permission from the beginning not to *have* to love them. It's that simple! Often, the only person telling you that you *must* love them is yourself. If your spouse has asked this of you, it's time to sit down and discuss reality. Explain the positive things you feel about your stepchildren and speak of your hope that the relationships will grow. Reassure your spouse that you accept them, respect them, and will try to be patient with them as you all adjust to your reorganized family. But make it clear that you cannot be burdened with the expectation of loving children before you even get to know them. This unrealistic expectation merely sabotages your stepfamily's chances for success.

The instant love myth sets another common trap: as a stepparent you might demand love and acceptance from the children and insist on family unity. Measuring family success in terms of harmony at all costs, you might dictate activities and deny free choices to family members, even diverting them from preferred activities so you can all be together as "one happy bunch." On the surface, family unity appears to have been achieved; under the facade, family members feel angry and resent you for forcing them to do things they don't want to do. Soon, to meet their own needs, they'll rebel, and the picture-perfect stepfamily hits crisis as you're forced to revise your expectations. This need for an artificial and early sense of unity seems to be most common for stepmothers.

Like a favorite book you read and reread, the rewards of living in a stepfamily grow as time passes.

Like all things of value, healthy stepfamily relationships take a long time to build. But, like a favorite book you've read and reread, the rewards of stepfamily living grow as time passes. Once your stepfamily begins to develop shared memories and a sense of a family history, you may find yourself liking your stepchildren, feeling a sense of pride in their accomplishments. And in many, many stepfamilies the liking eventually evolves to loving.

Struggling with Sexuality

Sexuality in the stepfamily affects all family members. It's very important to be able to discuss sexual issues because the home with a remarried couple is far more sexually charged than a first-family home. And, as they deal with their own emerging sexuality, teenagers especially are affected.

Chart 5

THE "INSTANT LOVE" EXPECTATION — DOWNHILL SLIDE TO TROUBLE

The problem begins with the unrealistic expectation itself.

It doesn't take stepparents long to realize they're not meeting the expectation they've set for themselves.

As they come to terms with this realization, many stepparents begin to feel inadequate and insecure. Some feel very guilty.

As the instant love expectation continues its destructive path, trouble brews between stepparents and stepchildren, leading to conflict between the couple.

In a further effort to erase guilt, many stepparents look for evidence that their partner doesn't love his or her own child.

When stepparents expect to love their stepchildren immediately, they set themselves up for disappointment and failure. This chart depicts the downhill course and relationship destruction that the unrealistic expectation of "instant love" takes.

Guilt often leads to resentment.

Resentment might lead the stepparent to find fault with the child and perhaps pick on the child unfairly.

In an attempt to ease this guilt, the stepparent might conclude that the stepchild is unlovable.

Treating a stepchild unfairly causes the stepparent to feel even guiltier than before.

This nine-phase progression is adapted from a model developed by Carolyn McClenahan, a marriage and family therapist in Los Gatos, California.

Family unity cannot be forced

Sexuality conflicts exist in traditional families too. Feeling sexual attraction toward family members is normal in all families, but biological bonds and the "incest taboo" usually prevent feelings from surfacing or being acted upon. But with no such social or psychological protection in the stepfamily, blurred boundaries and conflicted feelings are more likely to cause confusion, discomfort, and perhaps even inappropriate behavior. As they struggle with these normal feelings, many stepfamily members suffer from increased tension. When embarrassment keeps you from talking about your discomfort, these undisclosed sexual issues can threaten the very existence of your stepfamily.

Sexuality is especially apparent in stepfamilies for two reasons:

The children live with newlyweds. In first families, children don't think of their parents as sexual beings. But your new couple relationship, often passionate, makes it obvious that sexual intimacy is an important part of your lives. You may give each other lingering kisses, touch openly, or stay in the bedroom for long periods of time. Your children see you embrace and show affection for each other in ways they never saw with their parents as that marriage came apart.

Many young people are uncomfortable with these overt displays. Some are angry and resentful; others, embarrassed. When adolescents say they are bothered by their parents being "mushy," they're expressing anxiety about their own emerging sexuality.

You walk a fine line in your stepfamily! Your children need to see the tenderness you feel toward one another, and your display of affection provides a positive role model about relationships for your children as they develop their own concept of a marriage. Watching their parent and stepparent be close can also give your children a secure feeling. But to help them deal with confusing feelings, it's wise to minimize the sexual part of your relationship. When your children are present, it's best to keep your interactions nonsexual.

Boundaries are blurred. The second reason that sexuality issues may cause greater tension in the stepfamily is that children now live with people they haven't grown up with. Teenage stepbrothers and stepsisters may have been schoolmates; perhaps they were already attracted to one another. Although they're now in the same household as sister and brother, their feelings may suggest something else. With no incest taboo to control their feelings and behavior, some stepsiblings can become lovers.

Experiencing feelings is one thing; acting on them, another. In our society, an intimate relationship between family members is forbidden — indeed illegal. Those who become involved feel guilty, and as guilt and fear of being found out increase, behavior toward other family members changes. An unspoken trust has been broken. The entire family suffers.

Similar feelings may occur between stepparents and stepchildren, but research shows stepfathers struggle with it most. As their daughters begin to blossom into young women, some biological fathers deal with having sexual feelings about their offspring. These feelings are normal, and most men control them. Revelations about the prevalence of incest prove, however, that some don't. Incest is a tragic crime, severely damaging the victims and affecting everyone in the family. For stepfathers, dealing with sexual feelings toward teenage stepdaughters is often extremely difficult because stepfamilies aren't protected by the normal incest taboo.

Simple carelessness can intensify these difficulties. After living with their biological families for a long time, teenagers may have gotten used to casual living; walking around the house in underwear or skimpy nightclothes feels natural. Teenage stepchildren need to be told that this state of undress is inappropriate in your new family. Dress codes need to be established. While an edict to don clothes or a robe might embarrass some stepfamily members, this simple warning could prevent deeper problems in the future.

Teenagers' embarrassment often reflects anxiety about their own sexuality.

Intentional sexual behavior by stepchildren is more complex. As girls mature, many try out their charms on their fathers, dressing provocatively and flirting to get feedback. Boys often behave the same way with their mothers. Am I attractive? Will the girls like me? This behavior reflects normal adolescent development.

Some teenagers, too, may use their sexuality in retaliation. A young man, angry at his father over his parents' divorce and the daily absence of his biological mother, may begin to flirt with his stepmother. Or, his provocations might reflect a normal teenage competition with his father.

Stepparents are likely to feel both stimulated and scared by this seduction. A stepfather, while flattered by his stepdaughter's attention, also feels terribly guilty about his sexual thoughts and may begin to fear he'll act on them. Similar situations occur between stepmothers and stepsons too. In stepfamilies where sexuality isn't discussed, moving from fantasizing to acting on feelings does happen. A stepfather might rationalize his behavior by thinking, "She isn't really my daughter."

Even when actual physical involvement doesn't occur, the home atmosphere can become extremely uncomfortable when it's sexually charged. If your couple relationship is weak, and those involved cannot talk about what's happening, feelings of guilt, shame, and fear might prompt both people to protect themselves. In such a situation of discomfort, a stepfather may retreat and become overly critical of his stepdaughter, to create distance between them. But at this important time in her identity struggle, the teenager needs validation that she's not only okay but, indeed, attractive. She may try harder to gain her stepfather's attention; he in turn may retreat further. Not understanding why her stepfather, once playful and affectionate, has suddenly turned against her, she may feel rejected, interpreting his behavior to mean that he finds her unattractive or unlovable.

Many families never talk about sexuality. For some, it's embarrassing. Some fear talking about sex heightens issues and so they avoid it. Others may be unconscious of their feelings. Some think the incest taboo is enough. Thinking it's wrong to feel the way they do, and feeling embarrassed and ashamed, some keep their feelings secret. These families fail to understand the difference between feelings, fantasy, and behavior. Sadly, without open discussion, feelings may get out of control and lead to a regrettable situation.

Talk about sexuality in your stepfamily if you feel comfortable doing so. Everyone will be relieved. If you just cannot discuss the topic openly, seek help from a family counselor, a member of the clergy, or another uninvolved, nonjudgmental third party.

Guidelines for Addressing Sexuality in the Stepfamily

- Talk honestly and openly about sex and comfort levels. Discuss fears and feelings that might arise. Talk about and decide as a family what is appropriate behavior and dress.

- Recognize — as psychology and the law have made clear — that teenagers do not yet have adult judgement. It's necessary for the adults in the family to provide models of appropriate behavior and to set limits as needed.

- Anticipate and prevent situations where inappropriate sexual contact can occur. Assess whether teenage stepbrothers and stepsisters should or shouldn't be left alone together for long periods of time.

- Establish dress codes. Scanty lingerie and revealing jockey shorts are improper attire.

- Establish specific bathroom and bedroom etiquette. It's proper to knock before entering someone's room. Doors should be closed when someone is dressing or undressing, open when opposite-sex visitors are present. Bathroom doors can be locked, or an "In Use" sign hung on the door.

- Become aware of intense relationships or crushes between stepsiblings. Talk openly about the fact that such feelings are normal, so family members don't feel guilty. But also clarify what's acceptable in your home. Discuss the difference between feelings and behavior.

- Tune in when a family member expresses discomfort about sexuality issues. Don't brush the statement aside — it might be a plea for help. Encourage conversation.

- If you feel sexually attracted to your stepchild, recognize that such feelings are normal. There's no reason to feel guilty about your feelings. Realize, though, that *acting on* feelings by beginning a physical relationship — however "innocent" it may seem at first — is over the line, and will cause grief and guilt, delay the child's social development, and destroy your marriage.

Discipline — Again

We discussed the perennial topic of discipline briefly in chapter 7, and we'll treat it in depth in chapters 11 and 12, but we can't leave this chapter on "obstacles" without mentioning it again — briefly. It's important here to make note of what's different about disciplining other people's children.

In the beginning stages of stepfamily life, it's recommended that new stepparents leave much of the task of disciplining children to the biological parent. Here's why:

- *Children are used to their parent's discipline style.* Retaining continuity in this arena is important at a time when so many other changes are taking place for them.

- *Children adjust more easily to a new steppparent in their lives when you're not seen as an authority figure.* They need time to learn to respect and trust you in the stepparent role; only then will children respond to your discipline. It also gives you time to nuture bonds with your stepchildren.

- *As a couple, you need time to merge your differences*, find what works for you, and create a united front.

There are exceptions to these general guidelines:

- *When the stepparent is the only parent at home.* When you're left alone with your stepchildren and they misbehave, you shouldn't hesitate to take action. For this to work, however, the biological parent already must have transfered authority to you in front of the children.

- *When a child's misbehavior is directed specifically toward the stepparent.* Here it's your responsibility to manage the situation because it's between you and your stepchild.

Your first task as a couple in dealing with discipline is to learn what children are accustomed to and to set an atmosphere of trust and respect. Later, after bonds have developed between you and your stepchildren and, as a couple you've discussed and agreed on an effective discipline approach, it's appropriate for you to share this task.

As noted earlier, we'll get back to discipline in the chapters that follow.

What's Special about Being a Stepparent?

Why would anyone want to take on this role and such responsibilities? After exploring the many challenges of being a stepparent, you might be wondering about that. But special joys *do* come from being a stepparent. For the most part, the rewards can be long in coming, but when they do come, they're well worth the investment. Chapter 16 discusses these rewards in depth so, if you're feeling intimidated or discouraged, you might want to jump ahead and skim that chapter for encouragement.

Often a difficult and seemingly thankless task, being a stepparent can test your limits and your tolerance level. The challenges you face as a stepparent often unleash emotions that might otherwise remain buried within you. This can be very painful — and productive. In confronting these powerful feelings and working through them with your stepchild or spouse, surmounting the problems and savoring the successes, you cannot help but experience growth and feel good about yourself.

Remarried couples that persevere through the stressful times and finally achieve stepfamily stability speak of a strong sense of pride about their journey. As you work through problems and became closer as a couple, you'll earn respect from your children, who are witnessing a strong and positive role model for marriage.

Another possible reward — though not a promise — is developing a special relationship with a stepchild whom you see to adulthood. We all love our own children and hope to have that love returned; but with a stepchild, you may have a very special experience. Facing anger and resentment in spite of your best efforts, you may nonetheless struggle forward. Ultimately, you may have grown to care deeply about that child and perhaps even developed a bond of love. This very special love will have been earned, not through biology, but through respect, effort, and endurance. It happens for many stepparents. We hope it happens for you, too.

The promise of growth, the possibility of expanding the circle of love: these are the rewards you and your spouse can work toward together.

The Stepfamily Workshop

Session Five

Questions for Review

1. Of all the characteristics of an effective stepparent that have been discussed, which do you feel is the most important? Why?

   _____

   _____

   _____

   _____

2. What role do you play, or hope to play, in your stepchildren's life? How will you decide? Do you think the children agree about the role they want for you in their lives? Explain why you feel as you do. _____

   _____

   _____

   _____

3. Why might it be important for stepparents to choose their role rather than merely slip into it? _____

   _____

   _____

   _____

4. In which kind of stepfamily configuration do you live? What is your greatest stumbling block and why? What could help you transform that stumbling block to a success? _____

   _____

   _____

   _____

5. If you are both a parent and a stepparent, how do you manage to balance your time between your stepchildren and your biological children? _____

   _____

   _____

   _____

6. Have you had, or can you imagine having, a conversation with the nonresidential parent about your stepchildren? What do you want to share? What do you want to know? What are your fears? _____

_____

_____

7. What is your most important need as a stepparent? What is your partner's? _____

_____

_____

8. What was your most unrealistic expectation about becoming a stepparent? How did you, or might you, resolve it? _____

_____

_____

_____

9. Have you and your spouse clarified the levels of responsibility you have toward your stepchildren? Where do you still feel unclear? _____

_____

_____

10. What are some specific problems that adoption of stepchildren in your family might cause? _____

_____

_____

_____

11. How do you deal with sexuality issues in your stepfamily? If you've avoided discussion of sexuality, is there a reason? Where can you begin? _____

_____

_____

_____

Challenge to Conquer

Two weeks ago, Claire's 13-year-old stepdaughter Faith had her girlfriend stay overnight. As they watched TV with the girls, Claire and her husband Brad were feeling especially romantic. They began hugging and kissing and soon got up to leave. The couple headed for the bedroom, giggling, seemingly oblivious to the teenagers or anyone else in the home. Whispering intimately, they closed the door. A little later, Faith knocked tentatively on the bedroom door to ask about plans for the next day. "Go away," Brad shouted. When the girl persisted, Claire called, "Not *now*, Faith."

Since then, Faith will hardly speak to Claire or Brad. She's also stopped having her best friend over, saying she prefers to go to her friend's house instead.

1. What might Faith be thinking and feeling? Why has she withdrawn from the family? _____
   _____
   _____
   _____
   _____

2. How might Claire and Brad be feeling about Faith's behavior?
   _____
   _____
   _____
   _____

3. How can Brad and Claire empathize with Faith? What is she experiencing? What feelings did her parent and stepparent's behavior arouse in her? _____
   _____
   _____
   _____
   _____

Stepfamily Activities

(1) Take some time this week to discover differences and similarities in your individual values. Give each family member two index cards and have them mark one YES, the other NO. Then give each person five to ten pieces of notepaper on which they write questions they'd like to have answered about life in your new family. For example, "Should kids be required to share possessions with other family members?" Gather the questions together and then draw one at a time to which family members respond by holding up their YES or NO card. Discuss people's responses, *keeping in mind your goal is to express opinions and feelings and get to know one another better*. Ask further questions for better understanding: "Do you

think that's always true?" or "How did you come to feel that why?" Arguing, judging, or criticizing others' responses will defeat the purpose of the activity, which is to learn more about one another.

Here are some questions you might start with:

- Should you only get dessert once you eat everything on your plate?

- Do children have to do chores to get an allowance? Must some of it have to be saved?

- Should kids get to watch anything they want on TV and as much as they want?

- Can parents go away for a weekend without the children?

- Is it okay for kids to keep secrets from parents? For parents to have secrets from kids?

- Should parents insist on music lessons or church attendance when kids don't want to participate in these activities?

- Do parents have a right to spank children? Does the child's age make a difference?

- Do children have a right to point out mistakes that parents make?

- Should the "other parent" be invited into the house when they come to pick up the child(ren)?

- If you come home late without calling or planning ahead, should you still get supper?

- Must children pay with their own money if they break something that belongs to someone else?

- Is it all right for a stepparent to discipline a stepchild?

- Should parents tell kids how to wear their hair?

(2) Don't forget to add to your stepfamily history project. Maybe each family member could write two or three lines in your scrapbook/journal about how your roles have changed, or about the biggest changes he or she has noticed.

Understanding My Stepfamily

1. *Giving appreciations.* Think about some of the ways you appreciate your partner for helping you raise your children. A note of thanks for "being aboard" or a simple statement like "Khanh, I appreciate your willingness to help Eric with the model for the scouts' derby. I hope it was fun for you, too," will make a big difference to your partner. Take a moment to list the things you appreciate in your partner, the stepparent to your children. _____

   _____

   _____

   _____

   _____

2. *The misguided and the effective stepparent.* Complete the following.

   Here's something that I do now that's effective: _____

   _____

   _____

   _____

   _____

   _____

   Here's something that I do that I've come to realize is misguided:

   _____

   _____

   _____

   _____

   _____

   Here's what I plan to change or do differently: _____

   _____

   _____

   _____

   _____

   _____

Points to Ponder

- Stepparents can play several roles in stepchildren's lives: friend, confidant, another parent figure, mentor, role model. Couples need to discuss and agree about what role the stepparent will take.

- Remarried non-custodial parents with stepchildren often feel guilty about raising someone else's children when they cannot be with their own as often.

- Stepparents need validation and support from friends and family. Above all, they need it from their partner.

- Unchecked competition creates jealousy among stepfamily members that can hinder building bonds.

- The law cannot legislate love. Adoption is not a panacea for the stepfamily.

- The idea of "instant love" between stepfamily members is unrealistic. Refuse to believe this notion and give yourself permission not to have to love your stepchildren.

- Sexuality issues should be discussed in the stepfamily. Avoiding the discussion of this important topic can lead to serious consequences.

- Effective stepparents
  - Are able to empathize.
  - Are not defensive.
  - Avoid being judgmental.
  - Show acceptance.
  - Are open to change.
  - Have a strong sense of personal identity.
  - Believe in children's abilities and allow them to be responsible for themselves.

11

Stepfamilies and Discipline

Discipline is a challenge all parents face. In first families, money and sex are big troublemakers; in your stepfamily, dealing with discipline is your number one challenge!

Did you get a guidebook along with your new stepfamily? A *Dr. Spock for Stepfamilies?* Even this famous parenting expert, who guided millions of families in raising their children, faced plenty of challenges when he became a stepparent himself. Everything was different from what he knew and advised, he admitted, and many of his approaches to parenting had to be re-evaluated and adapted for his role as a stepfather.

Quite simply, your family life has become more complicated. From the start, there's my kid, your kids, our kids — all vying for attention to get their needs met. Since many of their issues center on how you manage discipline in your new stepfamily, fasten your seatbelt. Loyalty conflicts abound. Children often play one parent against the other, or the stepparent against the biological parent. Parents take sides with their biological offspring, often defending them. You might treat your stepchildren differently. Maybe you've never been a parent before and have ideas about how to parent children but they aren't well received by anyone. With so many different challenges, hurt feelings and resentment can make supporting one another on the discipline front hard.

Discipline Can Sabotage Your Stepfamily's Success

As a new stepparent, have you figured out your role yet? How do you fit into the discipline picture? Since early on your stepchildren won't accept authority from you and tend to view you as an outsider, what do you do? New roles and rules are unclear and, during these early stages of building your stepfamily, confusion is normal. As children move between two households, more scenarios emerge. Do they experience a totally different parenting style in their other house and get away with things that you'd never permit? As you're trying to get your new family launched, all of these discipline dilemmas challenge you.

This chapter clarifies some of the discipline issues you'll face in your stepfamily and provides you with some guidelines. We'll examine some typical scenarios that might occur and explain why they might be happening. As we explore specific discipline difficulties, describe parenting styles, and recommend approaches, this information will help you to understand what motivates children to misbehave and how to redirect those behaviors.

The Two Faces of Discipline

Effective discipline combines parental instruction and correction. It's about teaching children to live according to your family values and within your family rules and to prepare them for life outside their family. Discipline has two faces. One side is to nurture and encourage children; the other is to manage and control them so they can learn how to behave appropriately.

Nurturing involves giving affection, providing encouragement, building self-esteem, accepting, and focusing on positive behaviors. Nurturing reflects the 1001 ways a parent or stepparent says, "I love you. I care about your well-being" to your children. It's through the nurturing side of discipline that a strong parent-child bond develops. As this bond grows, so do trust and respect. Because no such bond exists between stepparents and stepchildren when your new family begins, nurturing is the most effective approach for you to take with your stepchildren. As part of a Stepfamily Living series of four booklets, the authors wrote *Encouragement and Enrichment* that focuses on this aspect of discipline. (See Stepfamily Resources and Training.)

The other side of discipline is to manage and control. Controlling involves establishing rules and routines, guiding choices, setting limits, and correcting misbehaviors. These appropriate behaviors help children learn to feel secure and that they belong — in the family and in the world. It is through the controlling aspect of discipline that your children learn how to behave.

Consistency is Critical

In all families, consistency in the discipline routine is critical. But consistency challenges a stepfamily for several reasons. First, the "instant" aspect of remarriage creates a dilemma. There's no grace period, no time for you and your stepchild to get to know one another well before the challenges start. Also, the luxury of time where you adults can explore a comfortable discipline style — one that works for both sets of children — simply doesn't exist. As you shared your vows, you became an instant family.

The concept of consistency also challenges your stepfamily because your children live in two homes. We'll discuss the two-household dilemma later in this chapter.

Yet another obstacle may exist. You and your new partner may already have developed some sort of an individual parenting style that you're each comfortable with; for you to change your approach, or expect him to, may seem to be an admission that what you did before was somehow wrong. Sometimes, new stepfamily couples war with one another about whose way is the "best" way. It's important to avoid judging one way right, the other wrong; you've simply had two different approaches before. Your task is to create a "united front" and to develop an "our" way to handle discipline. The best way to achieve this goal is to take a parenting class together early in your stepfamily's development together.

It's important for you to get on the same page about discipline early.

It's important for you to get on the same page about discipline early. If you continue to argue about which approach is right, no corrective actions are taken and the problems worsen. Children sense when this happens and they know they can get away with things. Once they see their parents being indecisive and inconsistent, kids start to manipulate situations so they experience few consequences for their misbehaviors. In the short-run, they have the advantage over you, the arguing and ineffective parents. They're in control. Some children in stepfamilies manipulate parents to avoid taking appropriate disciplinary action by playing the victim. These clever children evoke your sense of guilt and pity by acting, sad, forlorn, or defenseless. Their behavior signals "Look at me. I've been hurt by life, by my parents' divorce and remarriage. I'm fragile. I'll be damaged if you discipline me." If you don't take charge, you'll buy into the guilt for your child's apparent unhappiness, give in and do nothing.

Parenting Toolboxes

All parents need "tools" (skills and resources) to be effective. What are your tools? Where did you learn them? The important parenting tools that stepparents need are the same ones that all parents need to teach and manage their children. A good guideline is that whatever parenting style works for you, and is effective, will work for your stepfamily — as long as you're consistent. At the same time, you need to understand and decide which tools which parent person will use, and when — a much more critical issue in stepfamilies because of bonding and loyalty issues. (Tips in this chapter and the next will help you learn how to use some of those tools, and how to avoid the trap of being "consistently wrong"!)

When a challenging situation arises with your children, imagine a toolbox by your side. It holds the techniques and skills you'll use to solve the problem at hand. Like a skilled carpenter, who wouldn't use a screwdriver to drive a nail, your job is to learn which tool you think to be most effective in disciplining your children.

How did your toolbox get filled in the first place? Where did you learn how to be a parent and how to discipline? Most parenting tools are unconscious heirlooms, hand-me-downs from our parents. We repeat what they did with us; or for various reasons, we do the opposite. These parenting techniques may or may not have been effective for us, but for today's children, often those ways don't work. Because so much has changed in the world, you need up-to-date tools that work effectively with today's children.

Who Disciplines Which Kids?

In traditional families, either parent can deal with any child's misbehavior at any time. It simply involves choosing which tool to use and applying it swiftly and effectively. Not so in your stepfamily. Because your parent-child bond as a stepparent differs in length and strength from the biological bond you have with your own children, your discipline efforts will be received differently.

Earlier in this chapter, we defined discipline as two tasks: Nurturing and controlling. Since your child was young, as a biological parent, you performed both tasks. Early on in your new stepfamily, it's important that you continue to do both. Too often, a single-mom, weary from struggling to keep all the balls in the air, actually might anticipate turning over the controlling side of discipline to her new partner, a new stepfather. Generally, this is a mistake. That strong parent-child biological bond that existed for you and your children provided the foundation from which effective controlling and limit-setting had occurred. That won't work with a new stepparent!

Recommended Roles

At first, here's what works best! Early in your stepfamily's formation, it's best that each biological parent continue to focus on this part of discipline with his or her own children. And, as a stepparent, the best way to approach your new role is to find ways to nurture your new stepchildren in one of the roles described in chapter five: friend, support person, confidant, mentor, or model. While it may seem strange to deal with discipline in these two different ways, early on this "double approach" becomes important for several reasons.

- Stepparents have no authority to discipline at first
- Stepparents need to build a bond with stepchildren first
- Stepparents may have a different discipline style

These reasons reflect some of the ways your new stepfamily is different and why stepparents must avoid taking on the discipline role immediately — especially if your style is authoritarian. In traditional families, parenting begins with a great emphasis on the nurturing side of discipline. A young infant is cuddled, stroked, fussed over and its every need is fulfilled by its parents. Can you remember those days? As a new parent, you enjoyed your new infant and toddler. You and your partner had plenty of time to talk and share ideas on parenting and you proceeded with the control side of discipline slowly. Before you needed to say "no," or limit and control your child's behavior, a strong bond had developed between you and your child. Those "no" areas arose one at a time, and gave you time to decide how you'd handle each situation. There's a good chance that, together, you developed a consistent style of parenting that satisfied both of you and worked well. Regardless of the approach you took, or the theoretical model on which you based your parenting, you probably understood that consistency was the key to success. If you never agreed on a united front approach to discipline, or practiced consistency, maybe disciplining the children became problematic in your marriage.

A warning to new stepparents! Be careful. Even if your partner has yielded her discipline role to you willingly, after you carry it out, she may resent you. If your help doesn't mesh with a parenting style that she's comfortable with, your partner may judge your efforts as unwanted interference. Your stepchildren will certainly view it that way and rebel — especially adolescents.

Authority to Discipline

Early on, stepparents lack authority to discipline their stepchildren. That authority can only come with time and must eventually be transferred to you by your partner. After you've taken some parenting classes together and agreed on a discipline style that presents a "united front," your partner must indicate to her children — your stepchildren — that this change is taking place. It might sound like this. "John and I have decided that when I'm not around, he'll be in charge. If you misbehave, he has my permission to discipline you and I expect you to do what he says. If you choose not to, here's what will happen." Then you lay out a clear consequence if they choose to test him (and they will) that you must follow through on.

Another warning! Naturally, when you first attempt to implement your new role, being normal kids, your stepchildren will test you. This is where it's critical that your partner support you one hundred percent to display that "united front" you need to be an effective parenting team. If you don't agree about how the situation was handled, you discuss it privately rather than in front of your children. Work it out and, later, return to the children with your revised plan. A change of mind doesn't reflect flip-flopping or a weakness, rather it models for your children that it's okay to make mistakes. Even adults do so. It teaches them a life skill about gathering new information and adjusting their course. This overt transfer of authority is very important to understand because it lets your kids know that you agree. Once it becomes clear that you're on the same parenting team and that discipline policies will remain consistent, regardless of which parent is home, you'll have fewer problems.

Loving concern and consistency about discipline provides the sense of security and belonging your children need.

All children need rules, limits, and boundaries. Loving concern and consistency about discipline provides those and creates a sense of security and belonging. Your children and stepchildren deserve this feeling of safety, especially after all the changes they've been through. When your children from a previous relationship come to your house only part-time, you continue to carry out both the nurturing and disciplining tasks. That frees your new partner to develop a bond of respect and trust with your children by focusing on nurturing.

We all make mistakes. Sometimes this is when stepchildren need the most encouragement.

How Does the Other Biological Parent Fit In?

The biological parent in the other household has a strong impact on your stepfamily. Even if your children live between two houses in a joint custody situation, their other parent's approach to discipline is important because it can affect your household. Earlier in this book we emphasized the importance of integrating the other parent into your stepfamily. If your relationship isn't cordial, this can be challenging — especially if you disagree about discipline.

Understanding Inappropriate Discipline

Many parents whose children come for occasional evenings, weekends, or vacations may be lax with discipline. Whether guilt, fear, or the temporary nature of the visits motivates their behaviors, some completely sidestep the controlling side of discipline and only nurture. Of course, this lopsided approach wreaks havoc in your household when your children compare the permissive nature of their part-time visits to the reality of actually being a responsible part of a family. Reality can't measure up to a vacation atmosphere.

The brief and temporary nature of visits affects discipline decisions. Although fewer rules, routines, and consequences — essential with kids on a daily basis — work best for shorter visits, too often, fewer can get translated to none. When a child makes a mess on Sunday afternoon just before returning to their other house, it's easier for a parent to tolerate the disorder knowing it's not a fulltime situation. Besides, deep emotions around sadness and loss are coming up for everyone during this transition time. The parent often lets things slide because they don't want the visit to end on a sour note. Is it any wonder that children say "It's more fun at dad's house" where this laid back attitude toward discipline is taken?

Fear can breed anxiety for some part-time parents. They're concerned that their children won't want to visit if they seem harsh on them or make them do chores. Because they see little of their children, these anxious parents want the visits to be untainted by unpleasantness that might come from taking appropriate discipline measures. Others compete with new stepparents, and fear they might lose the love of their children to that person. As this imagined loss deepens their fear, they might avoid dealing with discipline and become a "Disneyland Dad/Mom." Such insecure parents ultimately cheat their child by not teaching responsibility.

Guilt also plays a role. Many parents without custody feel guilty about not living with their children and guiltier if they're helping to raise someone's children. Some may feel guilty about the pain they caused their child through the breakup, especially if it was a difficult divorce. By providing lots of nurturing, but little controlling and correcting behavior, they assuage their own guilt. While this self-serving approach to discipline helps parents who feel guilty feel better, it doesn't benefit their children.

Two-Household Dilemmas

Discipline dilemmas in the other household can increase problems for your stepfamily. As your children move between mom's house and dad's house, they may identify and complain about the differences. As parents and stepparents, avoid becoming defensive. If you start to compete with their other parent, and fear losing your stepchild's affection, you might also avoid taking appropriate corrective action. Then your children lose in both households.

Even when the other parent tries to discipline, that also can create problems. Maybe the tools in your former partner's toolbox differ from yours. You may dislike, or truly disapprove of, the way he manages discipline. You must remember that his discipline choices are something over which you have no control whatsoever. Indeed, different styles of discipline may have been a problem in your former marriage. If you have fairly good communication between the households, you could address your concerns about inconsistency, but be prepared for nothing to change. Above all, aim for consistency with discipline in your stepfamily — within your house and between you and your partner.

*Consistency **within** your household is critical, but expecting discipline to be consistent **between** two households is an unrealistic expectation that sets you up for trouble.*

Be careful! Here's where the notion of consistency challenges stepfamilies. While consistency *within* your household is critical, to expect discipline to be consistent between the two households is one of those dangerous unrealistic expectations that set you up for disappointment. Understanding this reality is important because you simply cannot control what happens somewhere else. How your former spouse deals with discipline in the other house lies out of your sphere of influence; and, if your relationship is poor, any attempts to try to make things happen in the other household may worsen things.

Most children, and especially teenagers, try to get their needs met any way they can. In your stepfamily, they might use the two-household conflict to pit parent against parent, or stepparent against parent. Don't get hooked into their attempts! Avoid such games by acknowledging and accepting the differences between their two homes. Simply don't enter into lengthy discussions with your children on these differences, but show them you are listening. For example, you could say, "Yes, I understand that you're allowed to do it that way in dad's house, but in our house this is what we expect." As you acknowledge the reality, affirm your children for managing their challenge of living between two houses. Children can, and do, learn to adjust and to cope with these differences. Except for the emotions these two-household transitions elicit in everyone, this challenge is no different from how your children learn to adjust in school where they confront the diverse discipline techniques of their teachers. Remind them of that.

Now that we've explored some reasons why dealing with discipline is challenging for stepfamilies, let's examine the possible styles of discipline available to stepparents.

Identifying Your Discipline Style

Successful stepfamilies depend on a strong couple relationship with adults acting as the CEO's of the family. The more compatible your individual styles of discipline are with one another, the more you can support each another. Faced with the security of your couple solidarity, your children will have less chance to pit one parent against the other. Your individual discipline skills and techniques in your toolboxes fall into three main discipline styles. The tools you use most often determines your personal style of discipline

To help identify your personal parenting style, you and your partner may find the following stepfamily discipline style quiz helpful. Don't compare answers until you've both completed it. Then score your quizzes to see how similar you styles are. Don't despair if they are diverse. It's important to analyze your parenting style and align with each other to develop a more effective way of dealing with your children.

Style of Discipline Quiz

1. For the third time this week, nine-year-old Suzie has forgotten her lunch. Mom should

   a. deliver it to her at school, assuring Suzie she doesn't mind.
   b. leave it where it was left, saying nothing.
   c. teach her not to forget things by making her go to bed 15 minutes early that night.

2. It's washday. Nine-year-old Billy left his dirty clothes on the floor, not in the hamper where they should be. As Dad does the wash tonight, he should

   a. pick up the clothes and wash them anyway. After all, a nine-year-old has more important things on mind.
   b. leave the clothes and wash those clothes in the hamper.
   c. rush to the living room, shut off the TV and demand that Billy pick up his clothes immediately.

3. Tim wants to go to the movies tonight but has spent his allowance. The 16-year-old asks Dad for the money. Dad should

   a. provide his son a handout. Why should Tim miss this chance to be with his friends?
   b. tell Tim he understands the difficulty of not being able to afford something you want to do, but that he is not in the loan business and there's nothing he can do to help.

    c. give Tim a lecture on the dollar's value and recount his teenage days when he had to work for a living. Tim looks so sad after the talk that Dad gives him the money.

4. Four-year-old Joan hates mom's supper casserole. She refuses to eat. Mom should

    a. leave the table and cook Joan a hamburger, which she loves.
    b. excuse Joan from the table, assuring her she'll be welcome at breakfast.
    c. force her to sit until she eats every last bite.

5. John, age 5, just hopped out of bed for the sixth time in 15 minutes. Dad should

    a. go upstairs, give him a hug, read another story and stay with his son until he falls asleep.
    b. ignore John completely. Dad should refrain from any conversation or interactions with him, acting as if his son weren't around.
    c. pick him up, put him in bed with a swat on his behind and a warning that if he gets up again he'll get a swat that he'll really remember.

6. It's 8:00 and the twelve-year-old twins have not done their homework. Mom or Dad should

    a. sit down and complete the assignments with them.
    b. say nothing at the moment. Tomorrow at dinner ask what plans they have to complete their homework each day.
    c. tell them they'll be failures in school unless they get at the homework immediately. Dad turns off the stereo, takes the kids by the arms, and leads them to their room to work.

7. At 7:30 a.m., Don still isn't getting ready for school, despite repeated warnings that he'll be late if he doesn't get out of bed earlier. Dad should

    a. plan on leaving for work a little later to drive Don to school if it gets very late.
    b. say nothing, get himself ready for work and leave at his usual time.
    c. remind Don every 5 minutes what time it is, threaten him that he'll have to walk if he missed the bus. If 30 more minutes pass and Don is in bed, Dad should rip off his covers and forcibly pull him up.

8. The kids are fighting again! You'd think that kids age ten and twelve would have learned how to get along with each other by now. Mom cannot stand it anymore. She should

   a. interfere, pleading with them to stop. She offers ice-cream as a reward if they'll stop.
   b. go about her usual tasks, ignoring the kids.
   c. threaten to tell their father about the fight if they don't stop. Dad will then punish by not letting them go outside with their friends after supper.

9. Eleven-year-old Jim dislikes bathwater. The family dinner is planned out and Jim doesn't smell too good. Dad should

   a. ignore the dirt and smell. He didn't like baths either when he was a boy.
   b. give Jim a choice of bathing and joining the family at a restaurant or not bathing and making his own dinner at home.
   c. take Jim by the hand, push him into the bathroom, and force him to shower before he is allowed to come out.

10. At 11:00 Saturday morning nine-year-old Laura still has not done her chores. Mom should

    a. do Laura's chores. It's easier than arguing.
    b. refuse to serve lunch until the chores are done.
    c. take away her allowance for the week.

Scoring the Quiz

The more A's you select, the more permissive your parenting style.

The more B's you select, the more democratic your parenting style.

The more C's you select, the more authoritarian your parenting style.

Understanding the Discipline Styles

The chart on pages 170–171 details the three styles of discipline. Take time to understand the concepts and to analyze your personal style. Is your approach to discipline getting you the results you want? Is it effective? If you're satisfied with your present ability to deal with your children's behavior effectively and, if you and your partner's discipline style are similar, there's no need to make changes. If not, or if a great deal of discrepancy exists between you, carefully study the styles. See which makes the most sense to you and read the recommendations.

Which Style for Stepfamilies?

Many parents were themselves raised by authoritarian parents. While it may seem natural to raise your children in a similar way, times have changed too greatly. Today, authoritarian parents often experience a great deal of difficulty raising their children — especially as children get older. Even if you both came up with an authoritarian parenting style in the quiz, this isn't the most effective method to deal with discipline in your stepfamily.

The authoritarian style is based on the absolute authority of the parenting figure. The problem starts with one reality that, in the beginning of your new stepfamily, stepparents have no authority with stepchildren. As discussed earlier, it only comes later when the authority to discipline is transferred to you by your partner. As a new stepparent, this starts with earning respect and trust by slowly building bonds with your stepchildren — the nurturing piece. This takes time! When you try to force stepchildren to behave and they refuse to honor your attempts at authority, a power struggle results. No one wins! Or, your stepchildren will withdraw and be unwilling to build a bond with you.

Negative Effects of Ineffective Parenting Styles

Some unwanted effects can show up. When you use an authoritarian approach, you can actually provoke your child to misbehave. This style fails to teach children to develop internal controls. When they're young, you can get children to do what you want, but they respond because they're afraid. Using adult power, you can use force and threat to temporarily make your child or stepchild do, or not do, something; but soon your child may strike out to get even. When children obey mainly from fear of punishment, soon they learn to lie and sneak to avoid getting caught. Behavior problems get worse. Since this negative effect isn't your goal, you'd be wise to examine a style that sidesteps creating revenge behavior in your children.

The permissive style is equally ineffective. As you try to merge two families, already enough ambiguity and chaos exists. Why intensify it by using a style of discipline that creates more confusion? Permissive parents tend to maintain few consistent rules and routines. Misbehaviors are managed as separate events. These parents tend to decide what to do on the spot, usually resorting to cajoling, prodding, and pleading in hopes the behavior disappears. Little consistency happens. Because permissive parents and

Chart 6

DISCIPLINE STYLES

	Authoritarian	
Role of the parent	• the boss	
Characteristics of the parent	• overbearing • dictatorial • inflexible • strict	• repressive • uncompromising • tyrannical • dominating
Role of the child	• to obey	
Who's got the power?	• the parent	
Home atmosphere	• tense • rigid • militaristic • oppressive	
Discipline tools	• yelling • commanding • ordering • rewarding • punishing • bribing • threatening	
Effect on the child	• obeys out of fear of punishment • subverts and manipulates, underhandedly • often out of control when parents aren't present; develops little self-control • retaliates, strikes out at times	
Quality of parent/child relationship	• fear • distance • coldness • resentment • rigidity	
Historical background	• most of us raised this way	

Democratic	**Permissive**
• leader; guide	• servant; bystander
• approachable • respected • reasonable • flexible • encouraging	• fearful, inconsistent • indecisive • yielding • passive • weak
• to think • to contribute • to cooperate	• to control others • to follow own wants and instincts
• shared between parent and child	• the child
• relaxed • orderly • consistent	• chaotic • uncontrollable • wild
• incentives • consequences • assertion messages • negotiation • conflict resolution • family meetings • automatic rules and routines established • requesting	• pleading • wishing • waiting • giving up and doing nothing • yielding
• develops self-discipline • can focus on the needs of the group	• becomes self-centered and demanding • fails to develop consideration of others or of needs of the group • develops little self-control
• close • open • sharing • respectful • communicative	• distance • resentment • child may feel unloved, uncared for • manipulative
• few prepared to discipline in this style • few raised this way • potentially can be taught to all parents	• some of us raised this way • often used when parents didn't want to be authoritarian and thought this the only alternative • some parents swing like a pendulum between this style and authoritarian style

stepparents keep hoping that things will improve with time, they take little direct action. You may even excuse the children's behavior by believing the problems stem from a "stage" to be outgrown.

In new stepfamilies, it's common for one adult to be permissive and the other authoritarian. Too often, the young stepparent without children of her own and no parenting experience, may take an authoritarian view of parenting. She may start by observing behaviors in her stepchildren that don't fit her ideas and points them out to her partner. While this "outsider" view can be helpful to a permissive biological parent wracked with guilt about the divorce, it can also backfire. The children connect the changes to the new stepparent. Her expectations that their parent fix things may create resentment and distance at a critical time when she needs to be building nurturing bonds with her stepchildren. Once you're aware that your stepchildren will rebel against and reject your input and authority as a new stepparent, you'll realize that this style of parenting won't be effective for your family.

Protect Your Marriage with Effective Parenting

How can authoritarian parenting breed resentment and hostility between you and your partner? Some parents may have a "hidden agenda" to find a partner who could "help her" with the children, one who can "take over" the discipline where she's had little success. If her unspoken wish is that her new husband successfully disciplines her kids, she may be setting him up for failure. Her expectation won't work because the children won't accept his authority. Enough time hasn't passed for him to develop the nurturing side of discipline. Without a strong stepparent-stepchild bond, the results are often negative — and destructive to stepfamily development. If you're a new stepfather trying this, you might become angry at the children and, perhaps also at your partner for putting you in this position.

As a biological parent, you'll need to continue your role as primary disciplinarian for your own children. They're used to the style that you've used with them in the past. With all the changes they've been through with the reorganization of their family, your children are more comfortable with what they know until you and your new partner can develop a "united front." If you've been a permissive parent, you'd be wise to slowly shift your approach to a more democratic style.

Before you enact any changes, it's important to announce them to your children, explaining what you are doing, why you are changing your approach, and how things will be different for them. Otherwise, they'll probably blame the changes onto your partner — their new stepparent.

Your challenge becomes that old ways need to be merged into an "our way" in a relatively short amount of time. You'd be wise as your stepfamily's CEOs to include your children in the process of setting up rules and routines, often very different in your two former households. Kids cooperate best when they have a say in how their family is run and can have input about setting consequences and limits for their behavior.

When you raise your children and stepchildren with democratic principles that promote positive communication and respect within the family, it raises their self-esteem. It also fosters self-discipline within your children and creates a relaxed, comfortable atmosphere in which family members can flourish.

Stepfamily Stresses Can Create a "Fishbowl" Atmosphere

Stepparents aren't alone dealing with discipline challenges. At times, all parents make mistakes. It's part of learning. But because your stepfamily lives in a fishbowl atmosphere — in which it feels as if others are watching every move you make — mistakes get magnified. Sometimes, as you're trying to get things off the ground, you might feel frustrated or even embarrassed about all the confusion. Such feelings might make it hard for you to take effective action to resolve problems and to correct mistakes with the ease you did in your first family.

Feeling as though you're constantly being observed adds yet another stress.

In the early vulnerable stages of development, you might feel as though everyone is watching and waiting to see if your new family sinks or swims. Old myths die hard and, unfortunately, notions that children who live in stepfamilies become troubled, or troublemakers, still persist. Feeling as though you're constantly being observed and judged adds yet another stress that you never had to endure in your first family.

Fear of Another Breakup

All stepfamilies form from loss. For at least one of you, your previous relationship has ended in divorce, or your partner has died. Your children also share this loss and, too often, they haven't been helped to cope with their sadness. Their dreams of a happy, traditional family have been shattered. For most children, one biological parent lives elsewhere; for too many, divorce brought the extra sadness of an absentee parent.

With time and good counseling, people adjust to their losses. As you adjusted to single parent living, probably you learned to manage well, providing a happy stable home for your children. In time, you considered remarriage and you're excited about having another chance at happiness. But remarriage struggles can sometimes activate the fear of another possible breakup. Because you've already experienced a major loss, you know it could happen again. This fear of repetition haunts many stepfamilies — especially children, and this unspoken stressor actually creates an extra pressure to succeed.

Denial Dents Your Chances for Success

This fear of failure pressure can intensify your discipline dilemma. You might ignore problems with the children, or deny them, because to recognize them somehow acknowledges that you could fail again. Rooted in fear, this pressure to succeed gives your children too much manipulative power.

Denial is all too common in stepfamilies — and very destructive. When problems are still relatively easy to resolve, you may deny them and they merely intensify. For example, in an effort to avoid "scenes," you might sidestep a confrontation or not deal with discipline when it's needed. If you're stuck in denial and wait too long to get outside help, you'll hit crisis; by then challenges are harder to resolve. You may try to maintain an outside appearance that all is well and, if your children sense that tension, and might try to take advantage of you. Soon your children learn that they don't have to pay a price for their misbehaviors. It's not long before this awareness becomes power and they're in charge!

In the following chapter, we'll take a look at the reasons children misbehave. You may be surprised!

12

Why Children Misbehave

Do you understand what your child is trying to achieve? Dealing with discipline effectively requires that you understand the purpose behind your child's misbehavior. Since children generally don't misbehave without some reason, tuning into what's going on is the start of changing it. Think of misbehavior as a message your child is sending to you when he or she isn't getting through to you in other ways. Once you learn the goal that your child's misbehavior is designed to achieve, you can follow the clues and redirect the misbehavior. You can teach her more positive ways to get her needs met. Your children need to learn this critical life skill.

Dr. Rudolf Dreikurs, in his classic book, *Children: The Challenge*, identifies four basic motivations for misbehavior. Children misbehave to *get attention*, to *show they're the boss*, to *get even*, or to *avoid failure*. When asked why he created only four categories, Dr. Dreikurs is purported to have replied, "I didn't make up these motivations. By observing children, these are the four I identified." The rest of this chapter is based on his approach to understanding and correcting the misbehavior of your children in your stepfamily.

Why is understanding these motivations helpful? In your stepfamily, as in any family, children exhibit lots of different and specific misbehaviors. By placing these behaviors into groups, you'll find it's easier to deal with them. Once you understand general strategies for dealing with behaviors from each basic category, you'll also be able to deal successfully with similar behaviors because you'll know they stem from the same motivation. When you can identify the basic motivation, you'll be less likely to choose the wrong strategy and, unknowingly, reinforce your child's misbehavior.

Chart 7

UNDERSTANDING THE FOUR GOALS OF MISBEHAVIOR

How do you feel?	*What do you usually do?*	*How does your child usually respond?*	*Goal*
Bothered, annoyed	Remind, nag, scold	Stops temporarily. Later, misbehaves again	Attention
Angry threatened	Punish, fight back, or give in	Continues to misbehave, defies you, or does what you've asked slowly or sloppily	Power
Angry, extremely hurt	Get back at child, punish	Misbehaves even more, keeps trying to get even	Revenge
Hopeless, like giving up	Give up, agree that child is helpless	Does not respond or improve	Display of inadequacy

Adapted from *Cooperative Discipline* (pp. 168–169) by Linda Albert. © 1996 American Guidance Service, Inc., 4201 Woodland Road, Circle Pines, Minnesota 55014-1796. Reproduced with permission of publisher. All rights reserved. www.agsnet.com

Needing to Belong

Everyone, adult or child, has a basic need to belong — to feel as a significant member of society. For children, that sense of belonging starts in the family. Every child needs to feel wanted and loved at home. As you read the rest of this chapter, when you read the word "belong," think *wanted, loved, important,* and *significant.*

One of the fallouts from a major family reorganization is loss and change and a shift in your children's sense of belonging. Where once they fit in and felt wanted simply for whom they were, now all the changes in their young lives cause confusion. It'll be a while until their sense of belonging gets re-established in your stepfamily. This takes time!

The more this need to belong is filled in your stepfamily, the less your children need to misbehave. Remember our discussion in chapter 11 of the two faces of discipline: *nurturing* and *controlling?* You can best influence your child's sense of belonging by nurturing. (For suggestions for increasing your children's sense of belonging in your new stepfamily, read *Enrichment and Encouragement* from the *Stepfamily Living Booklet* series by these authors. See the References for more information.)

Misbehaving for Attention

An attempt to get your attention underlies the first motivation for misbehavior. As part of belonging, all children need appropriate attention; but children who misbehave with this as their goal often seek excessive attention. They seem to forever keep their parents and stepparents busy noticing them and doing things for them.

In new stepfamilies, attention-seeking behaviors are common, and for some very real reasons. During the early developmental stages, many changes are taking place and many of these situations involve loss that might go unrecognized and unaddressed. While living with a single parent, your children didn't have to share their biological parent on a daily basis with another adult. Indeed, some parents develop "buddy" relationships with their children, becoming more of a friend than a parent. In an attempt to deal with guilt about the divorce, however, or to prove yourself as the "good parent," you may have become permissive without realizing it. If you were acting as a friend, disciplining and setting rules may have become difficult and, if single-parent living continued for a long time, this challenge increased.

When your stepfamily formed, this shift got harder. Your youngsters had to learn to share you with another adult again — and perhaps new stepsiblings — either on a part-time or full-time basis. You and your new partner have been busy creating a space for the stepfamily and building your couple relationship. During this confusing transition, maybe you haven't been able to attend to everyone's needs as you'd like. Perhaps your children feel left out. Some may even feel jealous of your new adult relationship, especially if your couple connection takes great energy. Attention-seeking behaviors may also signal that your stepchild wants a closer, caring relationship with you, but she doesn't know how to develop that appropriately. Children do the best they can. For many, it's easier to get attention by misbehaving rather asking for it directly.

Still another change may precipitate attention-seeking. As you put together two families, a change in birth order position may have occurred. How children learn to belong, in a family and ultimately in the world, is influenced by their position in the family. (More on this coming up in chapter 15.) When you made your stepfamily, your oldest child may have become a middle child. Or perhaps a youngest child moved into a middle position. When remarriage changes the birth order in a new stepfamily, children in shifted positions may feel insecure and unsure of how to relate from this new place. Until your child feels a sense of belonging in your stepfamily, and secures her place and feels comfortable in it, misbehavior may occur from a need for attention.

Children may seek attention when a stepparent is on the phone.

Recognizing and Redirecting Attention Behaviors

"How can I figure this out?" you might be wondering. You'll know that your child or stepchild is seeking attention if you feel irritated and annoyed when this misbehavior happens. You'll probably react by reminding, coaxing, nagging, yelling, or just plain asking the child to stop. Since those kinds of responses actually give attention to the child, even though it's negative, most likely the behavior stops — temporarily.

Here are some ways for you to learn to cope with attention-getting behaviors.

1. When kids demand attention inappropriately, avoid giving it to them.

2. At other times, and for no reason, provide abundant attention. Instead of fussing at them for misbehaving, "catch them being good" and affirm them for what they are doing right that pleases you and other family members. For instance, "Jane, how nice that you cleared the table tonight without having to be asked. I appreciated that time to talk with your father."

3. Ignore the attention-seeking misbehavior and continue what you're doing without voice or eye contact. Consider humming a tune so you can't talk and unwittingly give them the attention they seek. Try sitting in a comfortable chair and closing your eyes for a catnap. Look up an unknown word in the dictionary or do some yoga stretches. If you're unable to ignore the behavior, withdraw from the physical space of your child or stepchild. Without your presence, attention-getting behaviors become useless. Soon the child stops!

4. When children are not seeking attention in inappropriate ways, behave in a way that surprises them. Do something unexpected. Change the topic of conversation. Give them a hug. Get playful. Speak in a funny, high-pitched voice. Talk to the wall. Let your imagination devise silly and surprising behaviors that offer spontaneous attention without demand from the child.

5. Refuse to do things for your children that they can do themselves. When you're unsure of this with new stepchildren, check with your partner. When you do tasks for your children just because they ask you, you rob them of the chance to learn and practice skills. It lowers their self-esteem.

6. Send an "I-message." Here's a communication tool that's quite useful for new stepparents who have no history with the child. An "I-message" is made up of three parts that help you tell your stepchild what behavior bothers you and why: a *statement* of the misbehavior; your *thoughts* about it and the *effect* of that behavior on you; and your *feelings* about it. Clear messages — stated calmly and firmly — guide your children in how to succeed with you, since the focus is on how *you're* affected. The I-message sounds like this: "When you ____, I think ____, and then I feel ____." Be specific about only one behavior at a time, so you don't confuse your child. For example, if your stepchild is pestering you when you're talking on the phone, you might

say, "When you *interrupt me when I'm on the phone, I cannot hear my friend and figure out where to meet her,* and then I feel *annoyed.*" These clear and effective messages are part of an effective stepfamily's toolbox.

Misbehaving to Gain Power

A more common motivation — and more disturbing to parents and harder to redirect — is when children misbehave to gain power. When your kids seek power, they're attempting to prove that they're in charge. They want to be the boss. They'll do things in their own way, and from their own time frame. Their goal is to prove that no one can *make* them do anything — especially a new stepparent.

This stepfamily discipline challenge may be rooted in unresolved grief when children felt they'd had no say in what happened to their lives. To make up for the time when they had no power, and their lingering anger about their changed family, some children try to grab power whenever they can.

Power behaviors also could be leftovers from living in a single-parent family where children often are given a great deal of legitimate power, sometimes too much. Since most single parents work full time, youngsters learned to pitch in to help with household chores and they took great pride in their self-sufficiency and independence. Once they live in a stepfamily, things change. Role shifts have happened. Now, another adult is on hand to help and supervise. Children may view the stepparent as an intruder, an outsider, or as one making unwanted demands upon them — a common lament from stepchildren. Kids may blame you if they feel their freedom is curtailed. Worse, if you've attempted to discipline too soon, stepchildren may respond with hostility and refuse to accept your authority. Although we addressed these reasons earlier, you can begin to see how power behaviors may start.

A child's desire for power and to be in charge is not all bad. What's wrong with your children wanting to be independent, to have some control over their lives? Deciding for themselves? These choices are important stepping stones toward maturity. Problems start when your kids want to make decisions that are inappropriate for their age and maturity, or when they misbehave for power merely to force confrontations with you for unspoken emotional reasons.

Some children choose to stage power plays in public.

How Do Attention and Power Behaviors Differ?

How can you tell the difference? When you start to feel angry, defensive and frustrated, it's a clue that you're confronting power misbehavior. You might even feel fear, as though you've lost control of your child and the situation. When the misbehavior involves power, you'll experience much stronger emotions than the mild feelings of annoyance or irritation you felt when the behavior involved getting attention. Be aware! During the correction process, these behaviors don't stop quickly or easily. Often, power behaviors continue until your child figures out how he can save face; he needs to make it appear as though the choice to stop was his — not because you forced him to. Most likely, he'll verbally protest your corrective action.

Power behaviors are harder to correct than attention-getting behaviors. Your feelings of frustration and anger may get in the way of taking calm, swift, effective action. This is especially challenging if you haven't yet developed a bond that allows you the authority you need. Your frustration may result in your responding with power behaviors of your own: "I'm the parent in this house!" If you lose your temper, you might strike back with force or coercion and apply heavy punishment. Your effort might center on breaking your child's will and teaching a "good lesson" to settle for once and for all who is the boss — often the approach of an authoritarian parenting style.

Such efforts are doomed to fail! Parental power rarely influences children to make a permanent positive change. Your child might react to this style by increasing the intensity or frequency of his misbehavior; he might switch to revenge behaviors, discussed next. Most dangerous for your stepfamily's stability, power struggles with your stepchild might affect your relationship with your partner. Remember, because your marriage provides the foundation of your family, your couple relationship needs to stay strong. Don't let the children come between you!

Sidestepping the Struggle

The trick is to avoid power struggles with your children. Focus on your goal of solving the problem, finding a solution that both you and your child, or stepchild, feel good about. When you parent successfully, there are no winners and losers. Most of the time, effective discipline makes it possible for everyone to emerge from the heat of the battle feeling okay.

Most children are unwilling to relinquish power to a new stepparent — at least not at the beginning.

Learning to sidestep power struggles is especially important for stepparents. Most children are unwilling to relinquish power to a new stepparent — at least not at the beginning. "You're not my real mother (father) so you can't tell me what to do!" is a common response as children try to be in charge and rebel against you — the intruder in their family. If you try to defeat your stepchildren in a power struggle, you'll only damage the newly forming fragile bond you want — and will need in order to assume the role of disciplinarian later. Rarely does responding with power behaviors influence a stepchild in a favorable way. And it can create lots of distance!

When children try to engage you in a power struggle, the best thing to do is allow them some legitimate power. This decreases their need to misbehave in the first place. There are a number of ways to do this:

1. Give your children choices. Rather than commanding them to do something, give choices of "how" and "when" rather than "if." For example, if your young stepchild needs a bath, give her the choice of 7:00 or 7:30. You can allow other small choices:

shower or tub, bubble bath or not, color of towel. Still, she must take her bath. Giving your child choices allows her to feel powerful and competent without having to defy you. Choices are especially important in your stepfamily. Many things are new and different. A hard part of merging two households is managing to blend two different ways into one peaceable way — and eventually creates an "our" way. This takes time! When you present choices, you're respecting these differences, yet still setting boundaries and limits within which your children can choose to behave.

2. Include stepchildren in discussions about how rules and routines will be set up and about what consequences will occur when family members disregard or break them. Setting up new rules and routines without involving your children on some level invites trouble. They feel powerless. Whenever youngsters feel as though they have a say in how their household is run, they'll be more inclined to cooperate.

3. If specific misbehaviors get repeated often, you must establish consequences. You can all gather to discuss how recurring misbehaviors will be handled in your family. Group input is important because each set of family members might have different expectations about what discipline looks like, how it'll be carried out, and by whom. Your responses should be closely tied to the misbehaviors, *so your children can see the logical connection between their behavior and the consequence* they receive when they make the choice to misbehave.

Misbehaving for Revenge

Sometimes children misbehave to get revenge. They may break things or become physically destructive. Some children will defy values that a parent holds dear, or they'll say things they know will hurt your feelings. Some children go to great lengths to get even.

Why might a child resort to revenge? The motive might involve an attempt to even the score for some real or imagined injustice by a parent or stepparent. If a stepparent forces them to do something, their revenge response might be to make you feel miserable enough to cave in to their demands. As some children learn to manipulate their parents in a series of interactions, revenge becomes their perfect trump card.

Remarriage Can Set Up Revenge Behaviors

Several reasons underlie revenge behavior in stepfamilies. Once remarriage creates your new family, children finally must forfeit their dream of one day reuniting their biological parents. Now they have to share their parent with another adult and more siblings, losing the undivided attention they might have once had. And with a stepparent in the picture, your children face another authority figure, someone they had no say in choosing. Having an outsider's perspective, this new adult might actually notice things their biological parent hadn't, pointing out overlooked behaviors to their partner who then acts on them. During single-parent living, children may have gotten away with more misbehavior because of parental guilt, overwhelm, or a permissive parenting style. Now, rather than fault their own parent for ineffective parenting, they blame their stepparent and seek revenge.

Stepchildren also have to cope with the separation from their other beloved parent — long separations if the parent lives afar, shorter ones when they live between two households in the same community. If left unresolved and unspoken, this major loss and

A child who wants revenge will try to hurt parents and stepparents.

its attending sadness might contribute toward children resorting to revenge behaviors.

How can you tell if it's revenge? Your hurt and disappointment feel similar to what you felt with power struggle misbehaviors; only now, it's intensified with anger and frustration. A feeling of disbelief might surface. You wonder, "How could my own child do this to me?" While revenge appears similar to power struggles, the stakes are higher, the weapons heavier. Because of the parental hurt you feel, it's extremely difficult for you to remain calm enough to take appropriate action. But if you react emotionally and retaliate, you'll only worsen the situation. Retaliation contaminates the relationship with your child even more; then she'll feel justified and intensify her revenge behavior.

It may be harder for you to take appropriate action than it was in your former family. You may continue to deny that your children's problems are out of hand because, by admitting your troubles, it may seem as though your stepfamily is failing. As your fear of failure grows, stress builds. And when others witness your child's revenge behaviors, the fishbowl effect exacerbates the situation. Getting your children to stop revenge behaviors is difficult and, in many ways, the hardest behavior you'll deal with. Getting at the root of these misbehaviors might require help from a family therapist who understands the complexities of stepfamilies.

Correcting revenge behaviors involves using the same strategies you use when dealing with power behaviors. In addition, if your child has been destructive and caused physical damage to items, she needs to be responsible for the behavior and make restitution. How that gets accomplished could entail your child fixing something she broke, or paying all or part of the cost for the item to be repaired by someone else. This is not punishment, rather teaching a life skill about responsibility.

Reversing the Need for Revenge

When you're facing revenge behaviors, you need to separate the deed from the doer. While you take action and focus on correcting the behavior, remain friendly toward the child who has misbehaved. Direct your anger toward the behavior, not toward the child who did it. Remember, a behavior is just that — a *behavior*. Your child's act of defiance took only a few minutes; most of the rest of the time she behaves very differently. The best way to end revenge behaviors —

and this is especially important for new stepparents — is to build a solid, close relationship with your children so the need to get even disappears.

Behind your child's behavior may lurk hostility. It's doubly important that stepchildren be allowed to express hostility and negative feelings in *words* so they don't need to carry out revenge behaviors. Many children of divorce harbor intense leftover feelings they've been unable to work through. Your stepchildren may not have finished grieving the loss of their first family, and often this unspoken sadness is brought into the stepfamily. If these feelings remain internalized without a safe place to express them, they may come out in "crooked" ways, for example, in revenge behaviors. Make it okay for your children to express *all* their feelings. As they risk doing so, avoid criticizing, judging, giving advice, or talking them out of their feelings. Just listen. Be present.

One good way to provide a healthy safe space is to have a "family venting time" after dinner once in a while. This is a time when everyone has a chance to express their major feelings of sadness, anger, fears, and happiness about life in their new stepfamily. Use a large sheet of paper and let the kids record everyone's feelings as you discuss them. It might look like the chart on the next page.

Misbehaving to Avoid Failure

Is it possible your child fears failure? To avoid situations where they think they can't succeed, some children act helpless, disabled, or incapable. As they abandon any chance of succeeding, they want to be left alone. They withdraw.

This failure-avoidance behavior may show up when misperceptions and feelings of fear or guilt reign. Unless they're helped to work through emotions from their transition time, many children of divorce continue to harbor feelings that they might have caused the divorce. As long as they hang on to this self-blame, they wonder if their parents' divorce was because of some inadequacy or unknown failure on their part. Such inaccurate feelings may intensify when they hear you and your partner arguing in their new stepfamily. Any current couple conflict could retrigger thoughts and fears of another family ending and, rather than risk talking to you about it, your child may withdraw from the mainstream of stepfamily living at the critical time when you need to be strengthening new bonds.

Chart 8

FAMILY VENTING TIME

Sad	**Mad**
• That my parents had to divorce.	• That my parents still fight and put me in the middle.
Scared	**Happy**
• That this family might end too.	• That I have more brothers and sisters.

When your child misbehaves to avoid failure, most likely you'll feel helpless, inadequate, and defeated. You may give up on the child because, no matter what you try, he seems to repeat the misbehavior. This repetitive behavior frustrates parents and stepparents alike. Try to understand that your child chooses this behavior for a reason. It has a purpose!

You might unknowingly contribute to your stepchild's fear of failure in another way. Your standards might differ greatly from what he's used to. As he senses your disapproval, your stepchild might feel as though he'll never measure up. So why bother? His idea could be rooted in reality, or merely something he perceives. In either case, instead of trying and failing, the child is likely to give up and do nothing. To manipulate his environment and to avoid failure, he avoids trying.

Observing these helpless and incompetent behaviors, you may start to wonder if something is physically wrong with your child. You might even seek a medical diagnosis of the problem, a response that may trigger another process. When you take her to a doctor, your child may sense something is wrong with her; as she reacts to her parents' concerns, she acts even more helpless. The cycle continues once others start to believe something might be wrong with the child and thus start to excuse her misbehaviors. The longer you allow this pattern to continue, the more you reinforce her avoidance goal. She wins! (Really, she loses.)

Children who display inadequacy have given up. Often their parents have too. A sensitive stepparent might make a difference.

To stop this cycle, start by changing your view of your child and her avoidance behavior. Start to believe in your child, releasing any pity you hold. Encourage her to behave appropriately and to participate in the family. It's important that you hold expectations of your child, or stepchild, and view her as a capable person — no matter how she's behaving. Also avoid setting standards very different for new stepchildren than those they've been used to. Different or raised expectations might alienate them from you rather than bring them closer.

You can reduce, or eliminate, this fear of failure by providing a home atmosphere where *mistakes are accepted* as part of everyday living and learning. Mistakes provide opportunities to learn lessons. Replace criticism with constructive suggestions. Overlook minor mistakes and pick your battles. When your children make mistakes, discuss what lesson they have learned and what different choices they might make the next time. This is a great chance for stepparents to focus on the nurturing side of discipline and to work within the role of mentor or confidant in guiding their stepchildren.

Once children learn to use their mistakes as part of their normal learning, fear diminishes. Repeated success forms a solid base for confidence from which your children can try new behaviors without the fear of failure.

Beyond overlooking some mistakes, focus on your stepchild's successes and strengths. Recognize even small improvements. Affirm her. Notice when she's doing something right and comment positively. When you're trying to help build self-esteem, a child's "can-do quotient" is more important than her "intelligence quotient." Take opportunities to celebrate all the "can-dos" you discover in your stepchildren. It's part of the nurturing process. Discover what your stepchild likes. What's he best at? Then, and especially as a stepparent, provide the chance to repeat this success-over and over again. If you wait too long, or expect perfection, you might never get the chance to build your bond.

Keep in mind that dealing effectively with discipline is hardly unique to stepfamilies. Nearly all parents find it a difficult task. And although children will misbehave as part of their stepfamily adjustment, avoid interpreting every action in this light.

Your 12-year-old stepchild who displays a lot of rebellious behavior may not be showing hidden hostility toward you. The child may just be acting like a typical preteen, testing his own sense of power and control.

It's important to avoid viewing children's misbehavior as a sign that your stepfamily is failing. Use it as a signal that, to strengthen your stepfamily, you and your partner need to learn an approach

---

General Guidelines for Correcting Your Children's Misbehaviors

- Reject the behavior, never your child

- Correcting misbehaviors without giving clear direction confuses your child. Be sure to correct with clear, constructive guidelines.

- Be specific. State exactly what your child did wrong so that she understands clearly how to change it.

- Correct her behavior without adding more disapproving or disparaging comments to an already negative situation.

- Tell your child you appreciate her complying with the correction.

- For the future, reassert your expectations. "Let's talk about how you'll do it better the next time..."

Remarried couples who persevere through the stressful times and finally achieve stepfamily stability speak of a strong sense of pride.

to discipline that encourages children to cooperate and take responsibility for their own actions.

Many fine books and programs are available to parents who want to develop positive discipline methods. We like the approach of Drs. Don Dinkmeyer and Gary McKay in their *Systematic Training for Effective Parenting* (STEP) series and *Active Parenting Now* by Michael Popkin. You'll find those books and other suggestions in the References. The benefits of taking a class over simply reading about effective discipline techniques are many. A group setting offers stepfamily couples a chance to step back, explore their discipline techniques, and make a joint plan in an atmosphere that's supportive and encouraging. The group leader and other participants can offer valuable feedback during the process. For stepparents, who feel so isolated in their challenging roles, this peer support is very important. You'll find that you're not alone with these challenges! Classes give parents and stepparents time to try techniques at home and then return and discuss what happened. This valuable process will help you refine your parenting skills.

Our hope is that, fortified with solid information and effective strategies, you'll soon learn to deal with discipline in a way that works well for your stepfamily so you can fulfill your dreams of another chance for a happy and harmonious life.

Chart 9

DEALING WITH MISBEHAVIOR

Remember, to decide your child's goal, look at:

1. How you feel when the misbehavior happens
2. What you do about the misbehavior
3. How your child responds to what you do

Goal	Examples of Misbehavior	What Parents Can Do	Ways to Encourage Positive Goals and Beliefs
Attention	**Active:** Interrupting, clowning **Passive:** Forgetting, not doing chores, expecting to be waited on	Don't give attention on demand. Ignore when possible. Don't wait on child. Give attention for good behvior at other times.	Say thank you when child helps. Notice when child contributes.
Power	**Active:** Throwing tantrums, making demands, arguing **Passive:** Being stubborn, doing what parent wants slowly or sloppily	Refuse to fight or give in. Withdraw from power contest. If possible, leave room. Let consequence occur for child.	Give choices. Let child make decisions. Ask for help, cooperation at other times.
Revenge	**Active:** Being rude, saying hurtful things, being violent **Passive:** Giving hurtful looks, hurtfully refusing to cooperate	Refuse to feel hurt or angry. Don't hurt child back. At other times, work to build trust. Help child feel loved.	Be as fair as you can. Say thank you when child helps. Notice and appreciate when child contributes.
Display of Inadequacy	**Passive only:** Quitting easily, not trying	Do not pity. Stop all criticizing. Notice all efforts, no matter how small. Don't give up on child.	Focus on child's strengths, talents. Notice when child makes wise choices. Notice when child thinks of others. Give lots of encouragement.

The Stepfamily Workshop
Session Six

Questions for Review

1. Name the four motivations for children's misbehavior. _____
   _____
   _____
   _____

2. Why is it important to understand these? _____
   _____
   _____

3. As a new stepparent, what's the best approach for you to take
   with your stepchildren with regard to discipline? Why? _____
   _____
   _____

4. What if you and your partner have vastly different ideas about
   disciplining children? What should you do? Why? _____
   _____
   _____
   _____

5. Name some reasons why the democratic style of discipline is
   most effective. _____
   _____
   _____

6. What are some strategies to use when you realize your children
   are misbehaving to get your attention? _____
   _____
   _____

7. What might be two underlying reasons why your stepchildren
   exhibit power behaviors? What could be your part in it? _____
   _____
   _____
   _____

8. Why is the notion of providing a "united front" so important?

_____

_____

_____

Challenge to Conquer

For a long time, Maria raised her four children as a single parent. Often she felt overwhelmed. After leaving her alcoholic husband, she moved her family to another city to feel safe and start anew. Her children had little contact with their father and, after a while, they didn't talk about him much. Maria worked fulltime and managed the best she could, but she was always exhausted and irritable. She became more and more lax about making sure the children followed her few rules. When they were young, disciplining the children never was much of a problem, but when Roberto and Jorges became teenagers, they no longer listened to her. In attempts to get them to do their few chores and to honor their curfew, Maria cajoled, nagged, and bribed them. She felt completely frustrated.

Eventually, she married a man whom she'd met at work. During their brief courtship, Federico promised her he could shape up the kids so they'd respect her again. At first, she felt relieved to have Federico help raise her family. His three children lived in Mexico with their aunt since their mother died. As the new stepfather, Federico took over with Maria's children, encouraged by her when she admitted that she'd had lost control. He became the disciplinarian, "because their father wasn't in the picture," and he made many changes with his authoritarian approach. When Maria pleaded with him to be gentler with her children, the couple fought. "Look, you asked me to help you out with your out-of-control kids. I'll do it my way, the way my father raised me and, if you don't like it I can leave."

The couple fights constantly about the discipline dilemma. The younger children have withdrawn from the family and are doing poorly in school: the teenagers discount his discipline attempts and hang out with a gang of unsupervised boys.

1. What were some of the mistakes this couple made? What can they do? _____

_____

_____

_____

2. What's going on for the children? What are they feeling? What sort of motivations are behind their behaviors? _____

_____

_____

_____

3. Can Maria and Federico change the course of their stepfamily? How? _____

_____

_____

Stepfamily Activities

(1) Dealing with discipline is the major stepfamily issue. You and your partner can separately answer the three questions below. Then compare your individual responses and start discussing a shared discipline approach that will work best for your stepfamily.

A. Here's some ways that parents discipline their children. Check the techniques you now use:

___ yelling	___ nagging	___ reminding
___ giving choices	___ punishing	___ I-messages
___ negotiating	___ family meetings	___ spanking
___ rewarding	___ consequences	___ ignoring
___ establishing limits	___ requesting	___ bribing
___ involving	___ using incentives	___ conflicts
___ encouraging	___ resolving conflicts	___ threatening
___ setting up automatic rules & routines		

Compare your lists with your partner's. Are they the same or do they differ? Discuss steps you can take to begin to create common discipline strategies._____

_____

_____

B. Which techniques do you currently use that you'd like to stop? Why?_____

_____

_____

C. Which would you like to learn more about? _____

_____

_____

(2) When you add to your "history" project, consider drawing cartoons about a discipline challenge you've experienced. Have each person create one — and don't forget the captions. Encourage humor and positive outcomes.

Points to Ponder

- Dealing with discipline effectively requires that you understand clearly why your children choose to misbehave. Their choices have an underlying purpose: *attention, power, revenge,* or *to avoid failure.* Strategies exist for you to manage each misbehavior style.

- Wise stepparents approach their role as a friend and confidante who nurtures and establishes a warm relationship with stepchildren. Avoid taking on discipline tasks until you've created a bond with the children and your partner has given you the authority to discipline — and talked to the children about it.

- Stepparents need to assume the role of disciplinarian slowly; biological parents must support your efforts. Never disagree about issues in front of the children. If you decide to change a consequence a stepparent made, you can return to the children later and revise it. This models that it's okay to make mistakes and that, with new information, a change of mind is appropriate.

- Enrolling in a parenting class together is the wisest investment you can make in your stepfamily. Taking this step before remarriage, or early in your stepfamily development, truly shows your commitment to creating consistent discipline. It can curtail many challenges.

- Consistency about discipline *within* your household is essential; expecting consistency *between* the two households is an unrealistic expectation. This belief sets you up for disappointment and problems.

- The parent in the other household can affect you greatly. The better your communication and clarity about issues with the children between the houses, the more successfully your children can be parented in both.

- A democratic discipline style provides the best approach to discipline. Its clear rules, routines, limits, and consequences for misbehavior fosters self-discipline in your children and creates a comfortable family environment.

13

Your Stepchild's Challenges I:

Healing Young Hearts

Recently, I asked my six-year-old daughter what she wanted for her birthday. Looking toward her stepfather, Mitch, with an apologetic glance, she hesitated. Then she said, "'I want you and Daddy to get married to each other again." "Honey," I told her, "you know that can't happen. . . What else do you want?" This time her reply was quick and cheerful: "To go camping with you and Mitch. Can we do that, please?"

Childhood is a small part of one's life, yet what happens then influences the rest in important ways. Like the stepchild above, much has already transpired in your children's lives, causing them sadness and loss. Children *do* adapt to traumatic losses. But their adjustment depends on how well they're helped through the mourning process and how much you've supported them through all the changes they've faced.

Remember, the reorganization of their family wasn't your children's idea and most kids wish it had never happened. When you remarried, your children may not have completed their grief work. It's natural for them to carry some scars and confused memories into their new stepfamily. In fact, once they become stepchildren, anxiety over their loss may actually intensify and need to be revisited. As old fears resurface and new ones appear, stepchildren may feel surrounded with uncertainty. You may start your stepfamily with enthusiasm and high hopes while your children may respond with confusion and anger.

The questions children of loss rarely verbalize but carry heavy in their hearts often are rooted in fear. "Where do I belong? Will I still see my dad?" "If I learn to like this new person, will Mommy be upset?" While ultimately your remarriage can provide a new stability for your children, it won't calm their fears immediately. It'll take time to reduce their anxiety and rebuild their trust.

This chapter focuses on the emotional issues children in your stepfamily face as they adjust to stepfamily living. Exploring some of your children's specific concerns and relationships can help you see life in the stepfamily from their perspective. Soon you'll come to understand some of the reasons behind your children's actions. That'll put you'll a better position to respond in ways that help your children and your entire stepfamily.

Emotional Dilemmas — Grieving and Healing

Whether your first marriage ends through death or divorce, we hope that part of your personal healing process has included getting rid of anger and guilt and learning to trust again. Children, too, need to heal. Often, children in remarriages harbor many leftover negative feelings: anger, sadness, guilt, fear, and resentment.

Anger. Your children had no choice in the matter of the divorce or death. Their response to this lack of control in their lives may be anger toward either parent, but particularly toward the biological parent with whom they live daily. Their sense of security was disrupted when they lost regular contact with friends and relatives — or worse, their other biological parent. They may blame that parent for having to move. Teenagers especially need to feel they have choice and control in their lives.

Learning to trust again is difficult for children. They thought they could always count on their family; when the family as they knew it changed, they were dramatically let down. Such a loss may shatter their trust in adults, including their own parents, for some time. They may also come to distrust marriage and fear such a commitment.

Guilt. Guilt, the inability to forgive oneself, is another emotion your children struggle with. While guilt is common to all stepfamily members, in children it's usually buried and hard to detect. Many children blame themselves for their parents' break-up, sometimes even for the death of a parent. Such thoughts bring on feelings of unworthiness that can cause some children to set themselves up for failure. Retreating from friends and activities may be the way some children make up for what they believe they did wrong. Others may become overachievers in an attempt to compensate for their low self-esteem. Displeasing their parents adds yet another self-punishment that may help children relieve their imagined guilt. In short, they may mistakenly tell themselves, "I'm a bad person because I caused my parents' break-up, so I don't deserve to be loved by friends or family."

As parents you may have explained the death or divorce, and that it was not their fault; but if the explanation was unclear or hostile, children may have created their own stories for what happened. Their versions may be irrational and far from the truth. Unresolved, children live out their misperceptions in their stepfamilies and, later, in relationships as adults.

To help them understand, adults need to give children straightforward and nonjudgmental answers. Children are far better off living with the truth than complicating their lives with incorrect assumptions that must one day be cleared up. Most questions will concern what happened with the other parent. "Why did my parent leave? Why did our family end?"

While it may upset you to rehash your divorce, remember that your children's identity comes from *both* parents. When one is missing, an important part of your child is missing too. Speak honestly but discreetly as you fill the gaps. Remember, no matter how you feel about a former spouse, your child has an innate love for that person. It helps no one if you put down your former spouse. Indeed, bad-mouthing their other parent can backfire and turn your children against you. If you do, your children may fantasize about the other parent, to reconcile what they've been told with what they need to hear. Some fantasies can rival fairy tales. It's also a mistake to go to the other extreme, idealizing the missing parent. This can cause children to become caught up in loyalty conflicts and inhibit building their relationships with new stepparents.

Keep talking! Over time, chances will arise for your kids to talk and ask questions as they have a need to fill in the gaps. Let them take the lead and answer them honestly.

The best gift you can give your children is the permission to have a relationship with their other parent without your interference. The situation may be less than ideal. It may not be what you wish for your children; yet that relationship allows children to learn more about another part of themselves and sidestep some of the loyalty dilemmas they'd otherwise face. And, by maintaining positive ties with both parents, children gradually develop their own sense of justice and rid themselves of guilt.

Fear. Stepchildren fear losing another family. After all, they've been through that already. Any increasing conflict levels in your home, possibly even threats of divorce, may raise those fears again.

Often, juggling a job, family, and a new partner may leave you little quality time for your children. When this happens, your children may begin to wonder if you still love them. They may cling to you and avoid developing closeness with their new stepparent. Since their trust is already low and there's no guarantee the adults can make this marriage work, children tend to be slow to form bonds. They wait and see. They're seeking results and a sense of security.

The best gift you can give your children is permission to have a relationship with their other parent without your interference.

Your children may fear a shift or loss in their relationship with you and even feel resentful about your remarriage. This is especially likely if they're teenagers, already undergoing many changes in their own lives, or if you stayed single for a long time. Having lived together in a successful single-parent family, you and your children may have developed a special closeness. Now, they may not be eager to share time and space with another adult. They resent having to share you!

With their familiar family structure gone, and the new one not yet solidly in place, your children face the unknown. One way they may show their fear and confusion is through misbehavior. This is normal! Very young children might cling, have headaches or stomach pain, wet the bed, or withdraw. They have no words for their fear so their bodies speak for them. Sudden mood swings are common; so are tantrums and drops in school grades. Teenagers might respond by turning to sex or drugs. Until children find their place in the family and feel your remarriage is secure, they may test you — over and over — often with misbehavior.

Your decision to remarry may have been a wise one for all concerned. Released from an unfulfilling marriage or a life of loneliness, you started over, probably even becoming a better parent as you were able to provide your children with a happier family atmosphere. It's a mistake, though, to expect your children to feel as happy as you are about your remarriage. Such hope is a setup for disappointment! Yet, although experiencing death or divorce and remarriage is difficult, the loss can teach children how to adapt to changes and

> ### *Guidelines for Helping Children Through the Healing Process*
>
> - Be aware of all the changes in children's lives over which they had no control. Be sensitive to their feelings.
>
> - Ease into the newness of your stepfamily, realizing that your children's confusion and uncertainty is normal.
>
> - Be patient and answer children's questions honestly and carefully.
>
> - Accept grief and loss as part of life and encourage your children to face the reality of these losses. Empathize, rather than sympathize, with them. Help them to express their anger and sadness.
>
> - Encourage your children's relationship with their other biological parent. Never undermine that relationship.
>
> - Reach out with assurance of love and show continued caring. Nurture your children with extra hugs, "I love you's," and time together. Don't confuse nurturing with pitying, pampering, or overprotecting.
>
> - Confront misbehavior and take corrective steps. Don't make excuses for your children's inappropriate actions.

demands made upon them. As they learn to get along with people outside their immediate family, they develop flexibility. New role models with different values can teach your children a lot. As they come to terms with two sets of rules about life, your children learn to make better choices. Someday, after children work through their feelings, they may say, "Thanks for the fresh start." But it'll take a long time.

14

Your Stepchild's Challenges II:

Dealing with Differences

P icture your values and beliefs — all the information you impart to your children to help them make their way in the world — as a pair of prescription eyeglasses that you give them. Although some children may refuse to wear them, rejecting their parents' values, most tend to or will generally come to view the world through these or similar lenses.

In your first family, your children learned to make judgments and evaluations based on what you taught them. Your beliefs and behavior provided their frame of reference. When people responded in certain ways to their behavior, life became somewhat predictable; that predictability provided a certain security.

Enter a new stepparent with a different set of lenses. Children must now learn to use two separate sets of lenses to view the world. Asked to adapt to these new "eyeglasses," children may have a fuzzy, if not downright chaotic, view of life; they may respond with erratic behavior.

This "double vision" gets more complicated. As stepchildren move between mom's home and dad's, they cope with different beliefs and behavior in two households. First, they must deal with stepparents and stepsiblings in the home where they live. Then they must ease into yet another way of doing things in the home of their other parent, who may also have remarried. These two households may be very different.

Adjusting may cause difficulties, but they aren't insurmountable. Remember, your children already are accustomed to making a variety of adjustments. They adapt daily to different teachers, different sitters, the changing behavior of family and friends. The key is for adults to acknowledge, without judging, the differences children are experiencing and then to state expectations: "Yes, it *is* different between Daddy's home and Mommy's. But in this house, we do it *this* way."

Gradually, these adjustments are made. When you understand all the differences your children face, you'll be better able to help ease things along.

Children Face Differences at Home

Day-to-day living rooted in two separate histories will call for changes. When two sets of people with different backgrounds begin to live with one another, routine matters such as mealtimes, chores, personal habits and hygiene can come under scrutiny. While people have individual ways of doing things, family members who grew up together are more likely to do things similarly.

Do you eat chicken with your fingers? How do you hold your fork? Are pancakes large and thin, or silver-dollar-size? Do you fold towels into thirds and stack them, hems out? Do you towel-dry dishes, let them dry in a dish drainer, or rely on a dishwasher?

In first families, everyone knows what's expected and no one thinks much about these everyday routines: they're simply done a certain way. To get used to *new* ways, stepfamily members need time. Too much change too quickly upsets everyone. Problems begin when step-parents try to change things too quickly, discounting the way someone else has always done them. Some family members may feel attacked.

It's critical for stepfamilies to talk about the specifics of daily routines in former families — or in the other parent's home. Discuss mealtimes, dress codes, school, homework, morning and bedtime schedules, rules, responsibilities, and routines. Use such discussions for discovery, not for deciding which way is right. And then begin a new way that works for your stepfamily. Avoid criticism or ridicule of someone else's way. Where choices are necessary, make compromises. Above all, remember: neither approach to a task is *right* or *wrong;* each simply reflects a different way of doing things.

Children Face Differences Between Homes

As stepchildren move between two homes, they deal with even more differences. Children may be used to the way their biological parent in the other home has been doing things, but when that parent remarries, more differences complicate their lives. When caught between the two families, children may have a strong need to protect the parent with whom they live. They may criticize their stepparent, or be reluctant to bond. On the other hand, if children begin to develop a friendship with the stepparent, biological parents may feel threatened and talk negatively about that adult.

Differences in rules and routines will take some getting used to.

When you keep in mind that your children are family members of two separate households, helping them move between two homes becomes a little easier for all concerned. Family boundaries that are open and flexible work best. While basic decisions and authority lines need to come from the home in which children live most of the time, kids need to know they are loved by both parents and accepted in both homes — and have responsibilities in each.

Many benefits exist in stepfamily living. In fact, eventually, stepfamily members often find it ironic: differences that once caused problems become possibilities they'd never thought of before. Most also say that, after an adjustment period, they changed and became more adaptable. Experts find this to be especially true of *children* — *if* the children aren't burdened by their parents' unresolved problems. Change, when met without resistance or ridicule from adults, can enrich the lives of your children. Learning to view the world through different lenses gives them a head start on getting along with many kinds of people in their lives.

Having a Non-Custodial Parent

It's rare that a non-custodial parent is unimportant to a stepchild. Once a parent, always a parent; divorce doesn't diminish that reality. Dead or alive, parents are a shaping factor in our lives. When a parent dies, memories of that person linger in the child's mind forever; some very young stepchildren even fantasize that their dead parent might return. If divorce ended your marriage, the other parent is the person with whom the children and you or your new partner will continue to interact — a very good reason for doing it well.

Your stepfamily stability hinges on the quality of your couple relationship. But it's also affected by the degree to which the biological parent in the other household accepts, and is accepted by, your stepfamily. Your children have a right to relationships with both their parents. Since adults divorce each other but not their children, the other parent — a former spouse and symbol of the first marriage — remains a vital connection in the network of stepfamily relationships.

What about the quality of that relationship? Your children's visits with their other parent may be irregular. They may not represent the quality parent-child relationship you'd like. Still your children and stepchildren are better off for having contact with their other parent. While it may seem that day-to-day stepfamily living could be easier without continued contact with that person and the hassles it can create, closing off any relationship with the other biological parent ultimately creates more problems for your children. Everyone is much better off if you work out the unfinished emotional baggage that creates the challenges.

The other parent can be friend or foe to you and your stepfamily. If adult relationships are charged with unresolved hostility, this link between two families can create problems for stepchildren. Positive relationships, on the other hand, make the connection a source of strength that can help build and eventually stabilize your stepfamily.

Children adjust to seeing their other parent infrequently as long as, in some way, they are shown they are loved.

The secrets to being a successful part-time parent are *consistency* and *continuity*. Consistency means having a clear agreement to be firm, but fair, and faithful to established rules and limits. Continuity means keeping up an ongoing relationship by spending recurring meaningful time with the children. After a divorce, many biological parents play a diminished role in their children's lives. A person in this position isn't in any way less a parent, but not being involved daily makes it difficult to function like one. It takes hard work to cope with guilt about not seeing your children often; and it takes persistence to maintain a strong parent-child relationship in spite of time and distance constraints. Children adjust to seeing their other parent infrequently as long as, in some way, they are shown they are loved.

Love vs. "Stuff"

Some non-custodial parents feel so guilty about their diminished role that they try to make up for it during visits. Every stepfamily knows about the overindulgent biological parent. But, more than *presents*, children need *presence* from this parent they see so rarely. Although children welcome gifts as expressions of caring, *time* with their other parent is what children need and seek above all. Most children say they prefer getting time and caring from their parents to getting "stuff." This is especially true for children of divorce who need to know, above all, that they are loved.

Quality time is shared time! It doesn't need to involve a special event or high cost. Amusement parks and movies can be fun, but a steady diet of such activities sets up a poor long-term relationship with the children's other parent. Fixing a car, playing a board or backyard game, taking a hike, or even watching television (the weakest option) together all provide chances for parents and children to share — without making elaborate plans or spending lots of money. There are also many creative and inexpensive ways for non-custodial parents to remain an active part of their children's lives. Phone calls, tapes, letters, and postcards all remind stepchildren that, although they cannot be together, their other parent often thinks of them. A clever book, *101 Ways to Be a Long-Distance Super-Dad* by G. Newman (see References), shows mothers and

Guidelines for Helping Children Move Between Homes

- Let the other parent and your children and stepchildren know they can count on you for support.

- Be willing to talk over any problems that arise during the transition between homes. If you're still angry at your former spouse and cannot communicate directly, try dealing with your ex-mate's partner about transitions for the children.

- Visits to the other parent may be irregular, but when they're planned, help the children prepare emotionally. They need to know they'll be missed, but since they may already be anxious about going, avoid adding more stress by bringing up complaints about chores or messy rooms right before they leave.

- Simplify and neutralize transitions. Perhaps the other parent could pick the children up from school or the ballpark — some neutral spot. When children return home, avoid greeting them at the door; allow them time alone in their room to adjust. Don't give them the third degree.

- Be firm but flexible in your dealings with the other parent. Cooperation reduces tension.

- Adults should make the visiting arrangements among themselves, so children aren't caught in the middle.

- Be flexible. As children grow, their needs change. Their time becomes filled with friends and activities. Help them explain to their other parent why they don't want to come every weekend, even though the custody agreement decrees it. If you're the other parent, try to understand and accept your children's changing needs.

- With younger children, suggest taking along a familiar toy or game to help break the ice in the other household.

- Never use the children as messengers. Don't send lists of things you want the other parent to do or buy. Communicate directly.

- Allow children to talk about their time with their other parent if they wish, but don't pry. Just listen.

fathers creative ways they can maintain relationships with their children — even from three thousand miles away.

When Caution Is Required

Sometimes, a biological parent without custody is seen as unfit. Should children be allowed time with such a person? Unfortunately, situations do exist where parents need to protect their children from abusive parents or dangerous living arrangements. But many times a non-custodial parent is judged unfit either because of value differences or as a reflection of anger by the former spouse. As a custodial parent, it's important to determine whether your former mate is truly unfit and would endanger your child, or whether you're simply projecting unresolved hostility. Perhaps your former spouse isn't the ideal parent, but is this person truly dangerous or just a poor role model for your children? Or, in reality, do you still harbor intense hostility for being wronged? If there's concrete evidence of potential danger, a visitation supervised by a grandparent or legally appointed guardian is better than no visit at all.

Still Trying to Win?

A competition often exists between divorced adults. The contest's prize: your children's love and affection. Some kids use this explosive situation to get what they want from their parents. If your children cannot have what they really want — their family intact and the assurance that they are loved — they may try for "stuff." Since parents need to be loved, too, they too often say yes when no is most appropriate. By pitting parent against parent, children win prizes and privileges, but these make for a hollow victory. Until divorced parents cooperate rather than compete, your children may continue to maneuver you in this way.

Besides demanding material possessions, your children might use the "I'm gonna go live with Dad (Mom)" threat to get their way. By caving in to their threat, you'd be permitting children to avoid facing conflict and responsibility at home. If they're allowed to flee to the other home, your children learn only to run from difficulties and avoid responsibility.

Schools Can Help or Hinder

Another crucial adjustment and communication link can be working with the school. This important arena of your child's life can be a stabilizing force for children during divorce and remarriage — if teachers and parents work together. When educators are aware of stepfamily dynamics and the individual family's special needs, schools can respond by serving as partners in children's growth and adjustment.

But this partnership, like so many others, may suffer from an information gap. When communication between school and stepfamily is unclear or nonexistent — when educators don't know your family is reorganized and families don't know what to do to get the school's help — children's development can be hindered.

Today, many, many children in American classrooms under the age of 18 are involved in some sort of step-relationship. That figure continues to grow, because nearly half of all American children have experienced divorce and most of their parents remarry at least once. Most will become stepchildren. Yet, as common as remarriage is, often a school-stepfamily information gap still exists.

When school policies close out non-custodial parents or step-parents, the schools can pose a threat to stepfamily parent-child relationships. Forcing children to choose parent over stepparent, or parent over parent creates divided loyalties.

How does a child distribute the two tickets allotted for his school play? Who gets invited? Who gets left out? When teachers limit the number of presents made on Mother's Day or Father's Day, how does the child choose whether to give the gift to the parent or the stepparent?

Since language both reflects and determines beliefs, the words teachers use to refer to divorced and remarried families will affect their students. Uninformed teachers can use language that sabotages efforts being made at home.

 One child came home from school upset and insisted that his parent come outside and walk all around their house with him. He was looking for cracks because his teacher had said he came from a "broken home."

Children know most broken things don't work! Many single-parent families and stepfamilies, however, *do* work — very well. When children hear expressions like "broken home," "shattered family," "natural parent," or "failed marriage" they form a negative image of their own or their classmates' families. Many textbooks continue to portray only the never-divorced family. Unable to identify with the families in their schoolbooks, stepchildren may feel something's wrong with theirs.

If educators are insensitive to stepfamily dynamics, school conferences can create further difficulties. A teacher who feels uncomfortable with divorced or remarried parents may inadvertently shift the focus of the meeting from the children's progress to coping with her intrusive feelings — or those of hostile parents.

School counselors who understand a student's family configuration can better help that child. Unfortunately, only a few ask about a family's dynamics and may even consider it irrelevant to the child's school life. But emotions affect a child's performance in school greatly. How can children learn while their heads and hearts are in turmoil? As they worry about how they will fit in with all these new people, when and if they will see their grandparents, whether their new stepparent will stay, your children's concentration dwindles and their studies suffer.

Closing the Home-School Gap

If a gap exists between schools and stepfamilies, it only intensifies confusion for everyone. Closing such a gap begins with you. While schools have a responsibility to you and your children, they'll need your cooperation. It's up to you to let your child's teachers know about the changed status of your family and to work with schools to normalize within the classroom the image of stepfamilies.

It's up to you to let your child's teachers know about the changed status of your family and to work with your schools to normalize the image of stepfamilies within the classroom.

Contact might be through a formal letter or a telephone call. If you can do this before your remarriage, all the better because children often experience school adjustment challenges at remarriage similar to those at the time their parent divorced or died. When teachers have a clue to what's happening at home, they can approach classroom difficulties with knowledge and understanding and talk with your children to help lessen fears.

Clarify relationships and lines of responsibility. Let the school know exactly who has the right to interact with your child. Who can take your children from school? Your former partner remains a parent, and you'll want to work with the schools so that he's not left out of your child's life. Administrators who misinterpret the Buckley

Amendment from the Family Education Rights and Privacy Act or who are insensitive to stepfamily dynamics might view a non-custodial parent as a non-parent.

Ask teachers to integrate words like *stepparent*, *stepfather*, and *stepmother* into classroom conversations. Encourage schools to purchase textbooks and library books portraying a variety of family units and lifestyles and to let publishers know of this need. Talk with your children about their relationship with the school and ask them how they think stepfamilies could be better served. Tell them to speak out if they hear negative language about stepfamilies and to let you know if they fail to get the support they deserve from a counselor.

Don't Take It Personally

All children in all families have some basic needs that must be fulfilled: Above all, they need a sense of *security* and *belonging*. They need to feel *important* and *significant* as persons. Stepchildren who've experienced many losses and changes, often find it difficult to get these needs met. Inwardly fearful, anxious, or confused, they may react outwardly with behavior that baffles and upsets stepparents.

In turn, stepparents often assume responsibility for stepchildren's actions. "What did I do?" many ask. Usually, this defensive reaction just makes things worse. It's important to realize that stepchildren's behavior might stem from any number of sources having nothing to do with the stepparent. Adults who understand this reality can reduce their own negative reactions and become far more effective stepparents.

Do your stepkids ever behave like the children in the cartoons? If so, don't take it personally!

Remember our discussion in chapter 1 about how stepfamilies are different? As you see, the importance of those differences may be multiplied for children. The key to empowering your children to deal effectively with their new life is to talk openly and honestly with them about the differences, about what they may expect from others, and about the very normal feelings they may experience as a result. The suggestions in this chapter, and in the chapters before and after this one, will help. You'll find it well worth the effort.

Chart 10

IT'S NOT YOUR FAULT

A stepchild with whom you've had an excellent relationship may suddenly rebel and reject you. You didn't do anything. At some point, children have to cope with the reality that their parents aren't getting back together. As children release this fantasy and come to terms with this sadness, they often rebel.

Children who aren't given clear, direct permission from biological parents to develop warm relationships with stepparents often feel caught in loyalty conflicts.

Stepsiblings may feel jealous or resentful when they have to share their biological parent's time and attention. If they've lived with a single parent for a long time, the adjustment may be especially difficult.

Gaining a stepchild's trust takes time and patience. Stepchildren fear another loss: they have no assurance that their new stepparent won't leave them as their other parent did.

Very young children may fear that because one parent has gone, their other parent could also leave. This is especially true if a parent has died or abandoned a child. Some children even give up friends and play activities in order to cling to their remaining biological parent. Disconcerting as this may be to stepparents, it's a phase many children must pass through as they relinquish their grief and rebuild trust in a new stepparent.

15

Your Stepchild's Challenges III:
Coping with Changes

If most stepkids had their way, they wouldn't have stepparents or stepsiblings or stepanythings! They'd rather have both biological parents living together and things like they used to be. We know that isn't going to happen, so how can we help children to deal with the realities of their new stepfamily relationships?

Coping with a New Stepparent

The stepchild's wish for a return to the original family has little to do with the stepparent and a lot to do with their losses. But once a stepparent becomes a reality, your children must figure out where to fit this person into their complicated lives.

It starts with names. What should your children call their new step-parent? The terms *Mom* and *Dad* describe biological relationships and have strong emotional connotations; forcing children to use these words in reference to stepparents creates discomfort. Very young children might eagerly call stepparents Mommy or Daddy. Some grow into it. Older children prefer to use first names. Some children create different parental names for stepparents, such as Pop or Mama June. They may start by calling them by a first name and, when and if children develop an emotional bond with their stepparent, it might evolve into mom or dad. The final word about naming and introductions rests with how comfortable children are with the names; stepparents should feel content with them, too.

Choosing names is only the beginning. On a deeper level, children must ask themselves, "What can this stepparent be for me?" If a new stepparent is emotionally immature and demands a great deal of the biological parent's time and attention, he or she can become an intruder in children's eyes. First your children lost daily contact with one parent; now they fear you're unavailable. Their resentment can lead to power plays and triangles that threaten the stability of your stepfamily.

It's important to settle on a name agreeable to all.

By encouraging your children to begin building a relationship with your partner, you can help keep resentment at bay. Preserve your own relationship with your children by having special time together, apart from activities with the entire stepfamily.

Children form ideas about the role they want their stepparent to play in their lives. They assess many things — the kind of person the stepparent is, hobbies and interests the person pursues, age, whether the stepparent has children. They'll take into account their own needs, too, and have ideas about how they believe this new adult can help meet them. How children fit the stepparent into their lives also depends on their own age and development. The relationship they have with their own parents also affects their decision.

Such choices are rarely made on a conscious level. But, consciously or unconsciously, children do form expectations about this new relationship. They may cast the stepparent in one or more of the roles discussed in chapter 9: friend, confidant, parent figure, mentor, role model. It's important for parents and stepparents to be aware of each child's expectations and to consider how appropriate they are. What your children think they want may not always be in their best interests.

Guidelines for Helping Children Adjust to a Stepparent

- Recognize the importance of the other biological parent and respect children's right and need to love that parent. Support the time they spend with their other family and invite that parent and other family members to milestone ceremonies — recitals, play-offs, graduations. At such events, focus only on the children and put aside unfinished emotional business between the adults who are present.

- Never speak negatively of their other parent in front of your children. Control resentment you may feel, and work on letting go of it.

- As a stepparent, acknowledge the strong bond between your new spouse and his children. So children won't feel left out, avoid monopolizing your partner's time.

- Plan "alone time" with your stepchildren so you can get to know one another better. Invite them to do things with you — don't pressure them or make demands. And find out what they like to do.

- Understand that family life cannot always be happy. When conflict arises, it doesn't mean that your family is failing or that your stepchildren "hate" you.

- Give up your expectation of "instant love." Allow time for relationships to develop. Concentrate on learning to accept, respect, and like your stepchildren.

- Reject fairy-tale myths and unrealistic media portrayals of stepfamilies. Forgive yourself for being imperfect. Realize that you learn when you make mistakes. So does your partner, and so do your children!

Living with Stepsiblings

Stepsibling arithmetic seems simple enough: addition. With more children, there's more interaction, more rivalry and competition, more fighting — and more fun. But, at first, it mostly seems like more fighting!

Most siblings fight — to get what they want and to get their needs met. It's maddening but normal. When sisters and brothers raise the roof, sibling rivalry can drive most parents crazy. When children from two or more families come together, this rivalry often intensifies. Stepsiblings fight over the same things biological brothers and sisters do — parental favoritism, family position, space, time, and possessions. Mostly, they fight about having to share their parent. Learning to share a parent in a biological family is a tough enough task; learning to share a parent after experiencing loss and while trying to jockey for a place in the new family is extra hard.

Stepsibling Rivalry

Competition is common to all families. Sibling rivalry begins when first-born children must learn to cope with the addition of a new sibling who threatens their role and position in the family. Until their parents can reassure them that there's enough love to go around, your children may feel displaced or "dethroned." Older children who have a hard time sharing the limelight with the newcomer may display outright hostility. Troubles among stepbrothers and stepsisters, however, are more complicated than this. Stepsibling relationships give a whole new meaning to the term, "sibling rivalry."

Stepsiblings may resent one another. They're angry about the loss of time with their own parent whom they now have to share. They fear a loss of space and privacy and, often, this fear is justified. Sharing space means more adjustments; children may have less space for their belongings and no way to decorate a place exclusively as their own to create a personal identity. A loss of privacy means no place to be alone with friends. Worse, it means no place to be alone with oneself — to dream and plan.

When biological sisters and brothers fight, they share a loyalty bond that carries them through the troubles. Feeling loyal to their parents, their blood relationship, and their family, they know they must sooner or later resolve or accept their differences. Most

eventually do. Stepsiblings feel no such kinship; many don't even feel they belong to the family. With both sets of children feeling this way, what incentive do they have to get along? As the children jockey for their place in the new family constellation, sibling rivalry in stepfamilies can become extremely serious.

Guidelines to Help Support Stepsibling Relationships

- Help children accept the fact that things have changed for them. Help them come up with creative ways to make private space for themselves when they do have to share.

- Make it clear to your children that you expect them to live respectfully together.

- Model effective communication and problem-solving techniques so children see positive ways of coping with conflict.

- Teach children to say what they feel and avoid blame games. Help them express their feelings through I-messages: "I feel angry when someone uses my things without asking."

- Schedule a regular meeting time in which the entire family gets together to discuss routines, make plans, explore expectations, and air and iron out grievances. (See "Coming Together — The Stepfamily Meeting" later in this chapter.)

- Avoid interfering. As long as children aren't doing serious physical or emotional harm to one another, stepparents and parents are wise to let the kids work out their problems among themselves, without parental interference. Learning to compromise and negotiate problems is one of the important functions of sibling relationships.

- Above all, avoid being pulled into triangles, especially aligning with your biological children. Kids who work through their own problems learn from the process and end up being better friends.

- Remember that stepsibling affection cannot be forced. It develops slowly and naturally or not at all. Be patient as stepsiblings struggle to accept their new situation and move forward.

If only one partner brings children to the remarriage, sibling rivalry won't be *substantially* different from what it was before the remarriage. But in families with stepsiblings, adults need to encourage feelings of importance and belonging in all children and assure them that this new family is secure.

How do you do this? As a couple, you can make it clear to children that this marriage is a serious, lifetime commitment. Your children need to hear this confirmation so they neither worry nor harbor fears about another marriage ending — a possibility they imagine when they hear you arguing. Plan activities for your whole stepfamily that gives everyone chances to have fun together, get to know each other better, and to learn to solve conflicts creatively. Then children can feel secure that they are full members of the family. By arranging shared chores or special times during which parents do something together with two stepsiblings who need to get along better, you can encourage your children to interact in a setting that is limited and defined.

Kids need private time and space for daydreaming! You can help them find a space to sort out personal problems or just being alone. Families invent many ingenious ways of making private space for people. Creating a makeshift room divider out of a sheet or blanket they could decorate might be a project children enjoy. In homes with tight bedroom space, each child can have his own bulletin board or her private corner of the room to decorate. Left to their own devices, some children improvise to find space they feel they need.

If your child takes her toys off to the laundry room or gravitates to a dusty corner of the basement to do homework, become sensitive and alert to her efforts to find some privacy. You can support her right to this time alone and even help arrange seating or lighting to create a better space.

Putting two families together may mean more to your child than getting a stepparent! It can include new brothers and sisters too, and while that can be fun, it can also be unsettling. Who gets the biggest room? Who gets her way the most? Which favorite food gets cooked more often? Who gets more of dad's time? And what's my position in the family now?

Birth Order Reshuffled

A significant change for children in many remarriages is a shift in family birth order. A major force affecting the lives of all children is the position they were born into in their family. First child? Last child? Only child? In biological families, children have learned how to find their place and how to react; but when new stepsiblings enter the picture, many find their comfortable family position changed. As a firstborn or lastborn child tries to figure out how to function as a middle child, confusion about roles might bring about rivalry or misbehavior with siblings.

Although these transitions are confusing, also they offer new possibilities. The greatest of these is a new perspective. Your children can't always go out into the world playing the same role they played in their family. A changed birth order provides a "practice session," teaching an early life lesson: *Change* is what life is all about! And as stepchildren view and take part in the workings of the family from a new place, their struggles help them become more adaptable. Old ways of relating and behaving don't work; learning to cope with these realities ultimately creates their ability to adjust to life's changing situations.

As your children adapt to stepsiblings, it's important to avoid comparing them with one another. This is particularly true when there are two stepsiblings of the same age and sex. Having grown up in two different families, they may be very different.

Barbara and Ellen, for example, are both 12. Barbara likes to experiment with makeup, new hairstyles, and clothes. She talks about boys constantly. Sometimes, Ellen still plays with dolls and younger children. She's most comfortable in jeans, and talk about boyfriends sickens her. By supporting their differences and strengths, you can help both children feel accepted and reduce conflict between them.

As children struggle with a changed position in the family, take care that no one slips through the cracks. Be sure each child finds a way to be special and significant in the family. Avoid letting the child who took over the first position become the boss or responsible for the other children.

Thinking About an "Ours" Addition to the Family?

If you have a new baby, or plan to have one, it might be helpful to know that it's common for children to view this addition with anxiety and confusion. Newborns need lots of attention, and get lots of attention from outsiders; already, your children worry about sharing their parent. But a new baby also can serve as a biological

Chart 11

FAMILY CONSTELLATION CHART

Position	Typical Characteristics	Implications for Parents and Stepparents
First child	• Often takes responsibility for other siblings. • Gets along well with authority figures. • Likely to become high achiever. • Needs to feel right, perfect, superior.	• Avoid pressure to succeed. • Encourage fun of participating, not goal of winning. • Teach that mistakes are for learning. • Help child accept failure and not feel it's a reflection of self-worth.
Only child	• Unsure of self in many ways. • Used to being center of attention. • May feel incompetent compared to parents or others. • Likely to be responsible. • Often refuses to cooperate if fails to get own way.	• Provide learning opportunities with other children. • Encourage visiting friends. • Have spend-the-night company. • Use child care and nursery schools.
Second child	• May try to catch up with older child's competence. • May try to be older child's opposite in many ways. • May rebel in order to find own place.	• Encourage child's uniqueness. • Avoid comparisons with oldest. • Allow child to handle own conflicts with oldest.
Middle child	• May feel crowded out, unsure of position. • May be sensitive, bitter or revengeful. • May be good diplomat or mediator.	• Make time for one-on-one activities. • Include in family functions. • Ask for child's opinion.
Youngest child	• Often spoiled by parents, older siblings. • Often kept a baby. • Often self-indulgent. • Often highly creative. • Often clever.	• Do not do for youngest (especially on a regular basis) what child can do alone. • Do not rescue from conflicts (thus making a victim). • Do not refer to as "The Baby." • Encourage self-reliance.

Adapted from Michael H. Popkin, *Active Parenting: Parent Handbook* (Atlanta, GA: Active Parenting, Inc.), p.19. Used by permission.

connection to your separate families, bringing you all closer together. Beware of expecting older kids to baby-sit your new bundle of joy! If preteens or teenagers feel used, everything might backfire.

Jealousy — even when it seems unreasonable or extreme — is a child's natural expression of the fear of being replaced.

Stepsibs — The Special Bonuses

Unlikely as it may seem at times, stepsisters and stepbrothers may be one of the greatest gifts parents give their children with remarriage. As they learn to cope with each other's differences and fears, stepsiblings share many benefits. Friendship is one. Life lessons are another. Many stepsiblings develop life-long friendships, sharing common interests and problems. As they share abilities, hobbies, and opportunities, they learn from one another. Friendship, sharing, and learning to get along with others are a special bonus for only children who inherit brothers and sisters through remarriage.

A different or expanded point of view is another bonus. Learning to live with other children, kids might gain a new perspective on themselves, dumping old labels ("Jock," "Dummy," "Goodie-Goodie") that tie them to destructive patterns. Stepsiblings also teach each other new things, provide skills, insights, and a new system of beliefs.

Stepsiblings also can help one another learn to cope with life. From the ups and downs of stepsibling relationships, kids learn skills to better help them negotiate, cooperate, and accept. They become more flexible. Children who learn to adapt in stepfamilies may also learn to adapt to other life situations faster than children from traditional families. They've had more practice!

Grandparents and Stepgrandparents — Expanding Roles

For children, grandparents provide a vital connection between their heritage and their future. Contact with grandparents is valuable to children's development. During difficult times, this loving link can make a vast difference in easing your children's adjustment. When children's lives are being disrupted by divorce and remarriage, and their world seems topsy-turvy, grandparents can represent continuity. After the remarriage, too, grandparents may provide extra support to the stepfamily — if you welcome it.

But, for many grandparents, a divorce of their adult child that may cut ties with their beloved grandchildren can be devastating. Even if they've adjusted to the divorce and maintained contact, many grandparents go into an emotional tailspin upon their son's or daughter's remarriage. It arouses the fear that, although till now they haven't lost touch with their grandchildren, a major move or an adoption by a stepparent might bring about such a loss.

Grandparents worry about yet another alteration to the family tree: a new graft has been added in the form of stepgrandchildren. Suddenly, the older generation is expected to interact with children with whom they share no emotional or biological history. They have to decide how to treat these new children, how to handle issues from gift-giving to inheritance. As they cope with all these changes and decisions, many grandparents feel confused.

Coming Together — The Stepfamily Meeting

A family meeting is more than everyone finally getting together at dinner: it's a regularly scheduled, and somewhat structured, meeting of all family members. Its purpose is to encourage understanding and cooperation. Decisions and plans can be made, complaints and compliments shared, questions and suggestions clarified, and chores agreed upon. The stepfamily meeting provides a time to share positive experiences and good feelings about one another. It offers an excellent opportunity for children to listen and be heard. As this regular meeting creates harmony, it strengthens your stepfamily.

Begin by agreeing upon a time when all family members can come together. Invite everyone, but don't pressure someone who refuses to attend. When you make it clear that the decisions made during the meeting ultimately applies to all stepfamily members, the reluctant ones may join in. Organize the meeting with a "leader" and "secretary" and rotate those jobs from meeting to meeting.

Start the meeting by sharing thanks, appreciation, and successes so that everyone begins to feel warm and positive.

When problems are brought up, solve them together with this four-step process:

I. **Identify the issue.** It's important to clarify exactly what the problem is. Make sure everyone has a chance to be heard.

2. **Brainstorm possible solutions.** Allow for all suggestions, whether they seem realistic or not. In brainstorming, no idea is ever judged; all are accepted and considered.

3. **Evaluate the brainstormed solutions and choose one.** Work at this until the stepfamily can agree on one solution.

4. **Try out the solution agreed to.** Make sure everyone commits to following whatever plan has been made for a specific period of time. It's important that everyone share in the decision making, adults and children alike. As you make plans for your stepfamily, focus on the positive. Laughing and enjoying one another builds bonds.

Keep meetings short. Depending on whether your meetings include young children or teenagers, they might last anywhere from 15 to 30 minutes. Long, drawn-out meetings will become a turn-off.

In their confusion and wonder about where they fit in, many grandparents might treat their grandchildren differently from their stepgrandchildren. Biases become obvious at holidays or birthdays if grandparents give finer gifts to their biological grandchildren. Some stepchildren may feel hurt by this, and it's unfair. Already, these children have coped with so much sadness and loss that what they need is caring and a sense of belonging to help rebuild their self-esteem. Younger children tend to feel especially upset by unequal treatment. Older children can usually understand that grandparents might feel like doing more for children with whom they share a history; but even teenagers feel a tinge of resentment about second-class treatment.

This confusing situation is also unfair to grandparents, who may be expected to feel affection for stepgrandchildren whom they barely know. Grandparents aren't intentionally cruel; they simply feel different about each set of children. Their treatment of them reflects these feelings.

Like many people, grandparents may feel uncomfortable talking about their feelings. In this case, you or your partner may have to initiate a discussion of how their behavior affects your stepfamily. As always, by exploring feelings, you move closer toward understanding. Once they come to understand the effect their behavior is having, many grandparents will change their approach — especially when they learn that they're not expected to *love* the children, but simply to respect their feelings.

Grandparents are a vital connection between your children's heritage and their future. During difficult times, this loving link can make a vast difference as they help children adjust.

Sometimes, though, grandparents' confusion, brought on by loss and pain, may lead them to make a more profoundly negative response. Such decisions can have a destructive effect on your stepfamily. Some grandparents may not welcome your new partner and children at all. Some may not acknowledge your remarriage, or worse, may even try to sabotage it by forcing their daughter or son to make loyalty choices.

If this happens to you, you and your spouse must take firm action to keep your children and stepchildren safe from more loyalty conflicts. For the sake of your remarriage, you may have to distance yourselves, emotionally or geographically, from the grandparents until your family stabilizes. Although this situation isn't ideal for children, it spares them being caught in the middle. As time passes and the shock of the remarriage diminishes for them, grandparents often consider a different view. Then, carefully and gradually, you may all be able to heal old wounds and reestablish the relationship.

Guidelines for Enriching Relationships with Grandparents

- Recognize the importance of grandparents and the emotional well-being this connection provides children.

- Keep communication lines open. Help arrange times when children can be with their grandparents; reassure the grandparents of continued contact.

- Stay calm. If relationships become heated, don't threaten to cut off visits. Keep children's best interests in mind. Don't use your children to hurt your parents or those of your partner.

- Create opportunities for stepgrandparents to get to know their stepgrandchildren. Start with short visits. Keep your expectations realistic and give everyone time to deal with feelings.

- Include grandparents and stepgrandparents in your stepfamily's special activities.

Stepfamily Atmosphere — Easing the Adjustment

One of the ways children measure self-worth is by how people around them respond to them. From this response they feel loved, unloved, or anything in between. Losing a parent through death or divorce can be a serious blow to a child's self-esteem. The child wonders, "What was wrong with me that my parent left?" This irrational interpretation of the loss is a common one. As they make many changes, children in single-parent homes may feel different, as though they're not part of a "real" family. During these painful transitions their self-esteem may slip. Living in a stepfamily brings more confusion. Like many children of divorce, your stepchildren may suffer from low self-esteem. Sometimes, while everyone's adjusting to the new family, adults may overlook the contributions children make. Indeed, until they've come to accept their stepchildren, some stepparents may criticize, rather than encourage, them. Attacks on their already shaky self-esteem may lead some stepchildren to misbehave and heighten tension among stepsiblings.

You and your new partner have the chance to make a difference in the lives of your children. Building their confidence and sense of worth requires you to focus on the positive things they do rather than on what you dislike. At first, this may be difficult. But as you allow for individual differences and accept your stepchildren, nurturing and encouraging them feels good. The higher the level of self-esteem that each family member has, the more successful your stepfamily. So, fostering this in children contributes greatly.

Together, you and your partner can create a family environment in which your children and stepchildren will thrive. As a stepparent, one of your rewards will be a sense of pride from being important in the lives of your partner's children — perhaps even making a vast difference. As a biological parent, you'll know the satisfaction of having helped bring stepfamily members together, thus enriching their lives. In either role, with patience and understanding, you can guide all your children to believe in themselves and value all members of their special stepfamily.

The Stepfamily Workshop
Session Seven

Questions for Review

1. As children struggle to find their place in the stepfamily, what are some of their feelings? _____
   _____
   _____
   _____

2. How can you help children learn to trust again? _____
   _____
   _____
   _____

3. What's the major dilemma stepchildren face? How can you best help them? _____
   _____
   _____
   _____

4. What's the biggest problem your children or stepchildren have with their other biological parent? Do you play any part in that? What steps can you take to help ease this problem? _____
   _____
   _____
   _____
   _____

5. How can you influence schools to be a positive, supportive force in the lives of your children and stepchildren? _____
   _____
   _____
   _____

6. What causes stepsiblings to compete with one another? _____
   _____
   _____
   _____

7. How have you tried to create a feeling of belonging for children in your stepfamily? What works and what doesn't? Why?_____

_____

_____

_____

8. Have you begun regularly scheduled stepfamily meetings? What else can you do to improve communication and family relations?_____

_____

_____

9. Why is the link to grandparents so important? What can you do to help children, grandparents, and stepgrandparents build positive relationships?_____

_____

_____

Challenge to Conquer

For the past few years everyone in the stepfamily has been routinely spending the holiday at Marc's parents' home. Although Marc's parents think they treat all the children fairly, they continue to buy major gifts for his children and token gifts for his wife Shana's children. They explain by saying, "Their own grandparents will give them gifts." Marc's parents aren't intentionally cruel; they simply don't view their stepgrandchildren as they do their grandchildren. This year, Shana's children have refused to go to the holiday celebration at Marc's parents' home.

1. How might Marc's parents feel about Shana's children? About their refusal to come visit on the holiday?

2. What feelings might Shana's children be experiencing?

3. What might Marc and Shana decide to do? What will they say to Marc's parents?

4. What can Marc and Shana do to expand their options? How can they help ease the differences and resentment felt by Marc's parents, Shana's children, and by Shana herself?

Stepfamily Activities

(1) Identify those children in your stepfamily who have lost their original birth position in their family and help them to explore

ways to make their place in the new family comfortable — even special. Bring everyone together to discuss your children's original family birth position and where they fit into the new stepfamily they've become part of.

Younger children may enjoy making pictures of the family groupings. To do this you'll need several sheets of construction paper, a cardboard star pattern to trace, scissors, tape or gluestick, glitter or stickers for decorating, pencils, and felt-tipped markers. Help each child trace and cut out as many stars as there were children in the child's original family. Then write or have the child write the name of each sibling in that family, including his or her own name, on the stars — one name per star. Allow time for children to decorate their stars.

Next, provide each child a sheet of paper on which they'll represent their original family constellation. Ask each child to start at the top of the sheet and paste the star that represents their oldest sibling, next oldest, and so on from oldest to youngest. Share these pictures with the whole stepfamily. Then, together, make one picture using stars representing all the children who make up the new stepfamily. Be sure to include even those siblings who do not live in your stepfamily full-time. As with the first pictures, arrange the stars in order from oldest to youngest.

Talk about the different family forms and focus on those children whose place in the family changed when you formed your new stepfamily. You might use questions like the following:

- Whose position has changed? How do you feel about these changes?

- What's (was) it like to be an oldest child? Middle child? Youngest child? Only child?

- What do you like (dislike) about your position in our stepfamily? Is there another position you'd like better? Why?

- What do you think needs to happen so you'll feel good about your new position?

- Did you feel special in your other position? Why?

- Do you feel special in your new position? How do you feel special, or how would you like to feel special?

During your discussion, be accepting of feelings. Don't try to talk children out of them or judge them. Feelings aren't good or bad —

they just are. Your intent is to understand how each child feels, let then process their feelings, and gain insight into the dynamics of stepsiblings' relationships.

(2) Have each child draw a picture or write a brief entry in your stepfamily scrapbook that illustrates a particular dilemma that he or she has struggled with. Parents can comment on these in a different color ink, or write their own. Encourage one-liners that reflect lessons learned.

Understanding My Stepfamily

1. **What are children feeling?** Can you identify some of the feelings of children in your stepfamily? What losses does each child need to mourn?

Child's name	Feeling	Loss	How can I help?

2. **What differences are children dealing with?** Can you identify some of the differences children in your stepfamily are facing at home? Between their two homes?

Child's name	Issue	Way done in former/other home	Way done in our home	How can I help?

3. **How can you help your children with their transition to stepfamily living?** What specific things can you do? Or, if you asked them, what might they request?

Child's name	Issue	How can I help?

> ### *Points to Ponder*

- Kids have the right to a secure family life and continued contact with both biological parents.

- If your children live with you, they need special time alone with you and reassurances you still love them and they aren't being replaced by your new spouse.

- Children, like adults, need help — and time — to complete their grieving. Becoming part of a stepfamily may mean loss of friends, family, and familiar situations and places. Encourage children to express these losses.

- Confusion and uncertain behavior by your children and stepchildren is normal until you get to know one another.

- Stepchildren might have one idea of what role they want you to play in their lives; you might have another. It's important to clarify everyone's expectations about your role as stepparent.

- To get to know your stepchildren, plan time alone with each of them, allowing relationships to develop slowly.

- If you're the non-custodial parent or share custody, your children might encourage you to shower them with gifts and treats. What they really want and need is time with you, not "stuff."

- Schools can help or hinder stepchildren's adjustment. It's up to parents and stepparents to work with schools to gain support and cooperation.

- Stepsiblings are a big plus for kids as they learn from one another. An only child may gain sisters and brothers. Once they move from competition to cooperation, many stepsiblings become special life-long friends.

- A change in birth-order position provides new perspectives and teaches flexibility.

- Stepfamily meetings can help improve relationships among stepsiblings, give all stepfamily members opportunities to understand and enjoy each other, and provide a setting for solving problems together creatively.

- Grandparents are a vital link for your children — between the past and the future. Encourage children's relationships with grandparents and stepgrandparents.

16

Hope! The Heart of Your Stepfamily

Hope is at the heart of healing. Its positive energy helps you hold onto your forward movement and belief that you can do it — essential to your stepfamily's journey toward success. Hope requires faith and action that keeps you on track.

You are building a stepfamily! As architects of your new family, to create a strong foundation you'll need to integrate the reality of the past with your dreams for the future. With the element of hope, you can do that. The great American architect, Frank Lloyd Wright, said this:

> *The present is the ever-moving shadow that divides yesterday from tomorrow. In that lies hope. Hope enables us to share life's experiences with humor and compassion, accept what is, reflect without regret, and strive for what can be.*
>
> (*The Living City*, pt. 5, "Night is but a Shadow Cast by the Sun" 1958.)

Just as this great architect created innovative — and often controversial — projects, you're designing and building a different kind of family. You want it to withstand the tests of time just as Wright's great buildings have. His "organic architecture" used the land as it was; he didn't clear land and start over, as developers often do. His unusual designs incorporated the existing environment, building from what was already there, making his approach unique and exciting.

Likewise, you must build your stepfamily by honoring important parts of the past as you live in the present. You have hopes and dreams about what your family will be like. You accept your differences and wisely know that love, although it's important, isn't enough. Also, you know that hope alone isn't enough; yet, without it, no dream can ever be realized. And although information and skills are critical, you also must trust in the *process* of becoming a stepfamily.

This process takes a long time! As you've learned reading this book, working through your "stepfamily journey" takes most stepfamilies several years. Those who haven't prepared for remarriage get bogged down in the early stages and need support to move ahead. But once you accomplish this and commit to your family, you might describe feelings akin to the exhilaration of having built a unique house or having climbed a mountain. You've conquered the roots and rocks, weathered the storms, and finally stand together at the summit of success — proud for your perseverance in reaching your goal. Many people in stepfamilies say that, along the journey, hope was essential!

Hope provides the forward movement during your challenging journey. It helps you stick to your course and not give up. While its concept may be fuzzy, hope can help steady you when the normal pitfalls of stepfamily living endanger your chances for success. Hope can temper your fears so that, when you recognize challenges, you accept reality and have the wisdom to seek support and stay the course.

True hope has no room for delusion and denial. It demands action! Key elements of hope are belief and expectation, asserts Jerome Groopman in his *Anatomy of Hope*, as he explores how people prevail in the face of serious illness. When your beliefs and expectations are based in stepfamily realities, hope serves as a positive force — a domino effect. When we hope for something, Groopman says, we marshal our efforts and emotions toward a future event, a positive place. While hope isn't a direct cause for success, there is a connection; without hope, it's just too tempting to give up. After all, you reason, you didn't die from divorce before. But holding hope as your lifeline, step-by-step, stage-by-stage in your stepfamily journey, your focus on the big picture allows you to succeed so that you and your partner and your children can reap the many strengths and rewards it offers.

Stepfamily Strengths

If you're just beginning your stepfamily journey, or feel lost in the process, you'll wonder, what are some of those strengths? While it's important to be aware of the *pitfalls* in an effort to avoid them, that sole focus can become defeating and destructive. It's all too easy to identify only struggles! But by examining your strengths, you'll see possibilities and keep a positive perspective.

Many rewards come from stepfamily living. Some are short-term, most very long-term. Let's explore a few important strengths that will help keep hope alive during your challenging times.

Personal Marital Satisfaction & Family Commitment

Above all, a remarriage is a marriage! It presents another chance at love and the dream of a happy family life that has eluded you. Your first attempts disappointed you. It's scary to trust and truly believe you can achieve marital intimacy, especially when you'll be asked to confront and resolve harder issues than people in most families. But as you feel supported by your partner and learn to communicate well, your relationship strengthens. Your love deepens. You learn that nearly anything in your relationship, large or small, is forgivable and can be worked through.

You've learned an important lesson: although your daily roles as parents and stepparents are temporary, marriage can be permanent. As your children witness this excellent lesson, they can carry it into their young adult lives as part of their own healing. A commitment to your family involves much more than feeding and clothing your children. It's about being responsible for their long-term moral and educational development. You've taught your children and stepchildren values and how to cooperate and care for one another within the context of your stepfamily. When they move into the world beyond the family, they'll be equipped to become productive citizens and happy people because you've shown them what a commitment to family life looks like — and under some challenging conditions.

Remarriage presents another chance at love and the dream of a happy family life that has eluded you.

Your children learned early that conflict is part of family life and that their life journey won't always be smooth. They've come to know that, although they'll encounter mountains and valleys, they've also learned some of life's important lessons and have become stronger in character. They've also witnessed how clear communication, with negotiation and compromise at its core, can transform challenges into workable solutions Your children learned what it feels like to be in a family where its members are committed to one another. They've practiced respect. And they can relearn trust!

Positive Marriage Model for Your Children

Children learn by what they see you do! Once you get down to the business of building a strong marriage, it'll be a model that your children respect — and hope for themselves one day. As they've watched you master the challenges of stepfamily living, they've seen that, unlike their biological parents, you've made it work this time. They witnessed you fight for your marriage, making it a priority. They saw you reach out for guidance and learned that having the wisdom to seek family therapy isn't a weakness but a strength.

Your children experienced your struggle of shifting loyalties from your strong bond with them to deepening the loyalties to your couple relationship. Eventually, they came to understand that necessary shift didn't negate your love for them: it taught them that a solid marriage is the foundation for a strong, happy family.

Your healthy marriage model balances the negative one your children might have experienced in their original family. As they learn positive lessons about marriage, when they come to choose their own life partners your children will have a healthier reality on which to base their decisions. As the meaning of marriage came full circle for them, they can hand it down to their children — your grandchildren.

Role Models for One Another

With more people in the stepfamily, two families to be part of, and a larger extended family, most stepchildren have four parental models and extra grandparent figures, not to mention more aunts, uncles, and cousins. Each individual has some gift to share — a hobby or special interest. A skill. An expertise. A philosophy of life. Values. New behaviors and positive examples offer your children new lenses from which to view the world. These opportunities offer chances for your children to gain love and learn lessons they can carry into adulthood.

You can learn from your stepchildren too! One stepmother said her relationship with her stepdaughter, although sometimes stressful, changed her life. "I was a great homemaker. Creative activities, gourmet cooking, and entertaining were fun for me. But I'd never been involved with sports or outdoor activities. I'd always loved nature but limited it to gardening. Then my stepdaughter took me on a few short hikes. One day, after we hiked to the top of Mt. Washington in New Hampshire, everything shifted for me. Although exhausted, I was exhilarated and continued to keep hiking in my life in various ways. Small hikes, big hikes and, one year, I hiked the famous Milford Trek in New Zealand."

Her stepdaughter recalls her own struggles with being truthful when she was young. She'd learned by watching her parents' deceit and unethical ways and said she thought that's what was normal. As an adult, she now remembers the many talks she had with her stepmother about integrity (and the trouble she'd get into for lying) and how hard it was to change. "Now, as a mother myself, when I have to teach the same lesson to my daughter, I think of what my stepmother taught me about honesty. She was a great role model."

Another stepparent shared how delighted she was that her new husband taught her young sons many hands-on skills that their biological father lacked. "Their dad was very creative. He liked to paint and read but he couldn't build a birdhouse. Their stepfather taught the boys mechanical and carpentry skills and how to make things — a boat, an airplane." As young adults, today, both earn their living using those skills. They didn't have to choose, she says, rather they had an additional role model from whom to learn new things.

One young man said growing up in a stepfamily gave him "a spare dad." When his biological father died, he still had his stepfather to teach him things and support him.

Healed, Healthy Children

Healing takes a long time and goes in cycles. As your children grow and move toward young adulthood, continue conversations with them about your divorce or the death of their parent. Share the lessons you've learned. Discuss the hard path to forgiveness you've taken. Your openness to revisit what happened to them when their family changed helps them to continue to process their feelings and gives them chances to ask questions they might not have been able to ask earlier. Such dialogue gives them a chance to resolve conflicting claims and inaccurate stories they might have created. You may believe you did a good job of explaining that divorce was a grown-up problem to your children when it happened. The trouble is that your children were probably grieving

While not all negative effects can be reversed, with time, a healthy step-family can counteract many of the negative aspects of divorce.

and too young to understand. They might have been afraid. But as they mature, you can say different things, and from a more healed place yourself; and they can hear you differently.

As you integrate the past with the present, you can help keep memories alive for your children. Help them understand in a clearer, more mature way how your decision helped shape their lives, again reminding them that the past wasn't their fault. Teach them that loyalty to one parent doesn't need to mean they can't be loyal to you too. When you free them to love both of you, you help them to restore hope for their own future. Such ongoing conversations help them to heal, forgive, and move on. Your honesty may help them avoid mistakes that you've made so your children might have a better chance of avoiding the pattern of divorce. Without an understanding of what happened to them, and the chance to examine and process their feelings over the years, many children of divorce have a hard time considering commitment and marriage. They look to you for clues and guidance — and hope.

Recall the happy times! Continue to remind your children of the many positive experiences your family shared before the family changed. As they listen and remember, they'll learn that, with courage and hope, people can start over. They'll see it's not about forgetting, but they'll also learn that human beings who once hurt each other can forgive.

Your stepfamily is as capable of nurturing healthy human beings as your original family was, research shows. In some ways, perhaps more so. Your commitment to the ultimate rewards of stepfamily living holds great positive implications for your children. In a ten-year National Institutes of Health sponsored study of American stepfamilies, the research of Dr. James Bray revealed that a strong, well-functioning stepfamily can negate some of the detrimental psychological impacts of divorce on children.

This news provides another message of hope! While not all negative effects can be reversed, the study indicates that, with time, a healthy stepfamily can counteract many of the negative aspects of divorce. Bray indicates that a strong, stable stepfamily is as capable of nurturing healthy development as a nuclear family. He believes it can imbue values, affirm limits and boundaries, and provide a structure in which rules for living a moral and productive life are made, transmitted, tested, rebelled against, and ultimately affirmed.

Resiliency and Corrected Courses

In today's complex world, change is the only certainty! Stepfamily living prepares your children for this reality by teaching them resiliency that can help them overcome difficulties and manage life more successfully. One of your major stepfamily strengths has been your ability to become flexible and adaptable. It's become a necessity because living between mom's house and dad's house with a greater extended family often seems more like a "family forest" than a family tree. With the disruptions your children faced during a divorce or death of the other parent, often they've lived in a state of limbo as plans changed frequently. But they learned to adapt.

Many children ultimately develop the trait of resiliency. Researchers who study this important factor say that one of the most important buffers against divorce stressors for children is the guidance of a strong nurturing parent. But if two healed parents, and a stepparent, provide a loving and supportive co-parenting relationship, so much the better. Other adults — grandparents, neighbors, family friends — also can help children navigate troubled transition times. Children benefit from many supportive and consistent relationships and the greater stepfamily sphere provides many of those. The resulting resiliency is a strength they carry into their adult lives!

Children benefit from many supportive and consistent relationships and the greater stepfamily sphere provides many of those.

Extra sets of eyes and ears can be helpful! Stepparents can serve as sounding boards — and help children correct courses gone awry. Sometimes, during adolescence, children feel uncomfortable or even alienated from their parents. Many teenagers have a stressful relationship with their same-sex parent as they struggle with normal identity issues. As a stepparent, you can help fill in the gap and offer supportive advice that might really make a difference at a critical time in this young person's life. Having another parent person with whom to share ideas and garner information is helpful to stepchildren.

For example, one teenager said, "I can't talk to my mom about sex and drugs because she goes bonkers. But my stepmother is easy to talk with about these things. She gets me books and is patient with all my questions." This young man didn't have to turn to his peers where he might get inaccurate information or make poor decisions. A different opinion or a new option might be just what a stepchild needs to make a wiser choice and correct a negative course toward which they may have strayed.

If you're careful not to compete or undermine their other parent, being a caring confidant permits you to offer new perspectives. Your role may allow you to transmit important values and beliefs that contribute to a child's developing moral code, perhaps helping to encourage a course correction and greater resiliency. What a contribution to better prepare children for today's complex future!

Humorous Hindsights

A sense of humor is an important tool to strengthen your stepfamily. Finding the amusing or absurd within intense scenarios often can soften the hard edges of difficult realities-when humor is used appropriately. Throughout this book, we've used cartoons to illustrate typical stepfamily issues to lighten up common challenges. As some of these rang true, hopefully, you've had some good chuckles.

Humor helps remind us that the glass is half full rather than focusing only on what's missing. Providing this positive outlook on life to your children, who have experienced much loss and change, can be a great legacy. (Of course, it's important to teach them never to use humor at someone else's expense or in hurtful ways.)

One young man recalls a humorous moment in his stepfamily that, many years later, still makes him smile. He lived with his mother and stepfather on the east coast. When his California father came to visit, because everyone got along well, he stayed with the family. During one visit when the family was gathered for dinner, the young man recalls yelling out "Dad" to get his father's attention. "I remember both my father and my stepfather answering 'yes son ' at the same time. For an instant, it really felt awkward — until everyone began to laugh." What could have created a painful loyalty conflict for the young boy was softened by humor as everyone joked about it, helping the entire family to relax.

Special Sibling Relationships

Stepsibling relationships can evolve to lifelong friendships. Many stepchildren recall fond memories of growing up in a stepfamily; but they also say it wasn't easy in the early years. At first, they were merely strangers, thrust together because of their parents' decision to marry. They say it took time to build friendships. As they tried to find a sense of belonging in their new stepfamily, these biologically unrelated children shared many challenges — loss, sibling birth order shifts, shared space conflicts, and having to share time their parents' time with new people. Frequently these changes, and the confusion they wrought, created serious sibling rivalry with its accompanying resentment, competition, and tension.

Sibling rivalry is natural in all families. Having brothers and sisters is one important way that young children learn how to get along with others — and in the safety of their family. As they learn to negotiate and compromise, stepchildren have lots of extra complexities to work out. With time, as anxiety and anger dissolves, bonds of affection and appreciation begin to grow. As friends, they learn many things from one another — values and beliefs, skills and hobbies.

One set of grown stepchildren talk proudly of the strong friendships they continue to share — even years after the remarriage in which they grew up ended. Although scattered geographically across the country, these five young adults still create at least one annual adventure together. A ski trip to New Hampshire. A sailing cruise in the Caribbean. Hiking on Vancouver Island. They are genuinely fond of one another and agree that their lifelong friendships were formed by their stepfamily living experiences.

Learned Lessons

You examined your family issues courageously, made the necessary changes, and moved toward stability.

Stepfamily living offers you valuable chances to learn powerful lessons. If you've used your stepfamily crisis well (and there may have been several), you examined what happened, perhaps why it occurred, and decided on how to correct it. Maybe your teenager got hooked on drugs and was failing in school. A daughter got pregnant. Perhaps your six-year-old complained of headaches and stomach aches and didn't want to go to school. When you got support from a family therapist who understood stepfamilies, you learned that your children were acting out unresolved grief. Your stepson was angry because his biological father had left his life and he felt abandoned and betrayed by him. When your daughter heard you and her stepmother fighting, she began to feel afraid that your stepfamily was ending because she remembered that same sort of parental arguing preceded her mother leaving. As she turned to a boyfriend for emotional reassurance that she couldn't find in the family, she made poor choices.

All of these difficulties may have created crises in your stepfamily. But once your choice became to face them head on, you began to see the crises as challenges and opportunities for change and growth. Everything shifted. You learned some important lessons. With professional guidance, you examined your family issues courageously, made the necessary changes, and moved toward stability. You began to practice those lessons — not always perfectly at first. You may have encountered some setbacks; but, by this time, you finally understood that's all they were — setbacks. You no longer feared challenges because you knew that, eventually, they would lead to growth and strengthen your stepfamily.

Personal & Spiritual Growth

Like any adventure you've never before taken, some of your stepfamily journey was challenging! If you set out without the stepfamily "trail map" provided in chapter 3, this was especially true. You made lots of changes to succeed. But change, especially as it came during your "crazy time," had a way of cracking things open. You began to see things differently, respond differently and, ultimately, you were different — stronger and more centered. Your self-esteem strengthened! Your family relationships became fulfilling! Your marriage blossomed!

As you chose to do stepfamily living consciously, you and family members were forced to negotiate many difficult scenarios. Adversity and challenges strengthened you — even humbled you. When you reached out to your hurting stepchild, who was acting out toward you, and began to really listen and understand her fears, you practiced compassion. When you finally heard your own child's need to be re-connected with his absentee father who had hurt you deeply by leaving, you practiced empathy. As you released the regrets and resentments from your former relationship to transcend your hurt and make your child whole, you practiced forgiveness. As you and other stepfamily members dealt with many conflicting and complex feelings, and resolved them, you couldn't help but grow and change. Rather than let change threaten your couple relationship, you adapted to what needed to be done and made those changes. Now, you can reap the rewards of that personal and spiritual growth. Is this not soul work at its best?

What's Special about Your Stepfamily?

Your stepfamily is special! Not only is each person in it unique, but there is no other configuration in the world quite like the group you've created. Like Frank Lloyd Wright's innovative architectural designs, you've built a strong and interesting stepfamily. Change is no longer your family's enemy; it's become your strength

As your family members continue to work through the challenges, a core of mutual affection and concern develops. This caring begins with your remarriage — your fresh start in a happy, loving relationship. Together, as you and your partner weather the predictable stepfamily stages, you'll create security for your children. Above all, it's your strong marriage that provides the foundation for your successful stepfamily.

Your stepfamily is special. Not only is each person in it unique, but there is no other configuration in the world quite like the group you've become.

It's important to remind yourselves of this often. Rather than to get caught up with the stresses, it's more helpful to concentrate on your stepfamily strengths. Speak often of the appreciation you feel for one another. Gratitude is one of the great positive emotions.

There's a saying that's stitched on samplers and printed on posters: it says that we can give our children only two things — roots and wings. For many stepchildren, after their first families changed form, their roots become tangled and complicated. But, as new relationships take root and intertwine with the old, your children's spirit can blossom and thrive. With support and love coming from so many sources, children can branch out in many directions, forming a myriad of connections as diverse as they are strong.

And the wings? At first — for children who have known loss — confusion, guilt, and anger undermine their sense of self and security. Their wings may be as fragile as the newly emerged butterfly as it leaves its cocoon. But as time helps heal wounds and trust grows, your children not only take wing, but are released from the emotional baggage that's weighed them down. They can soar. You and your partner can feel a great sense of pride in their growth and achievements. And well you should!

Both stepparents and stepchildren speak of the warmth and closeness they grew to share. Most admit that, although building trust and commitment wasn't easy, they've reaped tremendous rewards. And most speak of how hope was at the heart of their stepfamily's healing and commitment.

As you continue to reap rewards and build wonderful memories, you'll share a joyful journey. For many people in stepfamilies, love will grow as well. And where there is love, most things are possible.

The Stepfamily Workshop
Session Eight

Questions for Review

1. In what ways has your remarriage given you a new sense of personal confidence and fulfillment? _____ _____ _____

2. How have you grown the most in your stepfamily? Which child have you noticed really benefited from your stepfamily experience? How? _____ _____ _____

3. Can you recall a time when you and your partner lost hope and felt discouraged about being able to succeed? Talk about that time of your journey. What turned things around? _____ _____ _____ _____

4. Was there a defining moment in your stepfamily, a crisis, that cracked things open? Discuss it. What made the difference that kept you moving forward? _____ _____ _____

5. Have you corrected some bad habits or character traits as a result of stepfamily living? Which ones? How did the changes come about? _____ _____ _____

6. How have you or your stepchildren been a role model for each other? What are some of the ways? Identify the one you think to be most important! _____ _____ _____

7. How will the adaptability and flexibility that your children learned living in this complex family help them in the world?

_____

_____

_____

_____

8. Which person in your stepfamily corrected a life course the most? Discuss it. What do you think was responsible for the turn-around? _____

_____

_____

_____

9. What special traditions have you established in your stepfamily? How did they come about?_____

_____

_____

_____

10. What's the most special part about your stepfamily?_____

_____

_____

_____

Challenge to Conquer

Maria's wedding is to take place in two months. She's excited about her marriage to Jorges but she harbors a great concern about her wedding day. Her parents had divorced many years ago and both remarried. Living between two households hasn't been easy for Maria because, for years, her biological parents continued to argue about money matters. Now they couldn't agree who would pay for what part of the wedding expenses.

Not only did this continuing money conflict trouble Maria, but she also hadn't decided who would walk her down the aisle: her biological father or the stepfather who also helped raise her? And which "father" should dance with her first at the reception?

1. What is Maria feeling above all? What should she do?_____

_____

_____

_____

2. Who do you think should walk her down the aisle? Do you have any creative ideas that might help Maria decide? _____

   _____

   _____

   _____

3. What would be the most helpful thing for Maria right now?

   _____

   _____

   _____

4. How has your stepfamily dealt with some of these ongoing issues in a creative way? What was most helpful? _____

   _____

   _____

   _____

Stepfamily Activity

As you continue to grow as a stepfamily, take out the stepfamily scrapbook or photo album history that we hope you created at the beginning of your Stepfamily Journey. Enjoy its contents and reminisce as a family. Notice any missing events and work together to fill those in. Ask extended family members if they have photos or mementos that might add to your stepfamily history. If you haven't made this family history project yet, get started and get everyone involved. At whatever stage you're in, have each family member write a brief tribute to your stepfamily and include those messages. Choose a theme. Our funniest memory. The scariest place in our stepfamily journey and how we resolved it. What I've learned from this new family. A trip I'd like our stepfamily to take. What I learned from living in a stepfamily. A dream I have for this family.

Over the years, take this history out once in a while to be reminded how, in spite of disappointments and setbacks, hope kept you moving forward. Feel very proud of your Stepfamily Journey!

Understanding Your Stepfamily

Creating a Chain of Hopes

Each of you in your stepfamily has brought certain hopes and dreams about how you'd like your family to be. Even if you've lived together a long time, you may not have discovered or discussed all of these. This cooperative activity allows your family members to express hopes, dreams, fantasies, and wishes for your stepfamily's future.

Gather colorful paper, pens, scissors, a glue stick, tape, or stapler. Cut paper into strips of any width that, later, will be looped into chains. As you do this, encourage people to talk about their hopes and wishes for your family. Trips you'd like to take. College and career plans. Activities you'd like to do together. Something you'd like to see happen or change. All wishes, no matter how big, small or realistic, are acceptable. Next, have family members write one wish or hope on each paper strip-as many as they can think of. You can create your own individual chain and later link it with those of others. Or, connect your loops of hopes with other family members as you go, sharing aloud what is written on each.

Hang the chain somewhere in your home. Or save it for your holiday tree. Occasionally, take it down after dinner and reread the expressed hopes. Encourage people to add a loop whenever they think of one.

Points to Ponder

- Establishing traditions and goals builds stepfamily unity.

- Many special joys and rewards result from living in a stepfamily.

- Hope is at the heart of your commitment to stepfamily living.

- When you create a strong marriage, you'll almost certainly have a happy family life.

- The stepfamily offers a place where children and adults can heal and grow.

- It's important to identify and focus on your strengths.

- You provide role models to one another.

- Having a sense of humor puts things into perspective, helps you over hurdles.

- Resiliency is a stepfamily reward that prepares your children for life.

- Stepfamily living provides many chances for personal growth and healing.

References

Ahrons, C. *We're Still Family: What Grown Children Have to Say About Their Parents' Divorce.* New York: Harper Collins, 2004.

Albert, L. & Einstein, E. *Dealing with Discipline from Stepfamily Living Booklet* series. Ithaca, NY: Elizabeth Einstein.

Berends, P. B. *Whole Child, Whole Parent.* New York: Harper Perennial, 1997.

Bernstein, A. C. *Yours, Mine and Ours: How Families Change When Remarried Parents Have a Child Together.* New York: Macmillan, 1989.

Bloomfield, H. H. & Felder, L. *Making Peace with Your Parents.* New York: Random House, 1983; New York: Hyperion, 1993.

Bohannan, P. & Ericksom, R. "Stepping In," *Psychology Today.* (January 1978)

Boss, P. *Ambiguous Loss: Learning to Live with Unresolved Grief.* Cambridge, MA: Harvard University Press, 1999.

Bozarth A. R. *Life Is Goodbye, Life Is Hello.* Center City, MN: Hazelden, 1986.

Bray, J. H. & Kelly, J. *Stepfamilies: Love, Marriage, and Parenting in the First Decade.* New York: Broadway Books, 1998.

Bridges, W. *Transitions: Making Sense of Life's Changes.* Cambridge, MA: DeCapo Press, Perseus Books, 2004.

Burt, M. S., and R. B. *Stepfamilies: The Step by Step Model of Brief Therapy.* Philadelphia: Taylor & Francis, 1996.

Cassell, C.,"The Role of Stepmothers: A Comparative Study of Stepmothers With and Without Natural Children." (Unpublished dissertation, University of New Mexico, 1981).

Carter, E. A., and McGoldrick, M. *The Expanded Family Life Cycle: Individual Family & Social Perspectives.* Old Tappan, WI: Allyn & Bacon, 2004.

Deal, R. L. *The Smart Stepfamily.* Minneapolis: Bethany House, 2002.

Deits, B. *Life after Loss.* DeCapo, Cambridge, MA: Perseus Books, 2004.

Dinkmeyer, D. Sr., McKay, G. D., Dinkmeyer, D. Jr. *STEP: The Parent's Handbook.* Circle Pines, MN: American Guidance Service, 1997.

Dinkmeyer, D. and Carlson, J. *Time for a Better Marriage.* Atascadero, CA: Impact Publishers, 2004.

Dreikurs, R. & Soltz, V. *Children the Challenge.* New York: Hawthorne Books, 1987.

Einstein, E. A. *The Couple's Spiritual Challenge* audiocassette tape from the *Stepfamily Living* series.

Einstein, E. A. & Albert, L. *Preparing for Remarriage* from *Stepfamily Living* series. See Stepfamily Resources and Training.

Einstein, E. A. *The Stepfamily Journey* audiocassette tape from the *Stepfamily Living* cassette tape series. See Stepfamily Resources and Training.

Einstein, E. A. *The Stepfamily: Living, Loving, and Learning.* New York: Macmillan, 1982; Boston: Shambhala, 1986; Ithaca, NY: Self-publish, 2004.

Einstein, E.A. & Albert, L. *Stepfamily Living: Pitfalls and Possibilities.* 2004. See Stepfamily Resources and Training.

Einstein, E.A. *New Connections: Preparing for Remarriage & Other New Relationships.* Work forthcoming.

Engel M. "Yours, Mine & Ours: Money in Stepfamilies." Presentation at Smart Marriages Conference, Orlando, FL, 2001.

Fisher, B. & Alberti, R. E. *Rebuilding: When Your Relationship Ends*, 3rd edition. Atascadero, CA: Impact Publishers, 2000.

Gordon, T. *Parenting Effectiveness Training: The Proven Program for Raising Responsible Children*. Three Rivers Press: CA, 2000.

Gottman, J. *The Relationship Cure*. New York: Three Rivers Press, 2001.

Gottman, J. *Why Marriages Succeed or Fail*. New York: Simon & Schuster, 1994.

Groopman, J. *Anatomy of Hope: How Patients Prevail in the Face of Illness*. Westminister, MD: Random House, 2003.

Halpern, H.M. *Cutting Loose: An Adult Guide to Coming to Terms with Your Parents*. New York: Simon and Schuster, 1990.

Harley, W.F. Jr. *His Needs, Her Needs*. Grand Rapids, MI: Fleming H. Revell, 2001.

Hendrix, H. *Getting the Love You Want: A Guide for Couples*. New York: Holt & Co.,First Owls Books, 2001.

Kornhaber, A. and Woodward, K. *Grandparents, Grandchilden: The Vital Connection*. New York: Transaction Publishers, 1984.

Kranitz, M.A. *Getting Apart Together: Couple's Guide to a Fair Divorce or Separation*. Atascadero, CA: Impact Publishers, CA, 2002.

Kubler-Ross, E. *On Death and Dying*. New York: Macmillan, 1969.

Lazarus, A.A. *Marital Myths Revisited*. Astascadero, CA: Impact Publishers, 2004.

LeShan, E. *Grandparents: A Special Kind of Love*. New York: St. Martin's, 1993.

Levang, E. *When Men Grieve*. Fairview Press: Minneapolis, MN: Fairview Press, 1998.

Lofas, J. *Stepparenting: Everything You Need to Know to Make It Work*. New York: Citadel Press/Kensington, 1985, 1996, 2004.

Luskin, F. *Forgive for Good*. San Francisco, CA: Harper Collins, 2002.

Markman, H.J., Stanley, S.M. & Blumberg, S.L. *Fighting for Your Marriage*. San Francisco, CA: Jossey-Bass, 2001.

Martin, D. & Martin, M. *Stepfamiles in Therapy: Understanding Systems, Assessment, & Intervention*. San Francisco, CA: Jossey-Bass Publishers, 1992.

Newman, G. *101 Ways to Be a Long-Distance Super-Dad*. Mountain View, CA: Blossom Valley Press, 2003.

Papernow, P. *Becoming a Stepfamily: Patterns of Development in Remarried Families*. Gestalt Institute of Cleveland Book Series, 1998.

Papernow, P. "A Phenomenological Study of the Developmental Stages of Becoming a Stepparent — A Gestalt and Family Systems Approach" (Unpublished dissertation, Boston University, 1980).

Peters, R. *Laying Down the Law: The 25 Laws of Parenting*. Emmaus, PA: Rodale, Inc., 2002.

Pickhardt, C. E. *The Everything Guide to Positive Discipline*. Avon, MA: F & W Publications, 2004.

Popkin, M. H. *Active Parenting Now*. Active Parenting Publishers: Atlanta, GA, 2002.

Ricci, I. *Mom's House, Dad's House: A Complete Guide for Parents Who Are Separated, Divorced or Remarried.* New York: Simon & Schuster Adult Publishing, 1997.

Satir, V., Banmen, J. & Gomari, R. *The Satir Model: Family Therapy and Beyond.* Mountain View, CA: Science and Behavior Books, 1991.

Satir, V. *The New Peoplemaking.* Mountain View, CA: Science and Behavior Books, 1988.

Sheehy, G. *New Passages: Mapping Your Life Across Time.* New York: Valentine Books, Random House, 1996.

Stahl, P.M. *Parenting after Divorce: A Guide to Resolving Conflicts and Meeting Your Children's Needs.* Atascadero, CA: Impact Publishers, 2000.

Taffel, R. *Nurturing Good Children Now.* New York: St. Martins/Griffin: New York, 1999.

Tavris, C. Anger: *The Misunderstood Emotion.* New York: Simon and Schuster, 1984.

Visher, E. B., & J. S. Visher. *Old Loyalties, New Ties: Therapeutic Strategies for Stepfamilies.* Philadelphia, PA: Taylor & Francis, 1991.

Visher, E. B., and J. S. Visher. *Stepfamilies: Myths and Realities.* New York: Kensington Publishers, 1980.

Visher, E. B., and J. S. Visher. *How to Win as a Stepfamily.* New York: Brunner-Rutledge, 1991.

Wallerstein, J. & Blakeslee, S. *What About the Kids? Raising Your Children Before, During & After Divorce.* New York: Hyperion Books, 2003.

Wittman, J. P. *Custody Chaos, Personal Peace: Sharing Custody with an Ex Who Drives You Crazy.* New York: Berkeley Publishing Group, 2001.

Stepfamily Resources and Training

Elizabeth Einstein, one of the country's leaders in stepfamily education, has a variety of stepfamily education resources available. She also conducts trainings for professionals and presentations for single parents and stepfamilies.

Additional Books

The Stepfamily: Living, Loving & Learning Paperback. Macmillan, Shambhala, currently self-published.

Stepfamily Living booklet series co-authored with Linda Albert. Four titles: Preparing for Remarriage, Pitfalls & Possibilities, Dealing with Discipline & Encouragement & Enrichment. Distributed by Elizabeth Einstein.

Audiocassettes

Stepfamily Living series audiocassettes with 5 titles. Preparing for Remarriage, Myths & Realities, The Stepfamily Journey, The Stepfamily's Spiritual Journey & Guiding Grandparents in the Stepfamily. Produced and distributed by Elizabeth Einstein.

Workshops

Strengthening Stepfamilies: A Developmental Approach is Elizabeth's creative one-day workshop for professionals. It gets rave reviews! Based on family systems and its developmental approach to stepfamilies, the interactive workshop has four major teaching segments. While her presentation is well-rooted in stepfamily research, she believes that people should have fun while they're training and learning. After an introduction to family systems, Elizabeth presents *The Stepfamily Journey* and moves on to *Teenage Trouble Spots*, examining major issues for adolescent stepkids. A teaching block called *Bonds, Boundaries & Stumbling Blocks* explores these issues and provides clinical guidelines. With one of her major mentors Virginia Satir, Elizabeth has adapted many of Satir's creative experiential techniques as teaching tools. Because stepfamilies are all about change — separation, divorce, single parent living, and remarriage — she teaches *Satir's Process Model of Change* in her workshops. This experiential piece is an exciting way to end a day of training!

You can contact her at:

Elizabeth Einstein
P. O. Box 6760
Ithaca, New York 14851
(607)272-2552
E-mail eaestepkid@msn.com
Website: www.stepfamilyskills.com

Index

101 Ways to Be a Long-Distance Super-Dad (Newman), 207

A

acceptance
and effective stepparenting, 121
ways to give stepchildren, 70
acting out. *See* misbehavior
Active Parenting (Popkin), 190
adopting stepchildren, 18, 32, 139–140
affection
stepparent's displays of, 144–146
ways to give stepchildren, 71–72
Alberti, Robert, 87
American Association of Marriage and Family Therapists, 63
Anatomy of Hope (Groopman), 236
anger
and children's revenge behaviors, 185
from divorce, unresolved, 43–44
against former spouse, 89–90
helping stepchildren to heal, 198
appreciation
showing in family meetings, 79
ways to give children, stepchildren, 71, 155
arguments and conflict resolution, 104–107
attention
misbehaving to gain, 177–183, 191
ways to give stepchildren, 69–70
author, contacting, 255
authoritarian disciplinary style, 169–170, 172

B

benefits
of being stepsiblings, 223–224, 233
children moving between two homes, 14–15
of stepfamily living, 206, 244–245
biological parents
described, 5
losing status, stability, 11–12
role as disciplinarian, 172
in stepfamily with children from only one partner, 130
birth order effects on stepchildren, 220–221
Bloomfield, Harold H., 88
Bohannan, Paul, 130
book, this
contacting author, 255

book, this (*cont'd.*)
organization of, 6–8
references, 251–253
boundaries
and discipline, 162
in new stepfamily, 58–59
and sexuality issues, 145–147
Bray, Dr. James, 240
Buckley Amendment, Family Education Rights and Privacy Act, 211–212

C

career commitments, issues to discuss, 116
Carlson, Jon, 104
children
See also stepchildren
birth order effects on stepchildren, 220–222
decision to have more, 96
disciplining. *See* discipline
growing up with biological fathers vs. stepfathers, 130
helping to adjust to stepparent, 217
and holiday arrangements, 73–74
issues to discuss, 116
living with newlyweds, 144–145
misbehavior. *See* misbehavior
moving between two homes, 14–15, 58, 204–206, 208
Children: The Challenge (Dreikurs), 175
collaborative law vs. mediation, 47–48
communication
conflict resolution and, 100–102
importance in marriage, 19–20
redirecting attention behaviors, 179–180
conflict
and competition in stepfamilies, 136–138
resolution, and communication, 102, 104–107
controlling, and disciplining, 158, 160–161
counselors, divorce and school, 28, 46, 63, 211
couple relationships
dealing with the past, 83–91
family and money decisions, 93–95
living arrangements, 95–96
taking time to grow, 108
custody, 20, 47, 62–63
Cutting Loose: An Adult Guide to Coming to Terms with Your Parents (Halpern), 88

D

decisions
  about family matters, living arrangements, 93–96
  disciplining children, 96–97
  mutual participation in, 106–107
denial
  and discipline issues, 174
  and resentment, 137–138
differences in stepfamilies, 9–18
Dinkmeyer, Don, 104, 190
discipline
  See also misbehavior
  consistency of, 159, 165
  guidelines for stepparents, 149
  identifying your style, 166–172, 195
  inappropriate, two-household dilemmas, 163–164
  issues in stepfamilies, 157–158, 173–174
  making decisions together, 96–97
  roles and authority, 160–163
divorce counseling, mediation, collaborative law, 46–48
divorcing adults
  creating 'lesson plan,' 39
  dealing with anger, guilt, 43–45
Dreikurs, Dr. Rudolf, 175

E

Einstein, Elizabeth, 54, 67, 89, 255
emotionally divorcing, 39–40, 51, 90
empathizing with stepchildren, 119–120
Erickson, Rosemary, 130
expectations
  about marriage and stepfamilies, 99–102
  moving from unrealistic to realistic (chart), 22–23

F

families
  See also stepfamilies
  birth order and child characteristics (chart), 222
  of origin, resolving relations with, 5, 88–89
  traditional, 5
Family Education Rights and Privacy Act, 211–212
family meetings, 75, 79, 225
fears
  exploring unexamined, 85–88
  helping stepchildren to deal with, 200–201, 214

Fender, Leonard, 88
fighting
  and conflict resolution, 104–107
  between stepsiblings, 218–219
finances. *See* money
Fisher, Dr. Bruce, 39, 87
former spouses, getting over, 83–91
friendship with stepchildren, 123–124

G

Getting Apart Together (Kranitz), 47
Gordon, Dr. Thomas, 101
grandparents' role in stepfamilies, 224, 226–227, 233
grief
  dealing with former losses, 35–43
  helping stepchildren to heal, 197–201
Groopman, Jerome, 236
guidelines
  for addressing sexuality in stepfamilies, 148
  for correcting children's misbehavior, 190
  for easing adjustment to stepfamily living, 132
  for effective stepparenting, 119–122
  for enriching relationships with grandparents, 227
  to help support stepsibling relationships, 219
  for helping children to adjust to stepparent, 217
  for helping children to heal, 201
  for helping children to move between homes, 208
  for sidestepping power struggles, 182–13
  for stepping through stepfamily stages (chart), 66–67
guilt
  and discipline, 164–165
  from divorce, letting go, 44–45
  helping stepchildren to heal, 198–199
  and raising other people's children, 133

H

Halpern, Marvin, 88
healing
  from former losses, 35–38
  process for stepchildren, 239–240
  stepchildren's hearts, 197–201
Hendrix, Harville, 89
holidays, deciding where children spend, 73–74
homes
  making living arrangement decisions together, 95–97

homes (*cont'd.*)
    children moving between two, 14–15, 58,
        204–206, 208
hope, and building successful stepfamily,
    235–236, 249–250
humor, using to strength stepfamily, 242

I

'I-messages'
    and good communication, 101
        helping with stepsibling relationships, 219
        redirecting attention behaviors, 178–180
Imago Therapy (Hendrix), 89
inadequacy behaviors, 188, 191
inheritance issues, 139
'instant love' myth, 140–143
International Academy of Collaborative
      Professionals Web site, 48

J

joint custody, 47
judging, and effective stepparenting, 120–121

K

Kranitz, Martin, 47
Kubler–Ross, Elisabeth, 42

L

law
    adoption issues, 139–140
    collaborative, divorce dispute-resolution,
      47–48
    getting help from legal professionals, 28–29
    legal relationships, stepfamilies with lack of,
      18
loss
    adjusting to, 174
    healing from former, 35–43
    identifying, 51
love, myth of 'instant,' 140–143
loyalty conflicts, 157

M

marriage
    letting go of former, 38–39, 83–91
    remarriage. *See* remarriage
McKay, Gary, 190
mediation, divorce, 46–48
meetings, family, 75, 79, 225
mentoring and effective stepparenting,
    126–127
military families, special situation of, 29

misbehavior
    dealing with (chart), 191
    discipline. *See* discipline
    and family venting time (chart), 186
    to gain power, 180–183
    to get revenge, 183–186
    for getting attention, 177–181
    helpless and incompetent behaviors, 188–189
    motivations and goals for, 175–176
models
    role, in stepfamilies, 127, 238–239
    Stepfamily Journey (Einstein), 54–55
money
    issues to discuss, 116
    making decisions together, 93–95
    and personal responsibility, 138
mourning lost relationships, 38–44, 50
moving children between two homes, 14–15,
    58, 204–206, 208
myths
    about 'instant love,' 140–143
    about remarriage, 56–57
    about stepfamilies, debunking, 21

N

names for stepparents, 215
newlyweds, children living with, 144–145
Newman, G., 207
non-custodial parents, 206–207, 209
nonresidential parents in stepfamilies, 12–14
nonverbal communication, 102
nurturing
    and discipline, 158, 160–161
    and feeling of belonging, 176
    in stepfamilies, 240

O

obstacles
    competing for attention, 136–138
    seeking recognition from stepchildren,
      135–136
    to stepparents disciplining children, 149
    taking personal responsibility, 138–139
On Death and Dying (Kubler-Ross), 42

P

Parent Effectiveness (Gordon), 101
parenting
    toolkits, 160
    tools, classes, 190
parents. *See* stepparents
part-time parents, importance of, 206–207

permissive disciplinary style, 169, 171, 172
Popkin, Michael, 190
power, misbehavior to gain, 180–183, 191
professional help, sources for stepfamilies,
        27–29, 46, 63, 211

R

rebellious behavior, 189–190
Rebuilding: When Your Relationship Ends
        (Fisher and Alberti), 39, 87
recognition, stepparents seeking from children,
        135–136
references to this book, 251–253
relationships
        couple. *See* couple relationships
        encouraging children to build with
            stepparent, 216–217
remarriage
        commitment to build positive model for
            children, 238
        and conflict resolution, 102, 104–105
        and continuing relationship with children,
            17
        expectations about, 104–107
        myths about, 56–57
        and revenge behaviors, 184–185
resentments
        children's, about remarriage, 200
        parent's, about former marriage, 39–40
        taking personal responsibility, 138–139
resources for stepfamilies
        American Association of Marriage and
            Family Therapists, 63
        books, audio, workshops, 255
        divorce counseling, mediation, 46–48
        parenting toolkits, 160
        Stepfamily Association of America, 29
revenge, misbehavior to get, 183–186, 191
rivalry between stepchildren, 218–219, 243
role models and effective stepparenting, 127,
        238–239
roles
        allowing stepchildren to discover their new,
            122
        changing partner, parent, 38–39
        of grandparents, stepgrandparents, 224,
            226–227
        parental, in stepfamilies, 238–239
        redefining as stepparent, 123–127
        stepfamily in which both adults are parents,
            131, 133
        stepfamily with children from only one
            partner, 127–131

roles (*cont'd.*)
        of stepparents, 83
        of stepparents in discipline, 160–163
        taking stepparents' too seriously, 87
rules and responsibilities, topics for new
        stepfamilies to discuss, 20–21

S

scapegoating to deny problems, 86
schools
        getting help from, 28
        and stepchildren's adjustment, 209–211
self-esteem
        building child's, 189
        easing stepfamily atmosphere, 227–228
        and personal growth, 109
sexuality issues in stepfamilies, 141–148
spouses
        getting over former, 83–91
        support for stepparent (chart), 103
stepchildren
        See also children
        adjusting to differences at home, between
            homes, 203–206
        adopting, 18, 32, 139–140
        creating family atmosphere for, 227–228
        disciplining. *See* discipline
        and effective stepparenting, 119–123
        helping to grieve and heal, 197–201
        misbehavior. *See* misbehavior
        rivalry between, 218–219, 243
        stepparents seeking recognition from,
            135–136
        ways to give attention, acceptance,
            appreciation, affection, 69–72
stepfamilies
        adding babies to, 221, 223
        benefits of, 206, 244–245
        building commitment in new, 64–65, 23
        children move between two homes, 14–15
        debunking myths about, 21, 24–25
        described, 5–6, 10–12
        development cycles, stages, 53–65
        differences in, 9–18
        discipline. *See* discipline
        expectations about, 99–102
        family meetings, 75, 79, 225
        grandparents' role in, 224, 226–227
        with lack of legal relationships, 16, 18
        misbehavior in. *See* misbehavior
        myth of 'instant love,' 140–143
        with nonresidential parent, 12–14
        with previous parent-child relationships, 15

stepfamilies (*cont'd.*)
    sexuality issues in, 141–148
    traditions, creating, 17, 72–75
Stepfamily Association of America Web site, 29
stepfathers vs. biological fathers, 130
stepgrandparents, 224, 226–227, 233
stepparents
    disciplining children, 149
    effective, guidelines for, 119–123
    importance of non-custodial parent, 206–207
    names for, 215
    roles of, 83, 124
    seeking recognition from stepchildren, 135–136
    and spousal support (chart), 103
stepsiblings
    benefits of being, 223–224, 233
    special relationships between, 242–243
    supporting relationships, 217–219
Systematic Training for Effective Parenting (Dinkmeyer and McKay), 190

T

talking
    about daily routines in former family, 204
    about sexuality, 147–148

talking (*cont'd.*)
    in family meetings, 75, 79, 225
teachers, communicating with stepchildren's, 211–212
teenagers and sexuality issues, 147
therapists. *See* counselors
Time for a Better Marriage (Dinkmeyer and Carlson), 104
traditional families vs. stepfamilies, 5, 9–10
training, workshops, stepfamily resources, 255

U

unfit parents, 209

V

venting time, and children's misbehavior, 187

W

Web sites
American Association of Marriage and Family Therapists, 63
International Academy of Collaborative Professionals, 48
Stepfamily Association of America, 29
'Who's Right?' game, 80
Wright, Frank Lloyd, 235

After Your Divorce
Creating the Good Life on Your Own
Cynthia MacGregor and Robert E. Alberti Ph.D.
Softcover: $16.95 (t)   192(t) pages
MacGregor and Alberti have prepared a friendly, straightforward manual of advice and suggestions that assumes every woman is capable of handling life on her own. Help for emotional recovery (MacGregor is a "survivor," Alberti is a psychologist), practical matters (finances, home maintenance), dealing with your ex (be assertive!), and much, much more.

Parenting After Divorce
A Guide to Resolving Conflicts and Meeting Your Children's Needs
Philip M. Stahl, Ph.D.
Softcover: $15.95   192 pages
Here at last is a realistic perspective on divorce and its effects on children. Featuring knowledgeable advice from an expert custody evaluator, packed with real-world examples, this book avoids idealistic assumptions, and offers practical help for divorcing parents, custody evaluators, family court counselors, marriage and family therapists, and others interested in the well-being of children.

Jigsaw Puzzle Family
The Stepkids' Guide to Fitting It together
Cynthia MacGregor
Softcover: $12.95   120 pages
MacGregor has created another warm and understanding resource for children of divorce which helps guide them through the challenges of dealing with a new stepparent... new rules in the house... new stepbrothers and/or stepsisters... living somewhere new. Dozens of practical and helpful suggestions for making stepfamily life better, gentle advice for understanding fitting into a blended family.

The Divorce Helpbook for Kids
Cynthia Mac Gregor
Softcover: $12.95   144 pages
The Divorce Helpbook for Teens
Cynthia MacGregor
Softcover: $13.95   144 pages
These warm and friendly guides by Cynthia MacGregor are designed to help teens or younger kids through the turmoil when their parents divorce: Why do parents get divorced? How will the divorce change their lives? What's going to happen next? Packed with helpful guidelines for making it all work.

<u>**Please see following page for more books with Impact**</u>

More Books with Impact

Your Perfect Right
Assertiveness and Equality in Your Life and Relationships (8th Edition)
Robert E. Alberi, Ph.D. and Michael L. Emmons, Ph.D.
Softcover: $15.95   Hardcover: $21.95   256 pages

Eighth edition of the assertiveness book most recommended by psychologists — fifth most recommended among all self-help books. Helps readers step-by-step to develop more effective self-expression. Psychologists Alberti and Emmons emphasize *equal-relationship assertiveness* — not the all-too-common "me-first" attitude. Includes materials on living in a multicultural society, appropriate anger expression, much more.

Calming the Family Storm
Anger Management for Moms, Dads, and All the Kids
Gary D. McKay, Ph.D. and Steven A. Maybell, Ph.D.
Softcover: $16.95   320 pages

Anger and confrontation are a part of our lives, like it or not. Every normal family experiences anger, but the reward for families that learn to deal effectively with it is a healthier, *happier* family environment. This practical manual offers helpful aids for handling the inevitable anger every family experiences. Helps families work on changes that will result in less anger, and a happier, more harmonious family life.

The Shelbys Need Help
A Choose-Your-Own Solutions Guidebook for Parents
Ken West, Ph.D.
Softcover: $16.95   272 pages

Parenting isn't easy, but learning parenting skills can be *fun* in this creative blend of vignettes and sound advice. Helps parents teach responsibility and the consequences of misbehavior by inviting their children to join in and help solve the Shelby family battles over waking up on time, dressing, fighting amongst siblings, eating, home-work, baths, bedtime, and more.

The Stress Owner's Manual
Meaning, Balance and Health in Your Life (2nd Edition)
Ed Boenisch, Ph.D. and C. Michele Haney, Ph.D.
Softcover: $15.95   224 pages

Stress is a greater part of our lives than ever before. Heightened awareness of our vulnerability, concerns about protecting children, fears of travel, terrorism, weapons of mass destruction, ongoing international conflicts, school shootings, natural disasters... all these and more have everyone's adrenaline pumping harder than usual. This book offers specific solutions to help you assess your areas of stress and shows you how to keep your life in balance, emphasizing *meaning* and *keeping perspective*.

Since 1970 — Psychology you can use, from professionals you can trust.

Ask your local or online bookseller, or call 1-800-246-7228 to order direct

Impact ✎ Publishers®

POST OFFICE BOX 6016 • ATASCADERO, CALIFORNIA 93423-6016
Free catalog of self-help and professional resources: visit www.impactpublishers.com
Prices effective September 2005 and subject to change without notice.